AF479169

HONOR FOR US

HONOR FOR US

A Philosophical Analysis, Interpretation and Defense

WILLIAM LAD SESSIONS

continuum

The Continuum International Publishing Group Ltd
80 Maiden Lane, New York, NY 10038
The Tower Building, 11 York Road, London SE1 7NX

www.continuumbooks.com

Library of Congress Cataloging-in-Publication Data
A catalog record for this book is available from the Library of Congress.

ISBN: 978-1-4411-8834-2 (hardcover)

Typeset by Pindar NZ, Auckland, New Zealand
Printed and bound in the United States of America by Thomson-Shore, Inc.

To Bill and Alice Sessions

CONTENTS

Preface   ix

Chapter 1
INTRODUCTION: ISSUES OF HONOR   1

PART I   CONCEPTS OF HONOR   **8**

Chapter 2
FIVE PERIPHERAL CONCEPTS   10

Chapter 3
PERSONAL HONOR   26

Chapter 4
PERSONAL HONOR, MORALITY AND RELIGION   37

Chapter 5
DEVIANT HONOR   44

PART II   HONOR'S REACH   **57**

Chapter 6
THE HONOR OF WARRIORS   62

Chapter 7
SPORTSMANSHIP AS HONOR   82

Chapter 8
PATRIOTISM AS HONOR   97

Chapter 9
ACADEMIC HONOR   113

Chapter 10
PROFESSIONAL HONOR   140

PART III   HONOR'S FUTURE   **154**

Chapter 11
IN DEFENSE OF HONOR   155

Chapter 12
HONOR FOR US   172

Selected Bibliography   192
Index   206
Index of names   209

PREFACE

"Dear Reader," I am tempted to begin — and then to ask, "Who might you be?" Anyone, I hope, who picks up this book with a ready mind and a willingness to think new thoughts about an old subject. But of course while writing I have often thought about more specific readers: fellow philosophers, to be sure, as well as my academic colleagues in other disciplines; my many students over the decades, who have taught me so much; and friends, relatives and acquaintances who have often asked me how I spend my summers. Beyond them, my fellow citizens of this faltering American colossus whose founders were so fond of their "sacred honor." And, finally, though not least, my fellow dwellers on this imperiled planet. To all I want to say: honor alone will not save us, but, properly understood, it might just help.

This is a book I would not, could not have written decades ago. I came to teach at a small undergraduate college in the Valley of Virginia in 1971, with little expectation of staying and even less awareness of what I was getting into. I did know there was a revered student-run honor system, one of the best of its kind, but I found many of the customs and traditions of "this old place," as a former president of the university called it, to be quaint and antiquated. I had a lot to learn — and still do — but I have come to understand those traditions, and others like them in other places, more deeply and sympathetically. Don't get me wrong. No one who knows me would mistake me for a Southern gentleman! I did grow up in the South, but it was South Dakota, and I neither can nor want to obliterate my Midwestern origins. Still, I have come to appreciate the importance of honor as a value in this community, and in the last decade I have studied some of the complexities of honor as a concept (or set of concepts) in any community. In 1999 I began a course brashly entitled "The Concept of Honor" — as if there were such a single thing! — in order to induce my students to reflect on their own understanding of honor — after all, they have to judge their peers' "honor violations," and by what lights? But when we started looking into the matter, pushing back beyond Robert E. Lee, president of this school after the Civil War, I found innumerable interesting philosophical questions on all sides, questions that no one else seems to be addressing today.

It is indeed a bit odd for a contemporary philosopher to be writing a book about honor, though perhaps it shouldn't be. Like most philosophical books written today, this one connects with an expansive and intricate scholarly literature. Unfortunately, that literature isn't a *philosophical* one, simply because philosophers today aren't working on honor. In my exploration of this nearly universal feature of human life, my resources — informants, critics, sources, discussion partners and intellectual fellow travelers — have been nearly all non-philosophers: historians, anthropologists, sociologists, literary critics, and the like. I wish it were otherwise. I wish I were joining a philosophical conversation instead of trying to start one. But the fact remains that philosophers in recent years simply haven't bothered to write about honor.[1] Perhaps this is just an accident; philosophers are as prone to fads as any other human group.

But perhaps the problem goes deeper, touching the very nature of philosophy. For most academic philosophers today, a philosopher is someone who considers important those problems and methods considered important by other academic philosophers; a philosophical problem is a problem professional philosophers currently think is worth thinking about. This is more than comical circularity. Philosophy has become domesticated in academe as one among many specialties (or rather a cluster of sub-specialties, or perhaps even a chaos of disparate specialized conversation groups), and so it must oblige with its own distinctive terminology, questions, issues, approaches, values and sense of what matters and what isn't worth scrutiny. Honor doesn't seem to fit into any current philosophical circle of conversation. I wish it did, I think it can, and I hope this book will help.

Still, this book follows another, older notion of philosophy: a philosopher is a person who considers *any* problem in a distinctive way — conceptually (v. empirically), normatively (v. descriptively), analytically *and* synthetically, clarifying pieces and comprehending all those things together: trying to see things clearly and to see them whole. In this view, there is nothing alien to philosophy; all the myriad reaches of the cosmos and all the depths of the human heart both raise and reward philosophical inquiry. I propose to study honor in this spirit.

So even though I am venturing into philosophically uncharted territory, I do want to survey it *philosophically*. In this I seek to go beyond the many scholars of honor who have skillfully, patiently and penetratingly examined particular examples of honor in various times, places and societies. These scholars — social scientists and humanists alike — have greatly expanded our understanding of honor, and I do not wish to disparage their inquiries. On the contrary, they have deepened our understanding of honor's ancient and global reach. But I worry that their methods, however adept in singling out certain aspects of particular cultures, have led them to think that the

---

[1] Philosophers from Plato to Schopenhauer not only used but frequently thematized the concept of honor. This stream of reflection dries up in the twentieth century.

particular outcroppings of honor they study are adequate samples of the entire bedrock. In a broader perspective, they have confused several quite different concepts of honor, and conflated particular conceptions with more general concepts. They have provincialized honor, encapsulated its normativity, and failed to find a general (and generous) overview of the manifold fields of honor. In doing so, they have tended to view honor as something exotic and alien — something "others" might find attractive, but with little application and no appeal to "us" — to what John Rawls in his last writings referred to as "you and I, here and now."

Contrarily, I have come to believe that honor is something deeply pervasive in human society, not confined to distant times and places and peoples but penetrating contemporary industrial societies just as it does those of heroic Greek warriors, medieval knights, Southern slave-owners, Albanian sheepherders, Pashtun tribesmen, or Bedouin nomads. Indeed, I find honor, in its various manifestations, to be deeply engrained in our American culture today, from academe and the professions to sports and the military; it is even reflected in deviant and marginalized groups such as criminal gangs (yes, there can be honor, of various distorted kinds, among thieves!).

But while I seek to explore honor's pervasiveness and to note its power to attract, let me make it perfectly clear from the very outset that I provide no blanket apology for honor. Many despicable things have been done in honor's name, and the carnage continues; it is no wonder honor has a bad reputation in some circles (i.e. is no longer honored, in one sense, by them). It is tempting, therefore, to follow the philosophical crowd and to ignore or shun or bury the contaminated concept. Thirty years ago I would gladly, if unthinkingly, have joined the burial party. But having lived amongst people who revere the spirit of a traditional academic honor system and seek to extend that spirit into all areas of life, I have come to discern and appreciate that there are other, more positive possibilities for honor, even in a (post) modern world that imagines it has outgrown all that. In the end, however, I aim neither to glorify nor to revile honor as a whole, though both attitudes are certainly appropriate on occasion. Instead, most fundamentally, I seek to understand honor's underlying structure and to project its potential salience for us.

Yet who counts as "us?" This question is not easily answered. Certainly I want to include not just philosophers or academics or intellectuals generally but all members of liberal democratic societies and enlightened citizens of the world as well. Even more: I am emboldened to think that the account of honor provided in this book is at least available and may be attractive to anyone willing to engage in thoughtful reflection on the matter. So, if you are reading this book with sympathetic understanding, you certainly are one of us, and I hope our numbers are legion. Here I return to my beginning: Dear Reader, I propose to study honor for us.

Honor is a formidably large and complex topic, and I only wish my talents were equal to the task of depicting it clearly. Perhaps my tentative explorations will inspire others — and I hope especially other *philosophers* — to do better.

I have more debts than I can acknowledge, and I apologize to those whose contributions I fail to mention. My biggest debt is to Washington and Lee — not only to the institution that has kindly provided time, environment and resources to work on this project, but especially to the community of honorable students, staff and faculty who have taught me about honor in so many different ways.

Portions of Chapter 7 are adapted from my article, "Sportsmanship as Honor," published in the *Journal of the Philosophy of Sport*, 31:1 (2004), 47–59.

Many people have been most generous with their time and attention to earlier versions of parts of this manuscript, and I honor them here:

Special thanks are due to Ed Craun, Nathaniel Goldberg, and John Schellenberg, each of whom heroically read the entire manuscript and provided extremely helpful comments that prompted many revisions, though not quite every revision recommended; they certainly made the final product better. In addition, Ed Craun has been a constant resource and treasured colleague over the decades.

Others also read and helped improve various parts of the manuscript: Rob Atkinson, Harlan Beckley, Alexandra Brown, Tom Burish, Bernard Chachula, Greg Cooper, Nicholas Dixon, Jonathan Eastwood, Ben Eggleston, Tony Hartle, Quince Hopkins, Suzanne Keen, Bill Klein, Jeff Kosky, Lash LaRue, Robin LeBlanc, Paul McClure, David Millon, Brian Murchison, David Newheiser, Joan Shaughnessy, Tom Shaffer, John Tucker and Mike Walsh. I thank them all! Members of the Murphy Institute seminar in December 2005, particularly Melina Bell, raised important questions and helped me understand my project more clearly. Faculty and students at Rhodes College asked fruitful questions of an earlier version of Chapter 8. In addition, I have received aid and stimulation from hundreds of Washington and Lee undergraduates in a series of classes on the concept of honor over the past decade. Karen Lyle has provided expert and efficient secretarial support. Finally, I'm very grateful to seven students who worked summers with me under the Robert E. Lee research program: Gabe Chapman, Taylor Gibson, Adam Hockensmith, Stephanie Jordon, Matthew Layton, Jessica McCormack and Susan Somers; they are all gems.

Of course, none of these people are to blame for the errors and inadequacies that remain; for those, I take sole responsibility.

I had the benefit of two sabbatical leaves from Washington and Lee while writing and rewriting parts of this book, and I am grateful to two universities in New Zealand (Otago and Canterbury) for providing me quarters, library space and intellectual stimulation during those periods, and to the persons who especially helped: Andrew Moore and David Ward in Dunedin, and Philip Catton and Carolyn Mason in Christchurch. I am also very grateful to our transplanted Kiwi daughter Laura Sessions for local arrangements, encouragement, and so much more.

The dedication honors my parents, William George Sessions (April 12, 1919–May 17, 2000) and Alice Billhardt Sessions (January 25, 1923)

Last, but never least, I am eternally grateful both to and for Vicki, whose friendship, loyalty and love has made it all possible — and worthwhile.

Chapter 1

INTRODUCTION: ISSUES OF HONOR

Honor pervades human history and contemporary cultures, not least our own. Yet honor is in trouble today. Dishonorable behavior is rampant, to be sure, but we are also confused about honor, about what it is and what it is not. Honor may well be ubiquitous, but the concept of honor is not well understood, either by those who live within honor groups or by those who view themselves as rising above any culture of honor.

Those living in honor communities certainly understand their own honor — they know intimately what their own community requires and forbids as matters of honor: they know quite well, even if they can't fully articulate, the particular code of honor and ideal expectations of their own honor group.

Yet they often don't understand the different senses of honor belonging to others, and almost certainly they don't view the concept of honor more comprehensively. Indeed, there may be something like an honor taboo restricting too much inquiry into honor: *as a matter of honor* an honorable person, however punctilious about living honorably, simply shouldn't inquire too closely into the concept of honor itself — its roots, its justifications and its connections with other normative concepts. Honor demands constant attention to matters of honor, but often excludes reflective attention to the concept of honor.

Those living apart from honor communities (or so they imagine) may be fascinated, dismayed, or even aghast at the spectacle of honor so fervently pursued by others — but always by others, never by themselves. These outsiders are not without some understanding of honor. Indeed the more scholarly among them may expend considerable energy examining the honor of particular groups at particular times and places.[1] But again their

---

[1] We will return to this theme in Chapter 9, but here will merely mention a few scholarly works on honor in various times and places: On so-called "Mediterranean honor," cf. Black-Michaud, 1975; Boehm, 1984; Campbell, 1964; Dubish, 1986; Gilmore, ed., 1987; Peristiany, ed., 1965; J. Schneider, 1971; P. Schneider, 1969; Walcot, 1970. In the sociology of American urban street

1

understanding is often defective because it is partial, mistaking honor found in one time and place for honor as a human universal.

Both insiders and outsiders frequently confuse some particular *conception(s)* of honor with a more global *concept* of honor.[2] The present study seeks to do more, to depict the concept — or, as it turns out, the several concepts — of honor as broadly and as deeply as possible. The focus is not on honor confined to some particular honor group at a restricted time and place, but on honor more widely exhibited — indeed potentially in any social group. This focus unavoidably entails abstraction from particulars, always a dangerous step, but this abstraction will be more a matter of suggesting preliminary patterns than of seeking Platonic forms. The broader and deeper understanding of honor I seek results in tentative generalities, not essential universals. Nevertheless, such generalization can help us describe and understand honor better than we currently do, even if we persist in thinking honor is still only for others.

But my account of honor aims at something even more ambitious than descriptive clarity with potentially universal scope (as if that weren't ambition enough!). By exhibiting honor as a *normative* concept, I hope we might come to see its value for us as well as for others. My account is therefore a philosophical rarity, for philosophers today share the general academic distaste for honor. For most Western academics, honor is a moral pariah, a concept recognized as important to others though not an idea to be taken seriously in one's own life. But there is an interesting twist. The last three decades have seen an upsurge of so-called "virtue ethics," where the moral life

---

gangs, cf. Adamson, 1998; E. Anderson, 1992, 1999; Horowitz, 1983; Jankowski, 1991; Katz, 1988; Nisbett and Cohen, 1996; Rodriguez, 1993; Vigil, 1988. In Biblical scholarship, cf. Campbell, 1998; DeSilva, 1995; Elliott, 1995; Hanson, 1996; Hobbs, 1997; Laniak, 1998; Malina, 1993; Malina and Neyrey, 1991; Moxnes, 1996; Neyrey, 1998, 1999; Schneider, 1972; Stansell, 1996. In the history of the American ante-bellum South cf. Greenberg, 1985, 1996; Nisbett and Cohen, 1996; Wyatt-Brown, 1982, 1986, 2001); on the American founders (Fischer, 1989; Freeman, 2001; Kennedy, 2000; McNamara, ed., 1999; Stevens, 1940); figures like Lincoln (Burlingame, 1994; Donald, 1995; Oates, 1984, 1994; Wilson, 1998), Lee (Thomas, 1995); Douglass (Harris, 1999); and even the Wild West (French, 1997; Tompkins, 1992). Classicists have explored honor in Ancient Greece (Adkins, 1960; Cairns, 1993; Engeman, n.d.; Fisher, 1979; Lloyd-Jones, 1990; Redfield, 1975) and Rome (Barton, 2001; Dupont, 1989; Lendon, 1997). Likewise there are studies of periods and regions in Europe (Dewey, 1968; James, 1978; Kollman, 1999; Reddy, 1997; Shapin, 1994); Latin America (Johnson & Lipsett-Rivera, eds, 1998); the Middle East (Abu-Lughod, 1986; Stewart, 1994); China (Kuo, 1996; Tomio, 1994; Zhi and Yiquan, 1987); Japan (Benedict, 1946; Hurst, 1990; Nitobe, 1907; Turnbull, ed., 2000); and especially medieval and Renaissance European studies (Cast, 1977; Christoph, 1995; Dutton, 1979; Fenster and Smail, eds, 2003; Kuehn, 1980; Neuschel, 1989; Trexler, 1978). Literary critics also find the concept vital (Ashcroft, 1994; Benson, 1992; Christoph, 1982, 1995; Collette, 1994; Council, 1973; Kalinke, 1973; Krueger, 1985; Mandrell, 1992; McNamee, 1960; Meyer, 1986; Mickel, 1975; Wasserman, 1980; Watson, 1960; Wisley, 1996). Since the reader's eyes are doubtless glassing over, I will stop here, hoping the point is well made: the scholarly literature on honor is vast! (More titles from other areas will be mentioned later.)

[2] These terms will be explained more fully in Chapter 2. Throughout the work I italicize words with special significance or technical meaning.

is viewed not in terms of rules or results but in terms of qualities of character, habits of mind and heart, dispositions to do and to feel.[3] Philosophers and their fellow travelers have written extensively about many particular virtues,[4] but not about the virtue of honor.[5] To be sure, anglophonic philosophers have written about honor in the history of philosophy,[6] in the US military;[7] and, all-too-rarely, about collegiate honor systems.[8] But there has been *no* serious normative examination of the concept of honor as such. It seems that philosophers, like other academics, are not much interested in honor as a living value in our society today.

Living values are norms, but it is not easy to characterize normativity. Still, we recognize normativity when we see it: normative concepts express normativity as they are used to make claims on those who accept them, involve and express commitment, guide belief and action and aspiration. There are many ways of bracketing the normativity of normative concepts: by relativizing them to a specific society or group of societies distant in time or space; by willfully suspending belief or disbelief; by disdainfully describing another's values with the clear implication that the depicter finds them confused, misguided, dangerous or even repulsive; or by ironically desiccating even the values of one's own culture, putting "scare quotes" around value terms and sucking out their normative juices so that there can be no claim on one's own life. Thus, for example, one might talk about the "honor" of a certain sociological class at a certain moment in history as if one were a paleontologist sorting through dry bones; or one might marginalize sub-groups within one's own culture by describing them almost as exotic life forms.[9]

Honor wears many normative faces. To many it is noble, inspiring, and even sublime. Declares Mowbray, in *Richard II*, I.i.181–182: "Mine honour is my life; both grow in one;/ Take honour from me, and my life is done." Or as

---

[3] On virtue ethics, see Crisp, 1996; Crisp and Slote, 1997; Darwall, ed., 2003; Foot, 1978; MacIntyre, 2e, 1984a; Swanton, 2003; Wallace, 1978.

[4] See recent works on gratitude (McConnell, 1993), humility (Richards, 1992), courage (Walton, 1986), integrity (Halfon, 1989; Carter, 1996), loyalty (Fletcher, 1993), civility (Carter, 1998), and reverence (Woodruff, 2001), as well as on correlative vices and associated conditions such as shame (Williams, 1993; Taylor, 1985), humiliation (Miller, 1993; Margalit, 1996) and embarrassment (Harré, 1990). This list only scratches the surface of a veritable cottage industry in the ethics of particular virtues and vices — with "industriousness" perhaps another, self-instanced virtue.

[5] Krause, 2002, and Welsh, 2008, are recent and welcome exceptions.

[6] Cf., e.g. Chereso, 1960; Cordner, 1997; Curzer, 1990, 1991; Heidsieck, 1961; Limbrick, 1981; Lloyd-Jones, 1990; Putman, 1995.

[7] Cf., among very many others, Axinn, 1989; Best, 1982; Fotion, 1990; French, 2003a; Gabriel, 1982; Galligan, 1979; Gray, 1959; Hartle, 1989; Holmes, 1989; Johnson, 1984; McGrath and Anderson, 1993; Sorley, 1998; Walzer, 1977.

[8] Beatty, 1992; Rosen, 1987.

[9] Irony of ironies, "marginalization" is shunning, and shunning is what honor groups do to those considered dishonorable. But of course those who marginalize honor don't wish to think they are doing so from a standpoint of honor!

an enthusiastic Washington and Lee alumnus once exclaimed: "Honor says it all!" To others, honor is hollow, an empty shell of reputation valued only by the vain. Here's Falstaff, in *Henry IV, Part 1*, V: 1, 126–141: ". . . What is honour? A word. What is that word honour? Air. . . . Honour is a mere scutcheon . . ." To still others it is a dangerous amoral idol, a source of evils great and small, including the evil of hypocrisy. As Emerson wryly notes in "Worship," "The louder he talked of his honour, the faster we counted our spoons."

We will not recount here the many superlatives piled upon honor, but note only that honor has inspired, and continues to inspire, many people to act decently, modestly, respectfully, civilly, hospitably, kindly, generously, gently, bravely and graciously. Honor is aligned with whole constellations of virtues, although the constellations vary over time and place. But we will seek to go beyond these traditional values in Chapter 12, to note some surprising potential merits of honor in the contemporary world — merits that are not always clear even to the partisans of honor.

Here it is necessary rather to turn to honor's "dark side," since so many in the Western world today, perhaps a majority of its intellectuals, are so alienated from the concept of honor. The following list of complaints against honor is not clearly divided, nor is it exhaustive; yet it registers most of the major concerns.

- Honor seems shallow, a matter of mere reputation. The worry is threefold: (i) The reputation may be mistaken or undeserved; despicable lives may be honored, and worthy ones ignored or dishonored. (ii) Honor looks like a gift — or an imposition — from others, not an accomplishment of the self. (iii) Even if those who award honors accurately track true worth, honor still resides only in their eyes, not in the person honored. Honor is external and incidental to a life, not something internal to it. Moreover, honor shackles an autonomous individual to a community's standards and monitoring. Honor induces conformity to others' expectations, not self-fulfillment; it stifles critical self-reflection and encourages hypocrisy.
- Honor seems dependent upon certain social conditions, and these conditions may no longer obtain in modern or postmodern societies, particularly industrialized liberal democracies.[10] Honor seems to be found only in traditional, homogeneous, hierarchical and warlike societies, and these are being displaced in the modern world. Honor is bound to societies with clear and often rigid status-roles that confer substantial identities to their members, in stark contrast to the "naked" selves produced by, and more comfortable in, more open modern societies. In short, honor seems

---

[10] Here I condense the main points of Peter Berger in his 1970 seminal article. Cf. also Tor Aase, 2002, who asks (p. 5): "Is honor a pre-modern weed in a modern garden of dignity?"

antiquated — almost quaint, if it didn't have such odious lingering effects in stubbornly traditional societies.

- Honor groups seem necessarily small, not suitable for modern mass societies. To be effective, honor requires mutual recognition and loyalty among members of the group, and this requirement appears to limit the honor group's size. Mass societies are too vast and impersonal to exemplify honor.

- Honor seems socially relative, and morality claims not to be, so honor seems amoral (or even immoral). Morality makes claims upon everyone, while honor claims only particular kinds of communities. Moreover, honor groups not only differ in their senses of honor, but also change over time, while morality is thought to be absolute and unchanging.[11] In addition, because of honor's relativity, persons may belong to multiple honor groups that tug in different directions, creating internal and external conflicts irresolvable in terms of honor. Honor divides and sets people against one another because it is manifold and relative, whereas morality unites because it is one and absolute.

- Honor seems inegalitarian and elitist, the offspring of ruling social elites and hence confined to their circles, their way of distinguishing themselves as "higher" from the "lower" classes and thereby, most importantly, their way of preserving their unjustified privileges. Honor thus is unmasked as an ideological front for unequal and illicit power. Honor groups have a sense of superiority that is often simply unwarranted, and anyway is incompatible with fundamental human worth and dignity.

- Honor is deeply complicit in violence. Honor has blood on its hands in such practices as: the so-called "honor killings" of women accused of sexual misconduct;[12] the "blood feuds" that stretch over generations in the Balkans even today;[13] the deadly duels over perceived slights in nineteenth-century Europe and America;[14] the ruthless violence that stems from "dissing" someone in American street gangs;[15] or the willing-ness of terrorists to "martyr" themselves in killing and maiming innocents. Born in the practice of war, honor cannot escape its ancestry. The honor of warriors in battle becomes extended to society in general, valorizing violence as an essential means of asserting and defending claims to honor. Honor dignifies a culture of self-assertive and vengeful violence.

---

[11] Honor's distance from morality also seems to follow from the first point: if honor lies in the eyes of others, it does not belong to oneself primarily; honor is social heteronomy ("other-law"), not moral autonomy ("self-law").

[12] Cf. Khouri, 2003, for one grisly example, though it may be more fiction than fact; Hirsi Ali, 2007, is more factual but equally grim. Such horrors are by no means confined to the Middle East.

[13] S. Anderson, 1999.

[14] Frevert, 1995; Kiernan, 1988; Peltonen, 2003; Wood, 2000.

[15] Cf. Horowitz, 1983; Jankowski, 1991; McCall, 1994; Shakur, 1993.

- Finally, the last straw, honor seems inextricably linked to patriarchy. Male warrior honor breeds peacetime male dominance, violently enforced. In honor groups, women are allotted only the prison of sexual purity, while men are free to gain honor by defending female honor, i.e. by controlling the sexual (and other) behavior of women. Women are reduced to lives of seclusion and oppression, so that men may have their public honor. Men may value honor's double standard, but it is not valuable to women.

This is a formidable bill of indictment, and many contemporaries doubtless think it settles the matter, enabling them to dismiss honor as a possible value for us. Were it truly proven, or fully true, there would be no question that we should welcome honor's obsolescence. In fact, so easy is it to agree with this way of looking at honor, that many will simply not even bother to consider the possibility that there might be something valuable in some of its forms. They will feel they do not need to pick up a book that considers even a partial defense of honor, for they already have consigned the concept to the outer darkness.

Yet I hope these cultured despisers of honor will reconsider. I have come to believe that their disregard of honor is deeply flawed and one-sided. Were the negatives just listed all that could be said about honor, I would not have written this book. Let me make it perfectly clear one more time that I am not an apologist for honor in all its forms and disguises; honor truly *has* caused much human misery, and it will not cease doing so even when it is better understood. Daily we learn of atrocities committed in honor's name: violent rapes, beatings, mutilations and killings; political acts of terror; and the subtler systemic damage of honor's complicity in social stratification, discrimination, elitism, militarism, patriarchy and machismo. No one who is honest about honor can deny the very great harms done daily in its name.

Even so there is more to honor than misery and domination, and there is more to be learned about honor — and also from honor. In these pages I lay out the following case:

Part I, "Concepts of Honor," is an essay in conceptual analysis. In it I distinguish among a number of distinct concepts of honor. Confusion about these different concepts is partially responsible for honor's eclipse today; in fact, at least six different concepts of honor may be distinguished (Chapter 2) so that we may better focus upon the central case: *personal honor* (Chapter 3). This latter concept is, I venture, something close to a human universal, though its various specifications, or conceptions, are not. This concept further needs to be distinguished from morality or religion (Chapter 4), and an exploration of what I call "deviant honor" will help us understand the concept via its internal standards of honorability (Chapter 5).

Part II, "Honor's Reach," is an effort at cultural interpretation. Here I consider personal honor's presence in and continuing relevance to a surprisingly wide swath of contemporary Western society, including war (Chapter 6), sport (Chapter 7), politics (Chapter 8), academe (Chapter 9), and other professions such as the law (Chapter 10). Surely something so pervasive deserves a closer look.

Part III, "Honor's Future," is a philosophical argument. I first respond to the prior bill of indictment, in light of the distinctions made in Part I and the range of relevance noted in Part II (Chapter 11). Personal honor is not cleared of all charges in all instances, but the condemnation is shown to be importantly incomplete. Finally, in the concluding chapter (Chapter 12), I explore honor's potential continuing worth and relevance to us. When suitably purged of unnecessary negative and local implications, I believe the concept of personal honor remains serviceable. Indeed, I think it holds great promise for all who wish to overcome dichotomies such as inner and outer, guilt and shame, individual and community, and who wish to deepen roots of self-respect as well as to strengthen bonds of loyalty and community in an increasingly fragmented and contentious age.

Doubtless even considering honor in today's intellectual climate will strike many as quixotic, almost literally so. But, unlike the man of La Mancha, I do not seek to re-live the romanticized values of a past now irretrievably lost. Rather, my hope is to recover aspects and dimensions of honor that have resonated with countless humans in the past and still may inspire us all today. There are dangers aplenty in reclaiming any traditional value, but we are not condemned, like Sisyphus, to simply repeat our dismal antecedents. As Alasdair MacIntyre has reminded us, ". . . when a tradition is in good order it is always partially constituted by an argument about the goods the pursuit of which gives to that tradition its particular point and purpose."[16] This book is an argument about the good of personal honor internal to the many traditions of honor. It is neither a whitewash nor a diatribe, but rather an honest effort to understand and to discern: to understand the full sweep of honor across human societies and to discern what enduring value personal honor might have for enlightened contemporary citizens of the world. It is therefore about human honor, as it might become *honor for us.*

---

[16] MacIntyre, 1984a, 222 (1981, 206).

Part I

CONCEPTS OF HONOR

Our study begins with the concept of honor — or rather with what we are seeking in a concept of honor. It will help to introduce a tripartite distinction among *concept, conception,* and *category*.[1] I will think of a *concept* as a characterization or set of features that can be variously instanced by more specific *conceptions.* Hence there can be many conceptions of the same concept. Complications arise, however, because there can also be more than one concept called by the same name, each with its attendant multiplicity of conceptions; so two conceptions nomsinally of the same thing need not be conceptions of the same concept of that thing. Where there are various concepts with the same name, it is an open question whether (and if so how) they can be brought into the higher unity I will call a *category.* The major possibilities are: (i) there is some systematic unity among all the concepts, perhaps some Platonic essential nature, so that there is a *univocal category*; (ii) there is no such commonality but only some looser relation such as Aristotle's "focal" analogy, Wittgenstein's "family resemblance," or paradigmatic cases, so there is an *analogical category*; (iii) the concepts share the same name only by sheer equivocation, and there is no true category at all.

I suspect concepts of honor, at least most of them, form an analogical category of some kind, but I don't want to argue that here; my concerns lie elsewhere. I have come to believe that part of the present disinterest, dismay or even disgust over honor is due not so much to lacking a clear category of honor as failing to distinguish among a number of rather different concepts

---

[1] I borrow the distinction between concept and conception (in part) from John Rawls, though not requiring that a concept must be characterized in terms of the role it plays (Rawls, 1971, 5); still, the roles honor plays in forming a certain kind of community are quite important.

each labeled "honor." Making their differences clear will help us address many otherwise intractable issues about honor, and it will help us see more clearly the instances of honor that we may find on every hand. Thus we need to embark on a short voyage of conceptual analysis, mapping the boundaries and contours of some concepts that should be at once familiar and unclear. I will distinguish among six important concepts of honor that surely occupy much of the logical space of any putative category of honor. Five of these, somewhat peripheral to my concerns even if prominent in popular regard, I will treat in the present chapter: *conferred honor, recognition honor, positional honor, commitment honor* and *trust honor*, but the sixth concept, *personal honor*,[2] my central concern, will receive a chapter of its own.

It is important to note that my map of honor's conceptual terrain is not the only possible one. Not only may there be still more concepts of honor to include,[3] but there may also be different points of view: perhaps one may devise different projections and highlight different distinctions altogether while mapping the very same territory I have surveyed. Here I can only ask my readers to consider things from my point of view, by trying out my analyses (Part I) and interpretations (Part II), before deciding that totally different concepts are needed.

---

[2] The term "personal honor" comes from Stewart, 1994, though I deviate from his characterization of this concept; in particular I construe it as a virtue and not as a right. It is important to stress at the outset that "personal" here doesn't mean "idiosyncratic," much less private: it is a person's commitment to a code shared with others as well as loyalty to those others. With personal honor, the personal is also, and essentially, social.

[3] For example, John Schellenberg has posited (personal communication) something he calls privilege honor, which is "what is referred to when, as so commonly, people speak of something they are experiencing as a great honor ('I feel so honored . . .', 'This is such an honor . . .', 'It's an honor to be here . . .') . . . .. [T]hey are referring to themselves as specially privileged." This is honor taken from the standpoint of the subject who feels honored, and it is a concept worth developing, though I have not done so here.

Chapter 2

____

FIVE PERIPHERAL CONCEPTS

I begin with two concepts of honor that are often difficult to distinguish in practice, even though I have sharpened their differences in the following account. Their distinction arises as follows. Consider any one of the myriad honors daily bestowed in our society: for example, the Academy Awards. The official account is that these annual awards recognize last year's finest achievements in various categories in the film business (at least from an American perspective!). The recipients, or winners, of the awards profusely express their gratitude for the great honor that has been bestowed on them, where the honor is clearly not the token presented at the awards ceremony (the actual "Oscar," the diminutive golden statuette), but what it represents: the recognition and approbation of their peers in the Academy of Motion Picture Arts and Sciences.[1] Everyone[2] agrees that this recognition adds value to his or her achievement by affirming its excellence publicly. But, as everyone knows, winners (especially of the major categories — best picture, actor, actress, director) are not always chosen solely on the basis of merit. There are sentimental favorites, rewards for pleasing personalities and disappointments for the unloved, paybacks for past (perceived) injustices, fads and fashions, etc. — a whole host of "subjective" criteria that are rarely absent, even if they do not always predominate. There is still high public regard (and its tokens), but now, as Academy voters if they were honest with themselves would admit, the basis for this regard lies (primarily) in the ones who honor and not in those honored.

The first kind of honor (others recognizing objective excellence) seems due, even when it goes missing — in hindsight, or at a distance, most can see the mistake. The second kind of honor seems a sheer gift, even when it is present. I call the first *recognition honor* and the second *conferred honor*, and

____

[1] The membership is only about 6,000.

[2] Well, nearly everyone. Some few refuse to accept the award — or even to attend the awards ceremony.

10

I will treat them in reverse order.

But first a word of caution: Pure cases of these and other kinds of honor are hard to find, as there are normally varying mixtures of each, and so it may be difficult in practice to disentangle the intertwined threads of conferred and recognition honor. The tangle is made even more complicated by the interested motives of both honorer and honoree: both have a need to believe that all is sheer recognition without admixture of conferring, when often something closer to the opposite is the case. Neither giver nor receiver of honor wants to think the basis of the regard of others is anything but the undiluted essence of objective excellence. When you have fans, or are one, you rarely ask probing questions about the basis of all this attention. Yet both are often self-deceived, in part or in whole. Still, it is worthwhile trying to distinguish in principle what we cannot always disentangle in practice.

I. Conferred Honor

The first, and most obvious, concept of honor I call "conferred honor." *Conferred honor* in the primary sense is the (sufficiently high) *regard* given by someone to someone else on some *attributed basis*. It is fundamentally reputation or even fame.[3] In a secondary sense, conferred honor is the token of this regard — gifts, rewards, attention and the like. The honorer must be a person or group of persons (perhaps a sub-culture, or even a whole society), and the honoree is normally a person or group of persons, though by extension honor may also be conferred on institutions (the Supreme Court), organizations (Amnesty International), artifacts (the flag), places (Thermopylae), or events (D-Day). The attributed basis consists of qualities the honorer believes are possessed by the honoree, in virtue of which the honoree should be shown high regard.[4]

Conferred honor is a relation, and indeed a relation that implies a certain dependence of the honoree on the honorer. The honoree does not have conferred honor intrinsically; someone else must confer it, and it consists precisely in that other person's high regard. If the honorer should cease to have high regard for the basis-properties, or should cease to regard the

---

[3] "Fame" is ambiguous among (i) simply being known by many; (ii) being well-known and also well-liked according to the values of the fans; or (iii) being well-known and also respected as worthy of fame according to (objective) standards of excellence. Only (ii) is conferred honor; (iii) is recognition honor (see below), and (i) is not honor at all (it is compatible with infamy).

[4] Complications arise where someone is honored because he is related to someone else who is the primary recipient of conferred honor — the basis is possessed by the latter, and may be less or even lacking in the former. Further, where someone is honored through another, the honor may diminish or vanish if the basis is attenuated in the second-hand honoree. For example, if the honoree is the son of a war hero, honored because of his father, the son's honor may diminish as the son is perceived to fall short of his father's heroic qualities.

honoree as having these properties, then the honor would be withdrawn even if the basis-properties should remain. Moreover, the honoree is not only dependent on but also inferior to the honorer. In noticing, selecting, and elevating someone for conferred honor, the honorer is implicitly elevating herself over the honoree. After all, the honorer's silent thought is: where would he be without me?

There is a basis for the honor — conferred honor is honor *for* something — but it is an *attributed* basis, something not only attributed but also valued by the honorer. Hence the basis need not actually exist, nor exist in the way supposed; all that matters is that the honorer supposes the honoree to possess that basis and that the honorer regards that basis highly enough.

In a sense conferred honors are possessions — it makes sense to say that the honoree not only receives but "has" them — but they are not ordinary possessions: they are not controlled by the owner nor owned by right. What is given may be withheld or withdrawn by the honorer, even when she has high regard for the basis-properties that she recognizes someone has. Conferred honor is not owed; it is a gift. So in a sense conferred honor is really owned by the giver, not by the recipient, even after it is given. Of course, the honoree may spend time and energy acquiring the basis-properties or calling the attention of the honorer to his possession of these basis-properties. But in the end, whether or not the honoree has conferred honor fundamentally depends upon another. Hence conferred honor is a possession only in the way that reputation is a possession.

Conferred honor is "external" to the person who has it, both in the sense that its conferral lies outside the honoree's control and in the sense that the person would remain the same person, though perhaps with diminished goods and self-esteem, should the conferred honor be withheld or withdrawn. This is not to say that conferred honors need be considered unimportant by the honoree; on the contrary, he may regard this kind of regard by others as vital. Still, few would feel their self-identity (as opposed to their self-esteem and happiness) is at stake in these matters.

Conferred honor, or at least its tokens, can in principle be quantified and counted; there are individual and aggregate conferred honors, so that one may speak of "an honor" or "many honors." An honoree may be the recipient of one or many conferred honors, and may accumulate a number of honors over a lifetime — more or fewer of them than someone else. Yet conferred honors also come in degrees or orders — some are "higher" or "greater" than others, in the sense that they convey greater regard by the honorer or regard by more honorers, are more rarely conferred, or are otherwise more highly prized. So honors conferred on one person may be greater than those conferred on another, and they may increase (or decrease) in degree as well as in numbers over time.

With conferred honor, appearance and reality coincide: to appear honorable is to be honorable, because how one appears to others simply *constitutes* one's (conferred) honor. Still, a secondary distinction can be drawn between apparent and real conferred honor: Since there is an attributed basis for the conferred honor, there can be mistakes of attribution. Perhaps the honoree lacks the basis altogether, or to the requisite degree, such that the conferred honor would be withdrawn should the honorer discover this lack. Baseless conferred honor rests on a merely apparent basis. Still, even a real basis is ultimately in the eye of the beholder — it is an attributed basis — and may be altered or withdrawn or replaced at the honorer's will. The reality of conferred honor remains in how it appears to the honorer.

Much of what gets called "honor" in our society is at least partially a matter of conferred honor. Consider the following diverse list: academic honors and honorary degrees, Academy Awards, appearances on "American Idol," celebrity banquets, championship trophies and rings, debutante balls, election to office, governmental appointment, literary and Nobel Prizes, MacArthur "genius grants," Medals of Honor, rock concerts, speaking invitations, and special appointments. Not everything in these honors is conferred, of course (Cf. Section II below). But none of these are pure cases of recognized excellence either. Often these honors bring material or financial rewards in their train — medals, prizes, awards and honoraria — but these are only *tokens* of the honor they express: winning a Nobel Prize is not so much receiving a large sum of money, like winning a lottery; what really matters to a scientific Nobel Laureate is the regard of fellow scientists (and perhaps of a wider public as well) on some attributed basis judged important.

Conferred honor has its attractions. Most people want to be well regarded by others, and the more the merrier. In addition, reputation transcends the limits of individual life — it is an immodest form of immortality. But at the same time conferred honor may be criticized in many ways. Agreeing with the criteria for high regard, one may doubt whether the honoree measures up ("he's really a coward," "her work is distinctly inferior"). Or one may quarrel with the criteria, considering the basis to be inadequate ("you call *that* important work?!") or unworthy ("she's the most outrageous talk-show host"). In a misguided and self-defeating egalitarian spirit, one might think no one should be honored without everyone being honored — "championship" medals for everyone! More deeply, one may sense there is something derivative and superficial about conferred honor: it originates with and is entirely dependent upon the values of the honorer. Conferred honor is indeed "in the eyes of the beholder." One should seek instead a sense of self-worth less chained to what others happen to believe and value about oneself; to live solely or fundamentally in the eyes of others is to be a mere reflection of a self, not a real self.[5]

---

[5] Mark Twain: "On the whole, it is better to deserve honors and not have them than to have

In sum, conferred honor is basically reputation, existing only in and through the regard of others. Were this concept all there were to honor, there would be very good reason for moral disinterest and dismay, perhaps even for moral disgust. But conferred honor is by no means the only concept of honor.

II. RECOGNITION HONOR

Recognition honor is public esteem of inherent qualities — I call them "excellences" — that merit or deserve such esteem. This recognition is at once awareness of excellence and also paying excellence its due, its appropriate tribute. It is showing, in a public way, through word and deed, that one not only notices but also reacts appropriately to excellence. There are four important, but debatable, components in this concept.

First, excellences are not constituted by their recognition but are prior to and independent of any recognition, and the person recognizing their excellence is aware of this priority; excellences are not made but found. This point is crucial, for if excellences were constituted by their recognition, then there would be no deep difference between conferred and recognition honor. By "excellence," therefore, I mean a value that exists independently of the recognition of others; excellences are in this sense "objective" values. But not just any objective values: excellences rise above the average of their kind, exemplifying their kind of value to a superlative degree.[6] Everything objectively beautiful has some value, for example, but only surpassing beauty rises to the level of an excellence; you may privately appreciate lesser beauties, but you should recognize those that are surpassingly beautiful.

Second, the notice and esteem are awarded at once to excellences, to their instances, and to their possessors, though in different ways. Excellences as such are the primary target, both as abstract quality and as exemplification: they are noticed, lifted up and praised for the *value* they have — or are — independently not only of the *valuer* (the one who values) but also of the *possessor* (the one who has this value). Now it may sound a bit odd to honor a value for itself; after all, that value is what it is regardless of what anyone thinks or says, and likewise its instantiation. Still, what recognition honor recognizes is not only that an excellence exists and is valuable, in *this* instance, but also that the value of the excellence exists, objectively and as

them and not deserve them."

[6] Friedrich Schleiermacher captures this notion nicely in his Christmas Eve dialogue (Leonhardt speaking): "One can extol or praise a thing in either of two ways: first in commending it, by which I mean acknowledging it and representing its kind and its inner nature as something good; but then also in honoring it, that is, giving prominence to its comparative excellence and perfection of its kind" (Schleiermacher, 1967, 70).

such, and has the surpassing value that it does independently of the recognition. The recognition is of the excellence as well as of its instantiation. A secondary target is the possessor of the excellence. If puzzle-solving is an excellence, for example, then the puzzle-solver as well as puzzle-solving (in general and in some instances) should receive recognition honor. But the possessor should not get too big a head: She is recognition honored only because of her excellence; her excellence is not honored because of her. Of course, only she, not her excellence, is *aware* of the honor. But that does not lift her above her excellence; on the contrary, the honors are given only because of and on account of her excellence.

Third, this notice and esteem of excellence (value, instance and possessor) is their *due*, not something gratuitous. Excellences are not persons, and so it may seem odd to think of them as due or deserving recognition, so perhaps it would be better to think of the recognizer as being obliged or required to recognize excellences; it is not the *excellence*'s due, properly speaking, but it is owed nonetheless. On what does this obligation rest? The basic idea is that recognition is required as the best, or the most appropriate, way to respond to great value, to align oneself with that value; recognition is a form of appreciation of value, the response appropriate to great value.[7] Recognition adds further value to excellence; although it is not a part of the excellence recognized, nor a completion of that excellence, it is a way for others to sympathetically share in that excellence. To fail to recognize excellence is either to fail to apprehend that something excellent *is* excellent or to fail to act appropriately upon that apprehension. Noticing but not recognizing excellence is not simply a lack but a failure, not only a lesser good but also a wrong, a fault of insensitivity, mean-spiritedness and smallness of soul.[8]

Fourth, the recognition requires appropriate *public* response. The honor required by recognition of excellence goes beyond correct apprehension to proper communication to others of that apprehension; recognition honor recommends an independent excellence to the attention and recognition of others. Further, there are restrictions on how that recognition is publicly conveyed: it should not be grudging but glad, not undercutting but fulsome, not envious but gracious.

Honor-seekers often confuse conferred and recognition honor, and they have strong ulterior motives for doing so: while basking in another's praise or notice, it is comforting to think that the honorer's criteria are objectively valid, that they are merely noticing an independent excellence. But the conferred honorer's attributed basis may be no such thing — it may only be

---

[7] Cf. Nozick, 1981, Chapter 5.

[8] If one thought that every wrong requires doing harm to someone, then the harm in this wrong would be self-inflicted; it goes to the person who fails to recognize excellence, not to the person who has the excellence.

something they happen to value in a manner similar to our own preference, and not something objectively excellent.[9]

Recognition honor has a motivational quirk that further helps distinguish it from conferred honor. Quite often the best way to get conferred honor is to seek it, to cultivate its potential donor and train up the qualities the honorer is likely to use as an attributed basis for conferring her honors. But pursuing excellence for the sake of recognition is often self-defeating: better to focus on the excellence first and foremost, lest one miss the mark. To be sure, being sensitive to excellence in others may spur one's own quest for excellence, but pursuing excellence only because others do is unlikely to be strong and focused enough to actually gain such excellence.

The recognized honoree need not be superior to the honorer (who may deserve recognition for the very same or other excellences), but is superior to many or most who lack the excellence (at least to this extent). Conferred honors may follow, but then they have a different basis: not the one attributed by the honorer but the one intrinsically possessed by the honoree. So the honorer is not in control of the honor; indeed, she is bound by the obligation to recognize excellence — the recognition is *due*.

There are, of course, difficulties with the concept of recognition honor. It shares the inegalitarian elitism of positional honor (see below), for excellences are as rare as top billing, even though recognition honor looks up to these excellences and not down from them (the traditional vantage point of the morally-dubious kind of elitism). The major concern is with the notion of objective value that crucially distinguishes recognition honor from conferred honor: some will doubt whether anything has value apart from someone valuing it, and excellences are constituted neither by the valuing of others nor by the valuing of the one who achieves or exemplifies them. Of course, if nothing does have this kind of objective value, then recognition collapses into conferred honor with its attributed basis.[10] Even if there are objective excellences, one still might doubt whether they can reliably be detected: perhaps we are all too prone to confuse what is locally admired with what is genuinely admirable. Further, one might question whether excellences ought to be publicly noticed; what's wrong with being content with private pleasure at something fine? Finally, some might worry whether recognition of excel-

---

[9] Abraham Lincoln wrestled with this issue, in different terms. At age 23, announcing his candidacy for the Illinois state legislature, he said, "Everyman is said to have his peculiar ambition . . .. I have no other so great as that of being truly esteemed of my fellowmen, by rendering myself worthy of their esteem" (Lincoln, in Basler, ed., 1953, 8). Was Lincoln more interested in conferred honor or in recognition honor, or did he conflate the two? I leave the answer to Lincoln's biographers.

[10] A pale after-image might still remain in the distinction between individual and social attribution: social attribution is antecedent to and largely independent of any individual's apprehension.

lence is a moral requirement; even if it does rise to the level of requirement, perhaps it's not a *moral* requirement. After all, not all excellences are moral goods: can it be a moral requirement to recognize non-moral goods?[11]

Yet despite all these difficulties, the concept of recognition honor remains distinct from conferred honor: the honorer controls conferred honors, while recognition honors are determined by the excellences of the honoree.

III. POSITIONAL HONOR

A third form of honor does not reside entirely, nor even primarily, in others' regard, even though it is often connected with conferred honor, nor is it necessarily recognition of an excellence, though excellence there may be. *Positional honor* is a matter of being, having or doing something that positions one "above" others in a group (culture, society). People with positional honor are society's "winners," in both literal and extended senses; they outstrip others in achievement or status; they are "better" (in some respect) than others; they are (or come out) "on top;" they have rank; they succeed. Gaining or occupying such a position is an honor quite apart from how it is regarded by others, though of course those with positional honor usually expect conferred honors as their due, and often receive them; at any rate, positional honor may be valued for itself, whether or not conferred honors follow.

Positional honor naturally divides into *achievement* and *status* honor. Achievement honor requires effort and accomplishment by an individual or group, while status honor consists in a certain relation to others, whether achieved, inherited or donated by others. The achievement may be a mere power-grab (dictators) but more often accrues in other ways: winning some actual competition (the Tour de France), completing a difficult and valued task better than others (Mozart), doing something extraordinary for the first time (Neil Armstrong, Edmund Hillary), displaying some particular excellence (Mother Teresa, Michael Jordan, Jane Austen, Bob Hope), and so on. Such achievement does require individual action, but it doesn't mean that great achievers are entirely self-made: although they normally have to train, practice and work hard (often very hard) to achieve their success, they typically parlay genetic luck, circumstantial opportunity, advantages of friends and family, assistance of others and gifts of fortune as well. Even so, they must fulfill their potential, seize their opportunities, take advantage of

---

[11] One further complication: perhaps some recognition honor is itself an excellence deserving recognition. To recognize excellence so excellently, so exquisitely aptly, so perfectly attuned both to the excellence apprehended and to the public to whom the apprehension is communicated — this recognition itself may demand recognition.

their advantages, and so on. Achievements are accomplishments on their own, but they also position the achiever above or ahead of others, and both aspects are independent of notice or applause by others.

Status honor, on the other hand, is social position or rank replete with influence, power and material goods, and may come through many sources: certainly achievement (getting rich), but also inheritance (daddy's genes, education or estate) and gift or recognition (the "honours list"). Status honor normally attends whole groups of people sharing certain characteristics (birth, wealth, talent, race, religion), though individuals may occasionally rise or fall in status on their own. Hence an individual's status is not always or entirely the product of the status of the groups to which she belongs.

It is difficult to disentangle status honor from conferred honor, as the "superior" social position wouldn't exist unless (most of) society agreed that those of certain qualities were indeed superior and then conferred (other?) honors on them. Nevertheless, it is useful to distinguish between the positional honor of *being* better (in oneself) and the conferred honor of *being considered* better (by others). Likewise recognition honor differs from positional honor: social position or achievement is not the same thing as excellence, or the only kind of excellence if it is indeed an excellence at all. Further, though both are relational notions, positional honor is viewed from the standpoint of the honoree, who is "above" the others, while recognition honor is taken from the standpoint of the honorer, who gives due acknowledgment of another's worth or value. Finally, there is this asymmetry: positional honor can exist without being recognized, but recognition honor cannot exist without excellence recognized.

Positional honor is relational or comparative. One who has it is "higher than" or "above" others; so without the others positional honor wouldn't be possible (Robinson Crusoe had no positional honor without Friday). As a result, positional honor is necessarily *inegalitarian* and *elitist*. Where there are winners there must be losers, and more of the latter than the former; this is as true of social position as of competitions and achievements. Not all are, or can be, equally positionally honorable; indeed, this inequality seems to be at the heart of positional honor: separating people into winners and also-rans gives the former something to be proud of (even to boast of) and the latter something to aspire to (or resent, envy or despair of).

But success tends to pride itself well beyond its actual status or accomplishments. Someone who wins a piano competition or a boxing title, for example, and thereby "rises to the top of the field," may view herself as superior to others in ways far beyond musical or athletic talent; Nobel Laureates may view their scientific success as a license to preach about political, social, philosophical or religious issues far beyond their expertise; and members of the inherited nobility may think they are inherently noble in character. But even when one confines pride to what is valuable in the actual positional honors attained, there can be an element of *hubris* through overestimation of the actual worth of the honor ("First Family of Virginia," "television personality," "celebrity"). In short, position is not necessarily an excellence that deserves recognition; positional honor is not recognition honor.

Unlike conferred honor, positional honor isn't quantifiable into discrete "honors;" rather, it comes in degrees or ranks: the best cook, one of the top golfers, a world-class economist, an influential commentator. One can of course mark individual successes along the way to positional honor, but just as one swallow does not make a summer,[12] so one achievement normally does not constitute positional honor — unless, perhaps, it is grand enough (witness Charles Lindbergh).

Positional status and achievement concern things that are generally valued in the society. Athletic prowess, beauty, intelligence, the ability to entertain or to make money — all are qualities enabling success in some domain (sport, media, science, Hollywood and Wall Street [sometimes!], respectively). Such success not only places one in a position superior to others but also is usually regarded highly by others: positional honor typically *generates* conferred honor. But this does not mean that positional honor *guarantees* conferred honor — after all, the superior performance may go unnoticed, and the winds of regard may blow in different directions — but rather that conferred honor normally does follow positional honor, because positional success is generally believed to be a proper basis for conferred honor. The prospect of conferred honor may in fact be why many seek positional success, but not necessarily; notoriously, one may climb the mountain simply "because it is there," not because others will notice and reward one for doing so.

Positional honor is not the same as social power, though the two are often closely linked. Those with higher position usually do have more power and freedom to pursue their aims ("power for"), satisfy their needs ("power to"), and compel or influence others ("power over"). But the connections are logically contingent. Status or achievement is not always recognized, and power may be "respected" more out of fear than admiration. Further, honor is a normative notion while power is not; positional honor claims to *merit* conferred honor, while power can only *compel* tribute.

Some might question whether positional honor is really *honor* at all, instead of de facto social status, achievement and distinction. But clearly positional honor is a normative, not a factual notion; it concerns rankings of higher and lower that are not simply reports of power differentials, and no merely factual property conveys its sense. The reason for thinking this normative concept is indeed a concept of *honor* is that while positional honor, unlike conferred honor, doesn't consist in others' regard, it is usually regarded as a proper basis of conferred honor, something that *should* be highly regarded.

---

[12] Aristotle, 1985, I.7.

Positional honor bedevils egalitarians. Absent some (frightening and anyway impossible) genetic and environmental leveling, people will always vary in their talents and achievements, and since there will inevitably be competitions, contests or struggles, it follows there will always be winners and losers in any society. Achievement positional honor therefore seems inescapable, and status honor follows in its wake. But at least some of the ill effects can be mitigated. Competitions need not have greatly disparate rewards (the "winner-take-all" syndrome); there can be social regulation of many kinds of payoffs. Further, not all competitions need be socially valued at all, and at the minimum persons should not be reduced in moral estimation to their positional successes and failures. Yet positional honor should not be universally deplored, for the success of some can benefit others, both in the extraordinary goods produced and also in the vicarious delight others take in the competitions and winning. Still, even if it is often worth having, or at least morally acceptable, positional honor is not an unadulterated moral good.

IV. Commitment Honor

A fourth sense of honor emerges when we consider such matters as honoring a promise or an agreement, or perhaps honoring a principle or ideal.[13] Conferred honor and positional honor, in their central cases, relate persons to persons, and may do so in recognition honor as well: the honoree receives regard from the honorer, has a status, makes an achievement, or receives recognition of his excellence that sets him "above" other persons. *Commitment honor*, however, relates persons to something more abstract — directly to principles and propositions, as well as to the illocutionary content of speech-acts such as promises and agreements, and only indirectly to the persons who exemplify or hold those principles. Commitment honor is honoring one's commitments to such principles, and thereby to the principles themselves, by believing and upholding them, keeping the promise, adhering to the pledge, etc.

Of course, the person must understand, in some minimal way, that to which he is supposed to be committed. One cannot honor a contract, for example, while ignorant of its provisions. Further, *depth* of understanding matters: commitment honor is increased by greater, deeper, more carefully nuanced understanding, while lack or defect of understanding betrays deficient commitment. Commitment to something certainly implies acceptance as well as understanding of that thing, but goes well beyond both — it also requires positive and negative support: positive in actively upholding and

---

[13] For example, John Rawls frequently speaks in Political Liberalism of honoring a political conception of justice or certain features of such a conception ("the proviso") (Rawls, 2005, 1).

promoting something, negative in refraining from disparaging that thing. Commitment is (optionally?) intensified if in upholding something one is also committed to bringing others to similar commitment, or at least to defending the object of commitment against others' deprecations. There are limits, of course, to most commitments, though religious devotion of one's entire life and self may stretch those limits.[14]

Commitment is manifest in speech but also, and especially, in action. Not only whether but also how (deeply, well) one is committed show themselves in what one says and in what one does. Commitment implies a fairly consistent pattern of behavior with respect to its object, not transitory adulation; it also implies a coherence of speech and action, for to say one thing and do another is hypocrisy, not honor.

Commitment honor is not always a good thing. Just as conferred honor may be objectionable if granted to an unworthy honoree or if the attributed basis is deficient; just as positional honor may be criticized if it reflects wrong or exaggerated or misplaced criteria of success; and just as recognition honor may be limited by ability and inclination to properly value excellence; so commitment honor may fall short, in several ways. Most obviously it may be *misguided* commitment, to a defective principle (e.g. National Socialism); but it may also be *inappropriate* commitment, according too much or too little regard to one principle in relation to others (forgetting to temper justice with mercy); or it may be *inadequate* commitment, binding oneself less than required for genuine loyalty (nominal assent, minimal follow-through).

Commitment honor is a limited concept of honor. It does not imply the kind of achievement that confers positional honor; it does not always attach itself to excellences deserving recognition; and few if any conferred honors are awarded to someone who merely honors his promises and agreements. Greater positional and conferred honor may be given to someone loyal to some grand principle, particularly if the principle is held in very high regard, if adherence to the principle is unusually difficult, or if someone is unusually deeply committed. Indeed, such unusual commitment may well be regarded as an excellence deserving recognition. But commitment honor does not usually rise to such levels.

---

[14] Cf. Tillich's "ultimate concern" (Tillich, 1957). I realize that some ultimate concerns may be lodged in persons, however extraordinary, but even so they typically concern that person as exemplifying some principle (virtue, excellence) to which he or she is committed. Even for Tillich God is the trans-personal "Ground of Being."

V. Trust Honor

A fifth peripheral concept of honor I call *trust honor*.[15] In fact, it just *is* a certain kind of trust of a person. In this form of trust we not only rely and depend on another, but we also *credit* that person as reliable and dependable, as worth relying upon, to varying degrees. Further, the credit is not private but a joint venture with others.[16] Such credit — i.e. the actual *crediting* — is a conceptually distinct form of honor. Trust honor is more than loyalty, sticking by a person; it is also upholding to others the trusted person as worthy of trust. It is likewise more than respecting a principle that someone instantiates (a form of commitment honor); it is respecting the person herself.[17]

Trust honor overlaps with recognition honor, but they are not the same. Crediting (trusting) someone may be based on, lead to, or result from recognition of some excellence in that person, but not necessarily. Perhaps trust entails some degree of perceived trustworthiness in its recipient, and hence some degree of perceived worth, but not necessarily any degree of excellence. Conversely, you may recognize someone's excellence without trusting her very much at all outside the range of her excellence (consider professional athletes and rock stars).

There are many forms of trust honor, but let me single out two for special notice: (i) We may trust someone to *act* reliably according to principles lodged deeply in character. While we may be unable to predict the trusted one's behavior with complete certainty, we can count on her actions conforming to principles ingrained in her character. She does what she does because she is who she is. Athletes can count on their teammates' support; buddies or mates have your back; combat comrades don't leave you behind. (ii) We may trust someone's *word*, in several ways. First and foremost, we may trust him to say what he believes and to believe what he says; he does not dissemble about his own self-perceived cognitive condition. He is truthful in speaking what he truly affirms or denies, or at least what he sincerely believes to be so, even if he happens to be mistaken about what is the case. Second, he acts as he speaks, whether in fulfilling promises made, carrying out announced intentions, or practicing what he professes to believe. A trust-honorable person, therefore, is worthy of being trusted because she can be counted on to speak truthfully and to act without hypocrisy or deceit.

---

[15] "To believe, to trust, to rely on another, is to Honour him; signe of opinion of his vertue and power. To distrust, or not believe, is to Dishonour." Hobbes, 1968, I: x, 153. Important works on trust include Gambetta, 1988; Shapin, 1994; Weber and Carter, 2003.

[16] Cf. Shapin, 1994, 38: "to trust is to join with others and to show estimation of their worth; to distrust is to disrupt cooperative relations and to dishonor."

[17] Complications: Honoring someone's rights combines commitment and trust honor; it is not simply commitment to an abstract principle of right — though it is that — but also loyalty to particular concrete persons; respecting the person through respecting her rights.

Trust is vital to all human communities, and not just ones that are labeled "honor groups." Without trust in caregivers, human infants do not thrive. Without trust in others, social cooperation and coordination are impossible, and a person is cut off from meaningful human relations. Without trust, as Steven Shapin has brilliantly argued, even human knowledge is severely impoverished; knowledge as we know it is actually a social concept, carrying us beyond our meager individual experience to the wider world of human fact and value, and trust lies at its foundation (Shapin, 1994).

Trust honor can be independent of the social hierarchies that constitute positional honor. Indeed, in some ways trust honor may undercut positional honor. Granted, members of social classes tend to trust one another more than they trust outsiders, and granted also, differences of all kinds, including ones of status and achievement, may hinder or block trust. Hence relations between social superiors and inferiors may be founded on repression or oppression rather than trust. But even so trust may spring up independently of position: even masters and slaves may come to trust one another in ways that subvert their fundamentally oppressive relationship. Of course trust establishes its own kind of hierarchy — based on degrees of trust — but this hierarchy may lie athwart the usual ladders of status and achievement.

While trust *is* the basis for many if not all human groups, such trust may also *have* a basis, whether in native impulse or in prior dealings. One may trust another out of a sunny disposition — trust is your default attitude toward others — or because that other has first done, or been credibly reported as doing, acts that seem trustworthy. One basis for trust deserves special mention: you may trust another because he has first trusted you. Here trust responds to trust, not diffusely or generally, but to specific trust given, received and reciprocated. Trust generates trust, and nourishes itself. We are all engaged both in spinning and in living upon a social web of trust.

Trust honor comes in degrees and amounts. We may trust someone more or less and with regard to more or less. Not everyone seems, or is, fully trustworthy, in all respects and on all occasions. One person may be a reliable team player on the field and at work, but you might not credit her with the courage to speak truth to power. Another may be trusted in solidarity with a group to which one belongs (political party, church, club), but not as a personal friend. Even experts have their limits, and unconditional trust should be reserved, it seems, for superhuman persons.

Trust need not be reciprocated, and so there may be mismatched trust as well as misplaced trust. You may trust another less or more than she trusts you, and your relationship may be a dynamic interplay of different kinds and ranges of trust, mistrust and even distrust. One-sided trust fosters inequality, but the advantages are not all to the trusted one, even a complete free rider. Receiving trust while not giving trust seems an effortless gain, but there may be unnoticed costs: the trusted free rider may overlook the ways trust enlarges capacity, builds useful and enjoyable solidarities, and enables future agencies.

Trust honor may be necessary for human interaction, but that doesn't imply that it is always desirable. Like commitment to principle, trust of persons may be *unguarded* (naïve trust), *misguided* (trusting the untrustworthy, or those limited in their trustworthiness), *inappropriate* (trusting one person more or less than others, or at the wrong times in the wrong ways) or *inadequate* (too little trust where more is warranted). Trust may become credulity or gullibility; it may lead to the confirmation bias of seeing only good in those one trusts; and it may simply get one into the wrong crowd. Trust is a good normally only when appropriately placed in someone trustworthy.

It is fruitful to compare and contrast the five peripheral concepts of honor. One important contrast is that conferred and positional honor magnify the honoree, while recognition and commitment honor tether the honorer, and trust honor does both. Of course, in sincerely conferring honor on someone the honorer presumably is committed to certain pro-attitudes and friendly behavior towards the honoree. But the focus of conferred honor is on the honoree: it is her qualities and person that are being honored. In positional honor status and achievement raise some above others; they are social rewards and advantages that normally elicit but don't require the acknowledgment of inferiors. In commitment honor the focus is reversed: of course the honoree is held up for regard, but the emphasis is on the honorer — does she have steady, faithful allegiance, or fitful, weak and limited commitment? Recognition honor likewise tethers the honorer to the honoree, but in different ways: recognition gives due regard to concrete excellence, commitment is loyalty to abstract principle. Trust honor is independent of conferred and positional honors, and overlaps recognition and commitment honor.

The opposites of the five kinds of honor also differ: the opposites of conferred honor are disrepute, disdain or disregard in the eyes of others; for positional honor, they are inferior status and mediocre or negligible achievement; for recognition honor, insensitivity, grudging acceptance, envy, and rejection; for commitment honor, betrayal (of principle or agreement) and indifference (lack of commitment); and for trust honor, suspicion, distrust and disloyalty.

Each of these five concepts of honor is interesting in its own right, and to some they all seem endlessly fascinating.[18] Nevertheless, they are distinct from

---

[18] One part of their fascination is connection with leadership. But honor and leadership are distinct, even if leaders are often honored, in various ways, and often rightfully so. A most important topic, rarely considered, is whether there is a connection between leadership and the concept of honor we will take up in the next chapter: do personally honorable people make good leaders precisely because of their personal honor?

and peripheral to the concept of honor that is central to this book — a concept I call *personal honor* — even though several of these peripheral concepts play central roles in personal honor: Those with personal honor necessarily belong to some honor group, and honor group members mutually *recognize* one another's excellence in personal honor, are collectively *committed* to the group's honor code and *trust* one another. These features, along with others, will be developed in the next chapter.

Chapter 3

PERSONAL HONOR

The sixth concept of honor, *personal honor*, differs significantly from the five peripheral concepts, though it incorporates several of them, particularly commitment and trust honor. It is a complicated but readily intelligible and surprisingly familiar notion, one that may be explicated in various ways. I will construe it from the standpoint of having an *effective sense of honor*, which is a *Janus concept.* Just as Janus, the Roman God of portals, had two faces, looking both inward and outward, so having an effective sense of honor has two kinds of feature that cannot be separated, though they may be distinguished: personal honor is a virtue of an individual in a certain kind of social setting.

First and foremost, an effective sense of honor is a matter of inner disposition, a trait of individual character. It is measured in terms of how deeply a person is able and disposed to live and interact with particular others in terms of a certain conception of honor — to what extent honor has become a personal *virtue.*[1] Such personal honor is more than mere integrity, self-consistency, commitment or responsibility; rather, it means adhering firmly to the *honor code* of some *honor group* and being loyal to its *members.* To use concepts previously introduced, personal honor requires commitment-honor to an honor group's honor code and trust-honor of the members of that group.

On the first point, having an effective sense of honor requires understanding what a group's honor code requires, prohibits and permits, being able to act according to the code, being motivated to do so, and effectively willing it. A person with a sense of honor treats her actions falling under her honor code as *matters of honor*, to be done *from* honor, motivated essentially by principles of honor, and not merely *according to* honor for other reasons or out of interests that have nothing to do with honor. She is committed to acting honorably as well as to acting as honor requires. Personal honor therefore has a deontological motivational structure, valuing commitment to principle above calculation of consequences.

---

[1] But not necessarily a moral virtue. Cf. Chapters 4–5 below.

Moreover, commitment to honor typically goes deep; a person with a full sense of honor regards her honor as one of her more important features, indeed as necessarily connected to her sense of self. Without her honor, she is diminished, defiled or ruined, perhaps even to the point of being unable to face the prospect of living in dishonor, so that exile or even suicide can seem preferable to a dishonorable life. Of course, not every part of an honor code runs so deep, as viewed from the outside. Rules of honor range from apparently minor matters of dress, speech and "manners" to more consequential matters involving harm and benefit to others. But persons of honor take their honor seriously and as a whole, and they will tend to be punctilious in all matters of honor. No matter of honor is trivial, and none may be ignored.

By speaking of an honor *code* I do not mean to imply that it is, should be, or even could be explicitly *codified*. It is, rather, a mixed bag of rules, principles and ideals guiding conduct, affecting motivation, and luring appetite. But these rules are not usually made explicit, for several reasons: the code is too complicated, subtle, nuanced, profound and comprehensive to be set forth in its entirety; often the rules may be minor ones which no one want to take the trouble to formulate; the code permits wide latitude of interpretation and explicit rules may constrain proper interpretation; explicit rules must not assume priority over implicit ones; reliance upon or undue interest in the explicit letter of the law casts suspicion on one's commitment to its spirit; and each person of honor is ultimately responsible for maintaining his own honor, not some legal authority.[2] Of course not all have the same level or depth of implicit understanding, and there will be occasional disputes about the proper application or adjudication of the honor code; in such cases there will typically be appeal to some authority. That authority, however, is never an explicit rule, but always someone's "local" interpretation of the code.

Typically an honor code contains rules of requirement and prohibition dealing both with insiders (other members of the honor group) and with outsiders. Rules for treating insiders will normally be more elaborate, for there the subject and object of action is a person of honor,[3] and honor is honed in interaction with those capable of recognizing and responding honorably to honorable treatment. But there are also rules for honorable treatment of outsiders: rules of hospitality, generosity, sanctuary and rescue. Why should there be such rules where there is no expectation that the recipients (aliens, strangers, fugitives, refugees) will be able or willing to reciprocate, appreciate or even recognize the honor given? Here honor is bestowed as a gift,[4] and that

---

[2] Outsiders may suspect a rather different ground: perhaps the honor code cannot withstand scrutiny if exposed to the light of day? But one cannot harbor this suspicion and remain a committed member of an honor group.

[3] I put aside complications of those regarded as honor group members who aren't themselves capable of acting from honor — the disabled, minors, incompetent, etc.

[4] That is, it is a gift from the standpoint of the recipient. But the honorable giver may see it as a

I believe is a clue as to at least part of its role. A gift-giver rises above a recipient of gifts, acquiring superior status and merit; the recipient is in the giver's debt, even if it goes unrecognized. An honor group's honorable behavior to outsiders is a way for the group to elevate itself above those outsiders — at least in the eyes of those who truly count, other honor group members. But rules for treatment of insiders are not gifts; they mark the respect due other members of one's honor group.

One might also divide the rules of an honor code into three parts (all codes will have the first part, most the second, but only some the third): (i) *the primary code* of requirement and prohibition, consisting of rules for which actions or omissions are required, prohibited and permitted to gain and retain honor in that group;[5] (ii) *the secondary penal code*, consisting of what must be done when someone breaks the primary code;[6] and (iii) *the tertiary redemption code*, consisting of what is required of those who, having broken the primary code and received the penalty, now seek re-admittance back into the honor group.[7]

But an honor code is not just a set of *principles*; it also contains, implies or at least coheres with *ideals*. The principles may be viewed as minimal standards, the floor for honor-space. They are dos and don'ts the violation of which renders one *dis*honorable. Ideals, however, urge or lure one beyond the minimum; they are the honor heights, the perhaps unreachable ceiling of honor-space. Ideals may be approached, more or less, but never fully realized; falling short renders one less honorable, but not necessarily less than honorable. Moreover, the honor-space may be more or less expansive: both principles and ideals may be demanding or easy, though ease of following or achieving is not a prime consideration for honor groups. To illustrate the distinction between principles and ideals, consider an academic honor "system": its principles will prohibit academic cheating, at the bare minimum, but its ideals may urge honorable behavior (intention, motivation) in other, perhaps even all, aspects of life (cf. Chapter 8).

Honor codes vary from honor group to honor group, but there are common

matter of honor, an obligation. The crucial point is that even so the obligation is to other honor group members, not directly to the recipient of the hospitality or other gift.

[5] This primary code in turn might be divided in two further ways: first, with one part of the code serving as entrance requirements and the other part as ongoing membership requirements; second, with rules for not insulting others (e.g. rules of courtesy) and rules for defending against insults (attacks on one's honor).

[6] Typically breaches of honor must be punished at least by loss of trust and hence of status in the honor group, quite often by exile or exclusion from the group, and sometimes by something worse. Detecting the breaches and adjudicating and administering these punishments is a group responsibility, even though various actions might be required on the part of individuals (e.g. calling out dishonor to oneself, dueling).

[7] There might even be further rules for recidivists, though not many honor groups would tolerate as many as two strikes; if it can be regained at all, honor cannot be regained easily.

elements. A warrior's honor code emphasizes bravery and loyalty under lethal threat; an athlete's honor code expresses sportsmanship; a theist's code covers honoring God as well as man; an academic's code regulates inquiry, argument and pedagogy; and so on, variously, for other groups. But all honor codes will require trust of and loyalty to other members of the honor group, commitment to the group's honor code, fidelity to one's word (at least to other members of the group), courage in standing up for the code and other members, and the like. There is a thin but recognizable common code of honor — not a full code, to be sure, but perhaps its core — across vastly different honor groups, as well as the structural similarities I am concerned to emphasize.

But recall that personal honor is a Janus concept. Even though it is indeed a matter of individual character and connects deeply with individual self-identity, nonetheless personal honor is intelligible only in terms of a certain social backdrop; it is loyalty to a community and commitment to that community's code. It involves belonging to a certain kind of social group, the *honor group*, consisting of all and only those members who recognize one another as sharing the same sense of honor.[8] This sense of honor has two sides: on the one hand, as we have just mentioned, it means understanding and being effectively committed to an honor code, the same code for all members of the same group; belonging to an honor group means adhering to a set of rules that is socially shared and publicly supported.[9] In this way personal honor contains commitment honor — commitment to the core constitutive principles of the honor group. This commitment is personal but shared.

On the other hand, a sense of honor also involves *mutual regard*[10] for the other members of the honor group: not only acknowledging their membership in the group and deferring to their prerogatives of honor but also monitoring and evaluating their behavior and character (according to the shared code); honorable people care about others' senses of honor. Here personal honor involves (but is not limited to) trust honor — trust in the other members of the honor group. In both respects (commitment and trust) personal honor is thoroughly public even though its locus is in individual character; it is enacted on a public stage that is a union shop, even if not everyone belongs or can belong to the local actors' guild.

---

[8] Certain capacities underlie this sense: a person must be honor-capable in being able to understand and govern himself by a code of honor, must be attuned to apprehending honor in others and defending it in oneself, and so forth. This is a complicated topic, but not central to our concerns. Note, however, that not everyone may have the capacities required to belong to an honor group, or to a particular honor group, and that even if they do have these capacities, they must actualize them through instruction and practice.

[9] Cf. Solomon, 1992, 221.

[10] This regard is not necessarily based on recognition in the sense defined above (giving excellence its public due). It is at once awareness of actual concrete persons as fellow members of the honor group, trust of them to be honorable (according to the group's code), and loyalty to them appropriate to their honor status.

Mutual regard contains an additional requirement: to be worthy of such regard by others entails standing up for oneself, asserting one's own honor. "Rightful honor (*honestas juridicum*) consists in asserting one's worth as a human being in relation to others . . ." (Kant, 1996, 29; cf. 210). Kant is speaking of moral worth, but a parallel claim can be made about honorable worth, what one might call *honorability,* or being worthy of being honored. Honorability is not a passive condition, but consists in proper self-regard manifesting itself in capable public defense of rightful claim. Self-regard (and assertion) and other-regard (and defense) are inextricable.

One may sharpen this sense of mutual regard by noting that it is a distinctive form of *respect,*[11] both self-respect and other-respect — and the one because of the other. Such respect is not *deference* depending on fear or favor, giving way to superior power or for ulterior ends. Nor is it the *esteem* that positional honor may attract — e.g. valuing someone, including oneself, because of her position (achievement, rank, status) is really esteeming the qualities she exemplifies, the attributed basis for conferring honor. You salute an officer because of the office, not the person. But the respect involved in personal honor is something more — positively valuing not only certain qualities and relations but also the person who has (or is believed to have) them. It is close to respect in Kant's sense (moral *Achtung*), regarding certain others as worthy in and for themselves, but without extending that regard to all — only fellow members of one's honor group are given such consideration. Moreover, this respect is nearly a primary social good in Rawls' sense (Rawls, 1971), one that it is rational to want more rather than less of independently of whatever else one wants — *provided* that one seeks to be a member of some honor group. Self-respect and the respect of respected others are normally deeply treasured, and constitute one vital source of honor's appeal.

It is worth re-emphasizing personal honor's *public* nature.[12] Belonging to an honor community is not simply joint commitment to the (abstract) principles and ideals of an honor code, nor is it that plus trust of the actual individuals comprising that community. It is also thoroughly public by requiring mutual awareness all around of all these forms of sharing: Each member is aware of the shared code and the other members' commitment to that code, and also of one's trust of those others and their trust of oneself; everyone is aware that everyone is aware of all this, and so on. Personal honor thereby entrains collective as well as individual responsibility: an honorable person is bound not merely to maintain her own honor but also to aid in communal housekeeping, such as detecting and ridding the community of dishonorable individuals. One might say that honor groups have a public

---

[11] Of course this respect is from and for those regarded as equals, not inferiors.

[12] Cf. Rawls, 2001, especially §9, on a fully public conception of justice and the notion of public reason.

solidarity that involves but transcends common commitment to code and trust in one another — binding both by public mutual regard.[13]

As with most communal values, *ancestry* is important to personal honor. The honor group and its code will have a definite history or tradition, typically extending back into the mists of time. This tradition, while continuous, is quite compatible with change, revision and development, though contemporary members of the honor group will choose to focus on the continuity rather than the changes. Personal honor as a *tradition* within the history of the same honor group constitutes the group as an honor group. Honor groups are not created in a day, nor ex nihilo by an individual, but require the nurture and devotion of generations. Some honor groups assign further roles to ancestry — e.g. counting "breeding" and "blood" as important determinants of honor — but this is to confuse positional (and perhaps conferred) honor with personal honor. Consanguinity may reinforce ties of trust, but only the latter are essential to honor. The true importance of ancestry for personal honor is that it expands the honor group over time: one's loyalties are to past as well as present members of the honor group. Even more, present members of the honor group are potential ancestors to future members. So an honor group extends forward as well as backward in time, thereby expanding but also blurring the requirement of mutual recognition for group membership.

Personal honor may be lost in various ways. Most obviously it may be lost through one's own doing — in words, deeds or their omission violating the honor code or betraying the trust of other members of the honor group — and to this extent it seems within an individual's control. But personal honor is not entirely up to the individual, for it may be challenged, diminished, and even lost, by others as well.[14] Honor is impugned by insult and offense, and both show the solidarity of honor, how it is lodged in both group and individual. *Insult* is a direct challenge by another, "calling one out" as dishonorable;[15] if there is no response, or the wrong kind of response, both label and reality of dishonor stick. The dishonor of an insult is not simply that one has failed to defeat its challenge, but also that someone else has succeeded in getting away with making the challenge, independently of whether it is true or false. *Offense* (in a somewhat technical sense) is an indirect challenge, where someone for whom one has honor-responsibility, such

[13] It follows that there cannot be an honor group of only one person, except as she is the isolated remnant of a formerly larger group. But the public condition also places a limit on the maximum as well as the minimum size: Mutual awareness is possible neither in a crowd of strangers nor in isolation.

[14] I put aside the loss of perceived honor, which is distinct from actual honor in the case of personal honor — though not in conferred and perhaps other types of honor.

[15] Note that the challenger must qualify: typically only members of the same honor group, or of another recognized honor group, can truly insult, not someone regarded as without honor. Someone "beneath contempt" is not a recognizable threat to one's honor.

as a family member, behaves dishonorably or is insulted by another. Here one's own honor can be preserved, or restored, only by rectifying (perhaps punishing or compensating for) another's dishonor.[16]

Dishonor, or loss of honor, links three quite different aspects of "inner" and "outer." First, dishonor involves the individual's *guilt* for breaking or falling short of full commitment to the honor code, and also his *shame* for betraying or falling short of trust in the members of the honor group.[17] Second, both guilt and shame may be noticed by the individual or by the group; the individual then *feels* guilty or ashamed, and the group blames or shames the individual. Of course the guilt and shame may be merely privately felt, if the dishonorable deed is undiscovered, but a person of honor will feel guilty and ashamed to the extent that her sense of honor is effective. Third, personal honor is therefore *both* self-regarding *and* other-regarding. Guilt bears witness to the honorable person's commitment to principles that are her own as well as those of her group, and shame to her loyalty to particular others. Dishonor is loss not merely of integrity but also of community — rupture not so much with an idealized kingdom of ends as with an actual group of honorable peers. Honor *is* a matter of "face," how one looks to others, but it is equally a matter of inner depths, one's hidden subjectivity, how one is to and for oneself. Once again personal honor shows itself to be a Janus concept.

Honor groups are fundamentally *egalitarian*, resting upon every member's presumed capability for personal honor and upon the mutual recognition, indeed respect, across the honor group. The mutual regard members of an honor group have for one another qua members is an *equal* regard for *equals*, in several ways: it extends equally to every member of the group; it regards those others as equally capable of honor; it regards them as equally willing to acquire honor (though not necessarily equally successful in actualizing this capability); it considers them equal in their commitment to honor and in their trust of other members; it is equal in both directions; and all members of an honor group are equally entitled to claim, indeed, are obliged to demand, such regard from every other member.

Of course, fundamental equality in honor doesn't mean equality in all things. Toward outsiders, honor groups are often elitist, and may be

---

[16] To the outsider, insults may seem gratuitous or self-serving, and on occasion they may indeed be nothing more. But they may be honorably motivated as well: to insult someone is to call her honor publically into question, and if she is in fact dishonorable, then others are honor-bound to notice and rectify that dishonor. So insulting someone may sometimes be precisely the honorable thing to do.

[17] There is a vast literature on the alleged differences between "guilt" and "shame" cultures. But I have found the distinction slippery and varying among different authors, and I think it a mistake to view whole societies as either one or the other. Rather, by adopting the distinction made here, I signal my belief that guilt and shame are integrally related to one another, at least in honor groups, however much one or the other is emphasized. So construed, guilt and shame are equally, and necessarily, connected to personal honor (for more on this topic, cf. Chapter 12).

superior (or inferior!) to outsiders in attainments, roles, status and the like.[18] Toward one another, honor group members may be unequal in several ways: they may have unequal offices (leaders or followers) by roles within the honor group; they may be unequal in actually achieving the honor of which all are presumed equally capable; they may be unequal in both capacity and achievement of *excellence* in personal honor; and they may fulfill the local ideal of honor more or less perfectly. Still, every member is equally bound by the code and by group loyalty, and regards every other member in this light. Outsiders who do not have the same sense of honor are viewed as deficient or even defective — they are sometimes deemed incapable of honor and so may lie "beneath contempt" (in terms of honor), whereas no member of the honor group is *beneath* contempt, however contemptible.

Personal honor is not status honor, a positional honor that usually comes automatically from membership in some group, but it does resemble achievement positional honor. It is a *personal achievement*, not something one has simply in virtue of innate, inherited, or other features beyond one's control or for which one is not responsible, but it is a special kind of achievement. First, it is not necessarily a competitive achievement; one person's gain need not be another's loss.[19] Second, its target is not an action but a state of character. Third, personal honor achievements are not permanent conditions; they may be gained, lost, and, sometimes, regained. Personal honor, therefore, is not a static condition nor an exchangeable possession, but rather an active personal attainment, something that requires considerable ability, purpose, tenacity and practice. One acquires personal honor by acquiring those habits of heart and mind that dispose and enable one thoroughly and intuitively to follow the honor code of one's honor group, and to recognize, respect and trust the members of that group. Honorable character is both learned through and expressed in honorable actions, and it is an individual's responsibility to achieve this character.

Personal honor is also intrinsically, sufficiently and effectively motivating for its possessor, not (only) something instrumental to something else, and not a weak or ineffective motive. Once an act or omission is seen to be a point of honor, for a person with an effective sense of honor it is not a matter of reflection or calculation whether or not to do the honorable thing. Of

---

[18] Since personal honor doesn't derive from status honor, it is not essentially tied to the traditional social roles that generate status, contra Berger (1970). Still, personal honor may be useful for performing those roles and maintaining that status, particularly if there is some need (or pretense?) of merit justifying the positional honor they have.

[19] Of course (as Nat Goldberg has pointed out to me), some honor groups may have codes requiring the humiliation of others to obtain positional honor in the group, so that achieving personal honor in these groups is a competitive struggle. But, as we shall see in Chapter 5, such groups are deviant from the standpoint of honor. Honorability certainly doesn't require zero-sum competition for honor.

course, discerning what honor requires in a particular situation may not be easy, and considerable reflection or counsel may be needed. But once an act is determined to be honorable or dishonorable, an honorable person qua honorable simply must do the honorable and avoid the dishonorable thing, regardless of other considerations to the contrary.[20]

At the heart of personal honor are two virtues, I will call *trustworthiness* and *loyalty*; they are really two sides of the same trait. An honorable person can be counted on both to be committed to the honor group's code and to remain steadfastly loyal to the other honor group members — and to do both without hesitation, question or calculation. The point is not simply predictability, but rather reliability — an honorable person can be relied on by others to act in solidarity *with* and *for* the other members of the honor group. An honorable person reliably and consistently guides her actions by her internalized sense of honor, and she is worth trusting because of her reliability. She is trustworthy to those to whom she is loyal, and she is loyal to those she regards as trustworthy.

Other virtues enter at this point as well. Courage, integrity, truthfulness, responsibility and the like are all often essential in living an honorable life. It is tempting to think of personal honor as a kind of meta-virtue that over-arches and encompasses such virtues as these.[21] But I think it makes more sense to regard personal honor as a distinct virtue — the disposition to be trustworthy and loyal — and to view the virtue of honor as closely allied to and supported by those other virtues.

Qualifications deemed necessary for membership may vary across honor groups, and they may not be applied flawlessly in any group; groups may err in thinking that some persons do not or cannot qualify for the group. Honor groups have traditionally used features such as sex, race, paternity, culture, religion and social class to delineate the set of honorable persons, but these marks may have little or nothing to do with what it actually takes to be honor-able according to that group's true sense of honor. What really matters for membership in an honor group is honor-capability, which includes not only cognitive and conative capacities but also actual motivation and determina-tion. In addition, there are frequently entry challenges and tests, as well as rituals marking rites of passage.

So any honor group likely has the potential to be indefinitely larger than it actually is. Yet there are important reasons why honor groups tend to be relatively small and exclusive — the size of Achilles' band of warrior-heroes, for example, or of Robert E. Lee's fellow landed Virginia aristocrats, or the

---

[20] David Luban captures a further point about excellence in honor-motivation: Oliver Wendell Holmes, Jr., he believes, ". . . displays the ultimate sign of good character: it never even occurs to him to be dishonorable" (Luban in Burton, ed., 2000, 46).

[21] Cf. Solomon, 1992.

students at a small undergraduate college.[22] The point of an honor group is to bond members who not only share the same sense of honor but also can and do *mutually regard* others who have the same sense of honor — who can and do verify others' honorable intentions and actions, can and do "honor" those others not only with trust but also with appropriate respect. The larger the group, the harder it is to regard, verify and reward others' honor. Size matters in honor groups because face-to-face regard matters. The anonymity of city streets may have many desirable features, but strengthening personal honor is not one of them. Unnoticed and even unnoticeable personal honor is headed down Peter Berger's garden path of historical "obsolescence."

Personal honor, like all virtues, is not all-or-nothing. It varies across societies and individuals. There is no such thing as an "honor society" pure and simple, but rather only varying degrees of importance attached to personal honor in that society. Some societies are greatly enamored of honor, even consumed by it, but no human society, I venture, is entirely without an awareness of honor, however dim, or without a concern for honor, however weak. Social groups likewise vary in their exemplifications of personal honor — or, if you like, in the degree to which they can intelligibly be viewed as honor groups. Similarly, some individuals are more conscious of and devoted to honor in their lives than are others, but few are insensible to honor's call, however faint. In short, personal honor comes in many kinds of *degrees*: societies and groups are more or less concerned with honor; individuals are more or less honorable.[23]

To this point I have said little about the concept of personal honor's relations to the five peripheral concepts treated in the previous chapter. In part this is precisely because these other concepts are *peripheral* in a normative sense: personal honor is the vital valuational center of honor, and the other concepts depend on it for their worth, at least they do so for us, in the following ways.

---

[22] Historian Emory Thomas claims that a collegiate honor system such as the one that descends from General Lee's Presidency of Washington College "is an elitist system that depends upon a relatively small, homogeneous student population" (Thomas, 1995, p. 397). There are three independent claims here: (i) I think Thomas is partially right about size, but wonder what he means by "depends upon;" I don't think there is a necessary or conceptual link, but only a contingent empirical dependency. For honor to work, mutual public regard and reward of honorable behavior and character are required, and it is hard to see how this can occur in too large a group. (ii) The homogeneity claim is ambiguous — it all depends on the kind of homogeneity in question: certainly an honor group cannot be heterogeneous in adhering to different honor codes, but there is nothing about honor that precludes other kinds of heterogeneity, including gender and race differences. (iii) The elitism claim depends on whether honor is moral or not (cf. the next chapter).

[23] Societies, groups and individuals may exemplify the concept of personal honor as I have explained it without necessarily making the concept explicit to themselves, much less using the word "honor" to name this concept.

- Conferred honor may be bestowed upon a person for her personal honor, but not always and not only; it entirely depends on who is bestowing the honors, and why. The mutual recognition of honor group members may resemble conferred honor, but its basis is a code shared by honorer and honoree, not a standard supplied (and controlled) solely by the honorer. The reputation of an honor group member is not only in the eyes of other members but rooted in the honoree's character in a way that preserves equality with the honorer.

- Recognition honor is a vital part of the mutual regard at the core of personal honor: public celebration of excellence is what those with personal honor take themselves to be doing when they hail one another. But there is more to each kind of honor than their overlap: recognition honor recognizes many kinds of excellence, not just personal honor, and personal honor's regard of other members of the honor group extends beyond recognition of excellence: it is all the myriad ways of respecting others who respect you, even if excellence is not involved.

- Positional honor may reflect personal honor, but often it does not. Human achievements are various, and they do not correlate well with personal honor; single-minded focus on achievement may even hinder proper concern for the recognition of others' honor. Likewise social status is not a reliable indicator of personal honor. However devoutly social elites have sought to convince others (and themselves?) that their success is a sign of virtue, it remains the case that members of the "nobility" are not always noble.

- Commitment honor is necessarily ingredient in personal honor: a person with personal honor is committed to the rules of her honor group. Keeping faith with others, being true to one's word, honoring one's promises are all essential aspects of personal honor. But personal honor is much more than commitment to principle — it also requires loyalty to honor group members — just as commitment to principle is found outside contexts of personal honor.

- Trust honor is also an essential part of personal honor: a personally honorable individual trusts the members of his honor group (including himself). But not all kinds of trust are incorporated into personal honor; and trust anchors personal relationships of all kinds. So trust and honor sometimes go their separate ways.

These peripheral concepts of honor lose importance for us if disconnected from personal honor. But can personal honor stand alone as the pre-eminent virtue of a human life? Is there nothing higher? Here we must trace the relations of personal honor to morality and religion, in the next chapter.

Chapter 4

PERSONAL HONOR, MORALITY AND RELIGION

The concept of personal honor embraces widely different conceptions of personal honor. Personal honor is an achievable virtue of individuals with the requisite capacities in a certain social context: it means someone possesses an effective sense of honor, understands and is committed to the honor code of some appropriately sized honor group, and openly trusts the members of the group, as they trust him, to act accordingly. Honor groups will naturally differ not only in their membership[1] and their (perceived) qualifications but also, especially, in what their honor codes require and prohibit, so that what is regarded as honorable and dishonorable by one honor group may not be so regarded by another. In short, personal honor is relative to time, place, and group.

I. Morality and Honor

Personal honor so construed seems on a collision course with morality. There are deep and possibly intractable issues here, but on many characterizations,[2] morality contains action-guiding prescriptions or principles that are, or at least claim to be, valid for any and all autonomous agents, and are also over-riding for them. No agent, it seems, whether in or out of any honor group, can avoid the requirements of morality, and these requirements trump all others, at least in crucial contexts. But only the members of a particular honor

---

[1] But not exclusively. Persons may be members of different honor groups at the same time or serially, and discordance may result upon occasion: conflict of principles or conflict of loyalties, and sometimes both together.

[2] Some construe morality differently. Alasdair MacIntyre, for example, holds that morality is relative to a particular kind of tradition of virtue, and on his view it will be impossible to distinguish honor from the morality of certain kinds of society (MacIntyre, 1984a, 1984b, 1988). Alternatively, Jonathan Dancy thinks morality doesn't require principles at all (Dancy, 2004). But these are minority voices, for whatever that is worth in philosophy!

37

group are subject to its distinctive code of honor, and however powerful the motive of honor may be for honorable members, its honor code is not over-riding for outsiders. It follows that personal honor is not necessarily moral honor, and this is plain to view: what honor codes require often lie *outside* of moral requirement and prohibition — in dress or manners, for example — and may even go *against* moral principle — such as snubbing, brutalizing or even killing non-members out of loyalty to the group, beating up or dueling with fellow group members in order to defend one's reputation, or wearing a mask of silence in covering up immoral group activities.[3]

Most honor codes do contain features that certainly *seem* moral. Consider, e.g. David Hume's characterization of honor as "keeping faith, observing of promises, and telling truth" (Hume, 1994, 294). These are doubtless features of moral significance, and they also belong to most honor codes. But what morality requires may be contained in an honor code without the code requiring it as a matter of morality. The primary commitment of a personally honorable person, as such, must always be to the honor group and its code, *whatever that code may be.* Truth telling and the like count as personally honorable *if, but only if,* they are part of the honor group's code. Unfortunately, there is no shortage of honor groups where lying, cheating and stealing are permitted, at least on occasion against non-members, and perhaps even against group members (e.g. when one has been insulted). So truth-telling and the like pertain to particular conceptions of honor only if they are included in or constrain the code of the particular honor group. The same holds true for other moral features such as respect, equality, fairness, duty and the like. Most honor codes require some kind of "respectful" treat-ment of other members of the honor group. But this is not necessarily a *moral* respect — it may just be equal regard only for other members of the group, not necessarily regard for everyone nor acknowledging the intrinsic dignity of anyone. So if Hume's "keeping faith" and the like are indeed universal features of honor they are not necessarily moral, and if truly moral they are not universal among honor groups.

Honor as a virtue, therefore, is not an unconditional good; its goodness is conditional on the ends and rules of the honor group, and these may conflict with morality. Only where the honor code essentially contains or is constrained by moral principle may we be sure honor does not stand at odds with morality, and this will not hold for all honor codes. Yet, I believe,

---

[3] An alternative, even more Kantian way of characterizing morality brings out the same contrast with honor in a slightly different way. Moral duty requires respect for all moral agents as ends in themselves and permits acting only on principles that are acceptable to all such agents (and that would be accepted by them were they fully rational). In short, moral duties are categorical. But honor duties are only hypothetical, requiring full respect only for fellow honor group members, with different kinds of regard (not necessarily full respect) for non-members. Non-members may be treated well, to be sure, but this generosity does not stem from a categorical imperative.

it is at least possible for an honor code to be not merely de facto consistent with morality but to be *necessarily* in agreement with morality. I will call this latter *moral personal honor* or, more briefly, *moral honor*, remembering that it picks out only one kind of conception among many different conceptions of personal honor.

There are two ways to construe moral honor. One is where morality is embedded *inside* the honor code. Here the honor code contains at least some moral prescriptions and these dominate non-moral ones — not in the sense that they take more time or energy or occupy the forefront of life but in the sense that they triumph in the case of conflict, ensuring that the morally honorable person, as such, cannot perform an immoral act in the name of honor. Moral rules are internalized within the honor system as rules of honor, and indeed they may be held more fervently and followed more scrupulously as rules of honor than as general moral rules.

The other way to construe moral honor is where morality lies *outside* the honor code but constrains or overrides it in cases where honor and morality conflict. Perhaps the code could contain explicit fealty to morality (for example, "these rules of honor hold only where all the moral rules are satisfied"), or there might be an implicit tradition of deference to morality by members of the honor group when conflicts do arise.[4] Members of the honor group might feel that their honor code is somehow ratified or even specially singled out for approval by morality, and so have extra ties to morality. But the important point is that while matters of morality are distinct from matters of honor, they do not conflict because they cannot conflict.

In both construals of moral honor, one should not suppose that apparent conflicts between honor and morality never arise or that, when they do, there is always some higher-order rule for settling all conflicts between them — just as there is none for settling apparent conflicts within the non-moral part of the honor code. Rather, what tends to settle such apparent conflicts for an honor group — if they can be settled at all — is some *honor authority*, some person who is, or is recognized by honor group members as being, in the best position and best qualified to adjudicate the matter.[5] This person may be the conflicted individual herself, but typically in honor groups it is some experienced (often literally battle-tested) elder with appropriate knowledge of the group's traditions and the particular circumstances. This does not mean that the elder's judgments are necessarily correct or even decisive, much less enforceable, though they may be so, but that they are generally regarded as wise and perceptive, (much) more likely than most to produce a solution to the matter at hand consistent with the honor

---

[4] Rarely would there be acknowledgment that morality is more important than honor.

[5] Recall that an honor authority may also be needed to settle disputes internal to honor groups over interpretation and application of matters of honor (cf. p. 27).

group's traditions. The elder speaks for the ancestors and tradition, for the continuity and integrity of the honor community over time.[6]

So while personal honor *need* not be moral (in all conceptions), it *may* be moral (in some conceptions), and in these latter it may be so *necessarily* — i.e. it may be consistent with morality because its particular honor code contains moral principles or is constrained by them. But what good is honor in addition to morality? Can't we just get along with morality alone? I believe that personal honor is worth having because it does add something to universal morality that even moralists might recognize as valuable. As a set of universally binding and overriding principles, morality is rather abstract and general, lacking in motive power. What moral honor adds to morality are social embeddedness, concrete power of motivation, possibly a sense of individual identity, and even a meaningful life (cf. Kateb, 2000).

First, all personal honor requires membership in an honor group with a shared sense of honor that is public, and this is crucial in the case of moral honor. Such honor is more than adherence to abstract general principles contained in the honor code; these principles more particularly express how to enact one's honor: in a sport, what constitutes sportsmanship; in war, what constitutes legitimate killing; in academic honor systems, what constitutes cheating; how to honor your parents, react to insult, etc. These specifications enable honor group members both to understand what they must do in particular situations and to be motivated to do what is required in those situations. Personal honor also requires concrete interpersonal relation — loyalty to a particular group of people who mutually notice one another's commitment to each other and to the sense of honor they all share. Living up to others' expectations is a powerful motive that may reinforce adhering to one's own principles; the power is multiplied when those expectations and principles are shared by self and other — for all members of the honor group.

Next, whereas morality anchors a sense of self to universal features, so that the moral self is in principle *any* self and hence verging on no particular self at all, honor embeds a sense of self in a particular community with a concrete code, so that the honorable self is in practice a very definite sort of self — and quite possibly a more enticing self. Finally, having a meaningful life involves having a sense of relatedness to a wider context — ultimately a sense of the whole. Honor groups mediate that holistic sense by connecting individuals to past, present and future honor group members and thereby to a set of background assumptions about human life and beyond. One may certainly live a meaningful life outside an honor group, but membership in such a

---

[6] Nothing in this paragraph implies infallibility, much less authority outside the honor group. Moral outsiders may have quite contrary views!

group can make meaningfulness concrete and compelling.

These, then, are at least some of the ways moral honor can add something important to morality.

Moral honor is not just following moral rules, nor even being a member of a group each of whose members follows the same moral rules out of the same internalized sense of morality; it also involves mutual recognition of particular others' commitment to the same rules and loyalty to the same people out of the same sense of honor. There is in moral honor a concrete particularity and therefore a vitality and depth of personal trust that undergirds commitment to the moral rules. A morally honorable person is committed to moral behavior in considerable part because she is committed to the honor code that contains or is constrained by moral rules, but also (and perhaps more strongly) because through these rules she is loyal to the honor group — loyal to particular people who are loyal to her and to the same moral rules. Moral honor therefore has at least the potential of deepening and enriching moral commitment — but only *moral* honor. Honor unhinged to morality has the demonic power of inspiring horrifically immoral acts, whether in the name of a supposedly higher cause (jihad) or in thrall to a perverted sense of morality (patriarchy or racial supremacy).

II. Religion and Honor

Personal honor is often intricately linked to religion,[7] but the connections I believe are contingent. Despite frequent and fervent belief to the contrary and despite common usage reflecting those beliefs ("my sacred honor"), honor is not necessarily religious, and religious requirements are not necessarily matters of honor. In this regard, honor stands to religion as it does to morality: frequent (though varying) close historical associations but no necessary conceptual connections. But also, just as there may but need not be moral personal honor, so there may but need not be *religious personal honor* or *religious honor* for short.

Religion is even more flamboyantly multifarious than honor, displaying such various and vibrant shapes that no single concept, much less category, seems to do them justice. Different forms of religious life might well have different affinities to different concepts and conceptions of honor, and conversely, and so it would be hopeless to attempt a blanket characterization of religion's relations to personal honor. Nevertheless, something of the general line that seems most plausible to me may be conveyed through glimpses of

---

[7] Elsewhere (Sessions, 2007), I have explored the (optional but useful) roles the concept of personal honor might play in theology; here we are concerned with the relations of personal honor to religion.

certain versions of *monotheistic* religion, religion that somehow incorporates belief in exactly one god.[8]

A monotheistic religious community may be structured as an honor group, with many of its rules of belief and practice construed as matters of honor and subject to a code of honor. This code may be considered divinely instituted and authorized, and the force of obligation to the code is therefore "sacred," construed as obligation to God and so taking precedence over all other requirements. God may also be construed as a perfect honor group member, upholding always and completely all the requirements of the honor code and respecting all honor group members unfailingly and unsurpassingly, and exemplifying fully the implicit honor ideals. Moreover, divine recognition defines the limits of group respect, for God observes not only what one publicly does but also what one privately believes and feels and desires; for God there is no distinction between what is and what merely appears to be personally honorable. All this makes being honorable before God not only very exacting and difficult but also extremely urgent and momentous: to be respected by God is the very summit of other-regard, and it is impossible to escape divine notice.

As in the case of morality, the relations of religion and honor vary. Sometimes religion is quite external or distant to an honor group, and sometimes the relation is merely contingent. But sometimes the relation can be necessary, again in internal and external ties: the honor group may internalize religious principles and make them overriding; religious belief may be a membership requirement; and religious obligations may be held as matters of honor. Or the honor group may defer, occasionally or generally, to religious principles or requirements, viewed as edicts from an authoritative source outside the honor group that trump all principles of honor. Religious honor ensures that the religious requirements will be satisfied, whether as matters of honor or as an obligatory deference to honor.

What do personal honor and religion (monotheistic religion at any rate) add to each other? What advantages are there to *religious* honor? The situation is not the same as honor's relation to morality — there honor augments abstract universal principle with concrete codes and definite relationships to particular persons — but the following relations may be suggested:

- Human notions of honor may lie at the root both of many religious communities and of their conceptions of God. In the history of human religiosity, concepts of honor may precede and condition theological ones, serving as one very important way of specifying divine–human relations. This is by no means antithetical to religious concepts of revelation, for

---

[8] I don't mean to imply all monotheistic religious traditions are the same in all respects; it is enough if many are at least similar in the ways I note.

God may well speak to a culture via concepts familiar to it, and may establish rules, practices and institutions that build on cultural antecedents.

- In a religious perspective, honor is elevated and deepened: seeking respect not just from other humans but also from God raises the stakes for being honorable. God is not just all-knowing but most high, the Creator and Ruler of the universe, and the self-respect that comes from divine regard cannot be equaled in height, breadth or depth.

- Viewing an honor code as religious duty (to God) strengthens its sense of overridingness, and may contribute to thinking that the honor code is universal as well: since there is one veracious God for all, an honor code established by that God is neither provincial nor provisional but universal and absolute. Such a sense of honor may displace or overwhelm morality (honor seems more important than morality), or it may be viewed (incorrectly) as morality itself. Here we are on dangerous ground indeed: religious honor may compete with morality or moral honor in claiming human allegiance. But it need not do so, for religious honor may be constrained by morality in the ways we have previously explored. Still, *moral religious honor* differs from moral honor and religious honor just as moral honor and religious honor differ from personal honor more broadly construed.

- Honor-bonding to other human members of the honor group is strengthened if it is viewed as divinely sanctioned, and this strengthens the religious community. In such a context, there may well be more fervent devotion to the code and greater loyalty to other members: *faithfulness* to other humans as required by personal honor dovetails with theistic *faith* in God, such that the two may even be identified, though they are not in fact the same.

Yet despite these religious connections to honor, it is clear that religion, morality and personal honor in general are only contingently linked: different religious communities have different codes, whereas morality is (or claims to be) universal, and different religious communities do not always regard other religious communities as true honor groups (outsiders are "infidels," "heathen," "gentiles," etc.), whereas no one is excluded from the moral circle, nor inferior within it. Likewise there may be non-religious honor groups, even though one can easily see how and why an honor group might desire divine sanction and blessing.

Chapter 5

DEVIANT HONOR

There is no honor among thieves — or so the saying goes. Thieves are devi-ants, and "[t]o the general public, the term 'deviance' refers to knavery, skullduggery, cheating, unfairness, crime, sneakiness, malingering, cutting corners, immorality, dishonesty, betrayal, graft, corruption, wickedness, and sin" (Cohen, 1966, quoted in Liska, 1981, 1). So how could deviants possibly be honorable? Still, we are often drawn to deviant persons and groups: the "thieves," after all, include pirates, gypsies, street gangs, and Mafiosi, among many colorful others. This interest might move us to re-examine the cliché: do thieves and other "deviants" truly lack honor? Or, do we only think they lack honor because they deviate from what *we* honor? In this chapter, I wish to explore some varieties of deviant honor. The result may disappoint those who want either a unified account of all deviance or an exposé (or perhaps exoneration) of particular deviant groups. Instead, I propose to examine some less-well-appreciated issues of deviance in relation to the concept of personal honor. My goal is neither to applaud nor to excuse deviance, but primarily to deepen our understanding of personal honor by seeing what deviates and what is deviant from it. We will come to see how the very criteria of honor as such — what I will call *standards of honorability* — point towards certain forms of honor as central and other forms as deviant *qua honor*. This will become important to the case I lay out in Part III about the kind of honor that can truly be "for us."

I. DEFINITIONS

Let's start by distinguishing some unfortunately like-sounding terms that are readily confused; I think I have captured ordinary usage, but if not, then consider these technical terms:

- *Difference* (variants *differ, different, differing*) is the widest category, embracing all varieties and degrees where one thing is not the same as another in some respect. Of course, if A is different from B, then B is different from A, and no value judgment is entailed one way or another by difference as such. Difference is not always value-free, but it is not necessarily value-laden.

- *Deviance* (*deviant*) implies a negative value judgment of some action, behavior, person or group that differs in certain respects from what is regarded as the standard or normal (in the sense of normative) case. With deviance, difference does entail (negative) value

- *Deviation* (*deviate, deviating*) is often confused with deviance, but it should be carefully distinguished. Deviation is difference from some standpoint but *without* disparagement.[1] Whereas difference can be valuable, worthless or indifferent, deviation entails that there is no value judgment one way or the other.

- *Derivation* (*derive, derived*) is difference that originates from one or another of the differing items. It comes in many sorts, including causal, historical, logical, semantical and symbolical derivation. Deviance and deviation sometimes derive from the standard case (perhaps even in conscious opposition to it), but this is not essential to either of them. Standard and deviant cases may have entirely independent origins.

To label something as deviant, therefore, does not merely note a difference or a deviation, nor does it primarily assign derivation, but rather it expresses the labeler's belief that the difference noted is sub-par, lacking, defective, or even dangerous in some respect(s).

[Some technical points: difference, deviance, deviation and derivation are all relations: no act, person or group can have any of these properties by itself; they are so only in relation to some other (one or many) act, person or group. In all these relations, the relation can be considered from some related item as a *standpoint*. That standpoint has varying significance: deviance's standpoint is regarded as a *standard*, something normatively proper or better (the deviant case is always {regarded as} worse than the standpoint); deviation's standpoint is only for comparison, not for evaluation; and derivation's standpoint is a temporally or causally prior *origin*. Only in deviance, therefore, is the standpoint a *standard* or *norm*. If A is deviant from the standpoint of B, then A is inferior to B; but if A deviates or derives from B, then either or neither may be superior to the other. So while difference is

---

[1] A similar distinction applies to the standard or norm according to which deviance or deviation is measured: it usually means a positive standard or rule (so that deviation is deviance), but can also, at least in statistical contexts, mean some kind of an average (mean, median or mode), with deviation having neither negative nor positive connotation. Likewise normal can mean either normative or usual — or often both at once!

a normatively symmetrical relation, and deviation and derivation are non-symmetrical, deviance is normatively *a*symmetrical.[2]]

Is deviance subjective? That is, does it exist only in the regard of the one who judges something to be deviant? Differences may be subjective or not, and likewise deviations, so long as the standard is not taken to be a positive value or norm. But the standpoint from which something is deviant *is* such a positive value or norm — or at least it is regarded as such by those who label deviants. Of course, without the labelers, there would be no deviance, and so deviance is relative to labelers, and subjective in that sense. At the same time, this labeling, when correctly applied,[3] is also objective, picking out real differences in deviant acts, persons, and groups. But the crux of this worry lies elsewhere: the deviant is judged inferior, lesser, substandard, misguided and improper. What about these values? Are they subjective or objective? I don't propose to settle this deep issue in a paragraph. I merely note that judgments of deviance are in no worse shape than any other value judgments: If (some) value-judgments can be objective, then so can judgments of deviance, in the same sense.[4]

II. Sociology

Deviance-theory, as I shall call it, is a substantial subfield of sociology, with enormous popular as well as scholarly interest. What does it have to contribute to our understanding of deviant honor? Perhaps less than one might hope. First off, deviance-theory embraces a vast array of phenomena as diverse as crime, delinquency, suicide and drug addiction, but also sometimes including mental illness and retardation, physical handicaps, sexual orientation, nudism, "infamous occupations,"[5] and even some aspects of racism, sexism, terrorism and the like.[6] There have been various attempts to construct a "general theory of deviance,"[7] but it seems unlikely that there is a unitary phenomenon

---

[2] A complication: Derivation is asymmetrical as such: If A is the origin for B, then B cannot be the origin for A. But this asymmetry has no normative implications.

[3] By "correctly applied" I mean that the labeler properly applies the objective criteria inherent in the label: she does not mislabel, does not apply the proper labels to the wrong things, e.g. by calling an arraigned or indicted but unconvicted person a "criminal."

[4] Social scientists, who are congenital social relativists, need to give more weight to the fact that those who make deviance-judgments do not often regard them as socially relative: quite often deviants are thought to be morally defective, and few moralists will concede that moral judgments are subjective or socially relative in their normative core. But still, this issue is far too large and complicated to be settled by such appeals.

[5] Not just prostitutes but also executioners, skinners, beggars, etc. Cf. Blok, 2001, p. 44 for a rather long list.

[6] For general introductions to deviance-theory, cf. Bridges and Desmond, 2000; Jensen, 2007; Calhoun et al., 2005; Downes and Rock, 1995; Goode, 2007; Kubrin et al., eds, 2009.

[7] Cf. e.g. Akers, 1973; Becker, 1966; Gottfriedson and Hirschi, 1990; Little, 1989; Schur, 1971;

to explain.[8] Some sociologists even seek to include "extraordinary" (positive deviating) behaviors and groups in this field of study,[9] but the dominant view conforms to our usage in Section I: the deviant is judged negatively from the standpoint of some presumed standard individual or group.[10]

Further, sociologists are not agreed on the very concept of deviance.[11] They do agree that deviance is normative deviation from social norms, rules or standards, not statistical averages; that deviance comes in degrees; that it is socially, culturally and temporally relative; that it cannot be viewed solely as an individual or arbitrary phenomenon but "reflect[s] patterns and processes of social definition" (Schur, 1971, 4). Beyond these points, most sociologists are content with the simple notion that deviance is violation of social norms negatively viewed and sanctioned by those holding such norms (cf. Goode, 2007, III: 1075; Bryant, 1990, xxi; Jenkins, 1998, 135). Some focus more on the social response to violations, whether it is mild "disapproval" (Smith, 1995, 178) or strong or even "hostile" reaction (Sagarin, 1975, 9; cf. Little, 1989, 3). Some de-emphasize the negative reaction, calling something deviant just if it "departs significantly from social situational expectations" (Dodge, 1990, 83). Others have more colorful labels for deviants: "the mad, the bad, the odd" (Downes, 1999, 232) or "nuts, sluts, and perverts" (Liazos, 1972, who is criticizing this type of view). Perhaps the fullest depiction, if not quite a definition, comes from Liska, who thinks sociologists agree that deviance involves departure from social forms (at a given time), violation of group norms, or straying from a standard, and is proscribed because it is somehow thought intolerable, with adverse treatment of people and behavior so labeled (isolation, correction, punishment, banishment); the two chief elements are norm violation and social labeling (and censure) (Liska, 1981, 1–4).[12]

Tittle, 1995; Wolfgang and Ferracuti, 1967.

[8] Downes and Rock, 1995, "hold that deviance cannot constitute a single problem with a single solution" but rather a "great kaleidoscope of theorems" (7). As a result, "the sociology of deviance has failed to be cumulative. It is an extended train of partially examined and partially exhausted ideas" (367).

[9] Kephart and Zellner, 1994. Dodge, 1990, Goode, 1991, and Smith, 1996, argue for a concept of "Positive Deviance," but this move is strongly criticized on behalf of the discipline by Sagarin, 1990, who takes "deviance" to be viewed in society as "negative, deplorable, devalued, disvalued, disreputable, undesirable, disgusting, frightening or in some similar manner" (101). Cf. also Best, 2004; Fogarty, 1990; Kanter, 1972; Kumar, 1990; Levitas, 1990.

[10] Of course, as many authors insist, this doesn't imply that the sociologist must agree with the judgment she describes; so abolitionists may be described as deviant in a slave-holding society without embracing that society's norms. Perhaps sociologists should put scare-quotes around "deviant" to neutralize the word's normal [!] normative force.

[11] Likewise the concept of honor: many sociologists seem to conflate it with status or reputation (what I have called positional honor and conferred honor, respectively), though some have a more nuanced understanding.

[12] Sagarin, 1975, in Part I, 'The Idea of Deviance', has a good discussion of what deviance is not (e.g. deviation, criminality, marginality, abnormality), though his positive definition (as "disvalued people and disvalued behavior that provoke hostile reactions") seems partial at best.

But even if there were a unitary phenomenon to be understood, and a clear concept in view, there seems to be disagreement about the kind of understanding sociology seeks: is it full-blown theoretical causal explanation of how individuals become deviants and/or how social groups construct deviance and grow, maintain and decrease deviants (cf. Smith, 1996; Kubrin *et al.*, 2009)? Or does sociology seek an empathic sense of what deviance means to both deviant and non-deviant groups and individuals? Those who pursue causal understanding are likewise divided; in one breakdown of the contending types of theory (Kubrin *et al.*, 2009[13]), there are trait theories ("the criminal mind," etc.), social disorganization and anomie theories (family breakdown, lack of meaningful work), functionalism (deviance maintains or undermines social stability), conflict and control theories (groups maintaining dominance through sanctioning and disciplining threatening behavior and groups), and labeling theory (deviants are made by the rules they violate, which are made in turn by dominant groups).[14] Add to these "the Chicago perspective" (social ecology) and "ethnomethodology" (phenomenology) (Liska, 1981, Chapters 3 and 6), among others. In another view there are different "levels" of explanation — e.g. biological, psychological and sociological ones (Liska, 1981, 8–13; cf. Little, 1989, 12). Doubtless there are other types of explanation, as well as different ways of partitioning the types, with various kinds of proposal to "integrate" the various types, which are not always consistent. In short, the explanatory field is unsettled at best, in chaos at worst.

Sociologists are also interested not only in promoting general theories of deviance but also in exploring other aspects of the phenomena: one concerns the ways in which persons or groups come to terms with the "deviant" label, and the psychosocial mechanisms at work. Another is the "deviantizing process" itself on a macro level — perhaps a "stigma contest" where different groups contend to label threatening others (Schur, 1980) or at any rate some kind of social process of constructing deviance and deviants. Another is the role that deviance-construction plays in social stratification, in conferring status and position for groups, as well as maintaining or disrupting social stability: "Crime and deviance are . . . the dominant censures of the day" (Sumner, 2004, 28). A fourth concerns how deviance connects with power,

---

Schur, 1971, Chapter 2, ends in the "working definition" that "Human behavior is deviant to the extent that it comes to be viewed as involving a personally discreditable departure from a group's normative expectations, and it elicits interpersonal or collective reactions that serve to 'isolate,' 'treat,' 'correct,' or 'punish' individuals engaged in such behavior" (p. 24, emphasis removed). Compare Lofland, 1969: "Deviance is the name of the conflict game in which individuals or loosely organized small groups with little power are strongly feared by a well-organized, sizable minority or majority who have a large amount of power." (Quoted in Schur, 1980, 12.)

[13] Bridges and Desmond, 2000, give an illuminating alternative classification: micro v. macro origin or reaction theories.

[14] Some would say labeling is more a "perspective" (Sagarin, 1975) or an "approach" (Schur, 1971) than a "theory."

particularly political power, but also "moral" power or authority (Schur, 1980). A fifth explores how deviance connects with identity, how one sees self and others, both from the side of the deviant and from the side of the standard person (Jenkins, 1998, 137f.). A sixth (and for some the most important payoff for study of deviance) is designing and evaluating public policies to address deviance regarded as a social problem.

These are all legitimate areas of study, and contribute much to our understanding of the pervasiveness, depth and importance of deviance in human societies; some of these concerns will connect with the following pages. But my present concerns mostly lie elsewhere. I am not seeking causal explanation, nor a general account of all deviance, nor connections with status, stability, power or identity. I am also not interested in exploring how people become, or avoid becoming, deviants, nor how deviance is socially constructed in concrete cases. Rather, I want to deepen understanding of (the concept of) personal honor. What I am exploring in this chapter are some of the boundaries of that concept, as well as some of its internal valuational structure. In the terms we have been using, I aim to clarify deviations from the central cases of personal honor, both beyond and within honor: when the deviation becomes something other than honor, and when it becomes deviant honor.

It is important to stress that the starting and enduring standpoint for our inquiry is not society at large, nor the dominant class or group that has the economic, social or moral power to label deviant groups and individuals, nor even the often contentious relationship between labeling and labeled groups, much less individuals however honorable or not. Rather, our standpoint is the *honor group* — some particular honor group when assessing other particular honor groups (and non-honor groups), or a generalized standard honor group when exploring deviations and deviants in general.

One final point about sociology: Sociological theory both guides and informs empirical inquiry, but quite often the study of particular deviant groups and behaviors results in thick/rich descriptions that read like anthropological ethnographies of "other" societies: richly detailed outsider glimpses into different (slices of) ways of life. These thick descriptions can be of great interest even if one doesn't share the explanatory paradigm (if any) of the researcher, and this is just as true in the sociology of deviant groups as in the anthropology and history of honor groups. One can come to understand — and perhaps to appreciate — the set of norms, values and assumptions of deviant groups, and why they are regarded as threatening by the dominant group that labels them as deviant, without necessarily sharing those norms and also without necessarily seeking to explain their causal conditions or effects.[15]

---

[15] Consider marginalized groups such as street gangs, Mafia, pirates, gypsies, and communes in the light of honor: to what extent, and in what ways, can these groups be regarded as honor

III. Deviations

In the next section, I will consider deviations that are deviant from the standpoint of honor — how far, and in what ways can they deviate and still are regarded as honor? Here I want to look more broadly at the possible kinds of deviation from honor, not all of them deviant. I am interested in cases that may well be outside the ambit of honor altogether, as well as marginal and deviant honor cases, and also cases where the deviations do not constitute deviance — they are just different forms of honor. Our standpoint, as usual, is personal honor, and so we begin with the concept of an honor group, some particular honor group or other. From such a standpoint, there can be deviations most obviously in membership or in code,[16] and these deviations are inextricably intertwined, for code-adherence sets boundaries for membership, while members choose the code and interpret its meaning, application and adjudication.

The membership of one honor group may include, overlap, or exclude the membership of another group. The membership of one group may have one or several sub-groups consisting of proper sub-sets of the members of that group ("inner circles," or "elites"); or two different groups may have some (not all) members in common; or the membership may be completely disjoint. As the membership differs, so do the loyalties (if not the rules), and so the senses of honor will vary. Of course, when someone belongs to more than one honor group, almost inevitably conflicts will arise, both between allegiances to differing codes and between loyalties to different persons. But also, sometimes the differing groups are not honor groups at all, and membership in some groups that are not (regarded as) honor groups may be such a deviation from honor as to call into question membership in the original honor group: consider insider trading, graft, betraying the trust

groups? For example, what is their code, their sense of honor, their mutual recognition, their loyalty, their maintenance of respect, etc? In this regard, I have found the following studies suggestive: Elijah Anderson, 1992, 1994, 1999, on Philadelphia street gangs; MacLeod, 1995, Jankowski, 1991, and Sullivan, 1989, also on gangs; Blok, 1974, 2001, on Sicilian mafia; Kanter, 1972, on communes; Horowitz, 1982, 1983, 1987, on Chicago gangs; Nisbett and Cohen, 1996, on skinheads; Vigil, 1988, on barrio gangs. I believe that looking again at these and many other groups in light of the concepts and distinctions of this book would be empirically fruitful as well as humanly insightful.

[16] Of course, there can be deviations in other respects as well: loyalty, respect, commitment, tradition, rituals, etc. I won't focus on such deviations except incidentally, though they are all valid avenues of exploring not only difference but also deviance. For example, there may be differences of loyalty deviating from equal commitment to and trust of all members, perhaps ones that mark hierarchical, cultural or religious biases, or ones that are based on expectation of reward instead of on mutual respect; or there may be differences of respect, such as assimilating respect to fear (where a group member "gets respect" by manhandling or terrorizing others). Some of these kinds of difference may constitute not only deviation but also deviance from the normative standards of some honor groups.

of others for personal gain. Further, membership in an honor group is not always clean and neat; boundaries may be vague, initiation (or re-entry) may be incomplete or on going, and mutual recognition may be obscured.

Honor codes differ in several ways. (i) Most obviously, the rules may differ, with one group having rules another lacks. (ii) The same rules may have different normative force, variously prohibiting, permitting, or requiring the very same acts. (iii) The rules may be more or less extensive, applying to wider or narrower classes of actions or perhaps to wider or narrower classes of agents. (iv) The rules may be more or less stringent or rigorous. (v) The rules may be variously ordered or prioritized, with different trumps in different groups. (vi) Even the same rules may be differently interpreted, or have differing procedures and kinds of authorities for interpretation. (vii) The rules may be differently enforced and adjudicated. (viii) Importantly for our concerns later, honor codes may be moral or non-moral. Finally, (ix) the codes may not be codes of honor at all because they serve some other end. There is no bright line between different ends, and the same rule may be held for reasons of profit, power, or self-indulgence, to name just a few, instead of, or in addition to, as a matter of honor.

All these deviations in membership and code serve to differentiate not only honor groups from one another, but also from other kinds of social groups. But they don't yet capture when deviation becomes deviance, for many deviations are mere differences, and others seem positive, perhaps even inspiring. Take any honor group as a starting point, and there will likely be other honor groups that are similar in code but different in membership, or perhaps subgroups that are similar in membership but somewhat different in code — and at least some of these will not be viewed negatively from the starting point. Just as in the *Iliad* Achilles and the Achaeans could look on their enemies, Hector and the Trojan coalition, as subscribing to the same heroic warrior code though with a different and deadly membership, so too medieval European knights could affirm the same chivalric code across different, often contending courts; and both would be able to see kindred spirits in Japanese samurai. So deviation isn't necessarily deviance; it may just be difference.

Moreover, it is tempting to view some groups such as benign religious sects or Utopian communities (e.g. Oneida, Harmony, Amana, the Shakers, Twin Oaks) as honor groups that not only diverge (and often derive) from ordinary honor groups but also exceed them in putting recognizable honor principles such as equality and respect into more perfect practice. It perhaps does such communities a disservice to call them "Utopian," for many are successful over many decades, and often serve as beacons — of guidance or warning — to other honor groups as well as to the wider society. So some divergence may be an improvement over many starting points; once again deviation from honor isn't necessarily deviant honor, much less no honor at all.

IV. Deviant Honor

So when *do* deviations from honor produce deviant honor? And when do such deviations produce something altogether other than honor? In short, what are the internal norms and the external boundaries of (the concept of) personal honor? These are obscure questions, and we should not expect precise answers. There is vagueness to the concept of honor just as to all (ordinary) concepts. Still, some rough guidelines may be drawn.

Members of one honor group can frequently recognize other groups as honor groups — regarding their members as honorable, their code as a code of honor — for a variety of reasons: perhaps because their membership is overlapping (potentially at least), because their codes are similar (particularly in what are regarded as essentials), because recognition of others' honor is reciprocated by them, or for other reasons. But none of this recognition entails regarding the other group as *equally* honorable. Honor groups tend to regard their particular way of honor as the best, if not the only "true," honorable life, and any deviations will therefore quite often be regarded as deviant. "Yes," an honor group member might say, "that other group is indeed an honor group, but still it's a defective one, a less than fully honorable one, since they lack an important rule which we have, or they have rules we (deliberately) lack, or they uphold the same rules less stringently than we do, or they take their honor less seriously than we do, etc. etc." This might be termed *subjective honor deviance* — one honor group privileges itself over other honor groups, making its own code and conduct the standard for judging others' deviation as deviance. But this kind of deviance settles few questions, for subjective judgments notoriously differ, and what appears deviant from one standpoint may seem quite the opposite from another.

So, are there more objective criteria of honor-deviance, ones that are internal to the very notion of honor and not imposed from without? Otherwise put, does the concept of honor contain, or suggest, an objective standard (or standards) for honor codes and groups, demarcating what is necessary or sufficient both for being an honor code or group as opposed to some other kind of code or group and for being a superior or inferior honor code or group, a more or less honorable code or group? In both cases we are on uncertain and controversial ground, but the following points may be hazarded.

Honor groups must, of course, have members who are committed to the same code, who recognize one another's similar commitment, and who are loyal to the other members; they live according to that code and with those others as a matter of honor. One form of deviance, therefore, is if a group, or some of its members, adheres to a code of honor but not (or not primarily, finally, or essentially) *as* a matter of honor. For example, perhaps some members are more deeply self-interested than interested in honor, or perhaps they are the agents of an outside enterprise, so that their adherence to the code is not, or not fully, a matter of personal honor. Connectedly, the pinnacle of honor is to place its concerns above all else, in particular above self-interest, and to be willing to act courageously to preserve and to defend one's honor. An individual deviates from honor to the extent that he is unwilling to put principles of honor above self-interest, and an honor group is deviant to the extent that it fails to live up to its own code of honor — to honor those shared principles. This internal standard of honor, then, is basically a matter of integrity or self-consistency: honor requires consistency of principle, motive, commitment, and action. But it says nothing about the principles to which one is committed. For all it says, loyal thugs are as honorable as obedient nuns.

Perhaps then we should turn from groups to codes: is there any way to extract a standard from the concept of honor, so that honor codes might be judged (objectively) as not only different but also deviant *with respect to honor*? Recall that there are two distinct issues here: First, what differentiates codes into those that are codes of honor and those that are not? Second, what grades codes of honor as more or less honorable — worthy to be regarded as better or worse *honor* codes? The latter is the more difficult question.

On the first point, codes of honor are Janus-faced, as is the concept of honor itself. On the one hand, the code faces outward, toward behaviors that can be recognized and judged by others; on the other hand, the code plumbs inner motivational depths. Honor codes require behavior that restricts unlimited pursuit of self-interest, respects others (at least other honor group members!), and acknowledges others' interest in one's conduct. But the code must be followed as a matter of honor, on principle and not for the sake of interests. Others are responsible for noticing and reinforcing one's adherence to the code, but the individual is also responsible not only for becoming and remaining honorable but also for ensuring that others see one as honorable. Regard for others pairs with responsibility for self.

We have, then, some minimal criteria to eliminate some groups from counting as honor groups. For example, if a group lacks principles of respect for others, at least the other members of the group (e.g. a partnership strictly "for business," a group of subway riders, mobs), or if it doesn't encourage individual responsibility but relies solely or primarily on extrinsic rewards or punishments (e.g. a press gang, paid informants, convicts, a gulag), then in that respect and to that extent it will not count as an honor group.[17]

Second, the more difficult problem is to distinguish degrees of honor among different honor groups — what might be called their level of *honorability*. But how is such honorability to be determined without begging the question — or rather, begging two questions? On the one hand, many

---

[17] Some may well think these and other deviations from honor groups as such constitute not just difference but deviance, but I will not assume this automatically, for there may well be worthy groups that are not honor groups, and honor groups need not regard them negatively.

members of various honor groups will insist that their own particular honor code should serve as the universal standard of honor. (Of course, since there is no agreement on which code should serve as the standard, who should determine honorability is not clear.) On the other hand, many (nearly all?) members of the large group of social scientists instinctively subscribe to some form of relativism,[18] thinking that values and norms — including honor codes — are just different and that there is no way of judging among them without taking an indefensible stand within some one of them.

So how are both groups to be answered? Only, so far as I can see, if we can discern in the very concept of honor some objective criteria of honor qua honor — what I will call *standards of honorability* — against which different honor codes or groups can be measured. I will assume there are no sound a priori arguments against the possibility of such standards; the difficult trick is to discern them. Let me propose four such standards:[19]

1   The code must be *other-regarding*, in several important ways. It must contain some important *duties to others*; it must assign a high, even pre-eminent value to *respect*, both giving respect to others and having (and also deserving) others' respect; it must give an equally high value to *loyalty*; and it must give importance to maintaining a *reputation* among other group members for respecting those others, being loyal to them, and adhering to their common code.

2   The code must make every individual member *personally responsible* for honor's maintenance. Each member must maintain her own (sense of) honor, adhering to the code for the right reasons, and each must ensure that others properly recognize her honor, while she monitors and recognizes the honor of others.[20]

3   Self-interest must on at least some important occasions make way for the (honor code) principles shared with others, both in assessing what to do and in motivating that behavior; such matters of honor may not be calculated in terms of self-interest, and they may on occasion require considerable *sacrifice* of those interests.

4   The code must imply or project an *ideal of life* as well as lay down minimal

---

[18] "It is sociologically axiomatic to say that deviance is relative." (Jenkins, 1998, 157)

[19] I realize I do not provide much evidence to support these proposed standards, relying only on my own general sense of honor groups across time and cultures, and appealing to a similar apprehension on the part of the reader. I am certainly open to other versions, or to other standards altogether. But I also think the difficulty of finding such standards is not insuperable.

[20] Complications: Honor groups may differ about the relative importance of internal and external honor, as well as the means of maintaining either. Notoriously, some honor groups seem to value the reputation for honor more than the virtue of honor, and many resort to violent tests and "proofs" to sustain that reputation. But I don't think this latter tendency follows from (and indeed I would argue it conflicts with) the internal criteria of honorability proposed above.

requirements.[21] In this, of course, an honor code is rarely explicit and never codified, but it is nonetheless deficient if it is just a set of rules, like a legal code, the following of which keeps one free of censure or blame. An honor code must inspire as well as require.

To the extent that any of these (or perhaps additional) criteria are not met, the honor code is defective, inferior as an honor code, and in that sense we may say it is *honor-deviant*. Moreover, the more criteria it fails to satisfy, or the greater its failure in each, the more honor-deviant it is (there are degrees of honor-deviance). If it completely fails all tests, or if the tests are irrelevant to the code, then it no longer counts as an honor code at all.

This complex standard of honorability means that we can assess codes, and thereby the groups that hold them, in terms of factors intrinsic to honor, at least to a limited extent. There are therefore better and worse codes of honor *qua honor codes*, just as there are codes that are not honor codes at all. An honor code that meets all the criteria is better than one that meets only some, and it is also better if it satisfies the same ones more fully; standard honor codes are therefore superior *in terms of honor* to deviant ones. A code that satisfies none of the criteria is not an honor code at all. Comparing honor groups is a bit more complicated because groups are rarely as good, or as bad, as their codes: One honor group may be better than another group with an inferior code (according to the above criteria), but the other honor group may fulfill its inferior code more fully. Groups that have no honor code, or that make no pretense of following an honor code they supposedly have, are not honor groups at all.

I will not attempt to apply these criteria to concrete cases, though that would be a worthy enterprise. Instead, I close with a forward-looking remark. Earlier I distinguished between moral and non-moral honor codes: *moral honor codes* either include (overriding) moral first principles or are constrained by them, while *non-moral honor codes* do neither (recall that "non-moral" is not the same as "amoral"). Now, I contend that moral honor codes are, all things considered, more likely to conform to standards of honorability than non-moral ones. This is because the standards of honorability pick out at least some of the features that morality also selects (other-regardingness, personal responsibility, sacrifice of self-interest, ideal of life), though morality wants them to hold universally and not just for some particular group.[22]

---

[21] Scholastic "honor codes" that are merely behavioral rules imposed by administrators or faculty are misnomers, not only because following those rules is not a matter of honor at all but also because there is no projected ideal of honor, only rules and punishments (cf. Chapter 9).

[22] One reason why honor is often confused with morality rests on this point: honorability is very like a particularized version of morality, like morality restricted to some local honor group. But honor is nothing without this particularity, even while it also contains the seeds of something more universal.

If so — if moral honor codes are indeed more honorable than non-moral ones — then there are important consequences for the argument of this book. In the last part, Part III, I will attempt to make a case on behalf of "honor for us" that not only rebuts the many charges laid at honor's door but also shows how honor can provide positive benefits for contemporary thought, action and character. My conclusion would be reinforced from an unexpected standpoint — that of the concept of honor itself — if honor for us also exemplifies to a high degree the criteria of honorability we have just proposed. It would be a most happy result if honor for us were also the acme of honor as such, not deviant honor or fake honor.

Conclusion to Part I

The concept of personal honor is importantly distinct from the five peripheral concepts of honor, although it is often confused and conflated with them, and even though there are indeed interesting connections and associations. All six concepts of honor, I believe, are *descriptively* universal, or nearly so, in two ways: They apply to just about any case of honor in any human society, and since honor of one sort or another is quite common in every human society, they apply throughout human life. But not all these concepts, and not nearly all conceptions of them all, are *normatively* universal — i.e. express values which (nearly) all will embrace. Some concepts of honor (like conferred or positional honor) seem inherently peripheral in normative terms, however, common they may be in actual practice. If honor is to be a defensible value for us today, it will most likely be lodged in some conception(s) of personal honor, with its included commitment and trust honor. Distinct from morality and religion, personal honor has intriguing relations to both of them: from the (different) standpoints of morality and religion, personal honor often, though not always, looks desirable, furthering many of the independent ends of each.

In the next Part, we will examine personal honor in more particular manifestations — and we will look not far but near. Leaving to historians and anthropologists the exploration of other cultures, we shall consider *our own* culture — various areas of contemporary life where the concept of personal honor plays important, often vital roles. Personal honor provides a unique vantage point for viewing our own culture in unusual and surprisingly compelling ways. Thereby we may come to appreciate something of the ongoing vitality of this concept for understanding human life. It will be a further step, one we shall take only in Part III, of seeing whether personal honor not only is pervasive but also should be embraced as normative: whether any form of honor can truly be "for us."

Part II

HONOR'S REACH

Scholars of honor most always study the honor of and for others — honor held dear in social groups distant in time or place or deviant in our own time and place. Such honor is not our own because we wouldn't want to live in those ways, even if we could, which usually we can't. There is nothing inherently wrong with the study of honor for others; indeed it's an excellent way to gain greater insight and appreciation of those others, and we may be surprised at how revealing is the perspective of honor. Honor reaches both widely and deeply in human history. Yet studying the honor of others has this danger: it may lead us to think that honor is *only* a concept for others, that it has no roots, relevance or attraction for our own lives today.

To counter this misapprehension, in Part II we shall explore honor's wide salience not to others but to ourselves, to various important aspects of our contemporary Western culture, in ways that often go unnoticed or unappreciated. We will concentrate on personal honor, with occasional mention of the other five concepts of honor as needed to keep our focus sharp. Each chapter in Part II rests on the concepts distinguished and analyzed in Part I; but each chapter is also independent of the others in this Part, even while each strengthens the over-all case for honor's ubiquity. Of course, ubiquity is not normativity. Just because a concept has wide descriptive application doesn't mean that we should welcome it as a guide to how we ought to live. Still, the pervasiveness of honor even in modern liberal societies should give us pause. (We will resume pursuit of the question whether honor *should* be "for us" in Part III, "Honor's Future.")

In exploring honor's reach, we will not only be describing a wide range of cultural phenomena, but proposing that personal honor is an appropriate, useful and illuminating standpoint for understanding those phenomena.

In the light of honor we can see new things, and we can also see familiar things in new ways. To view such things as sportsmanship, patriotism and professionalism from the standpoint of personal honor is to gain fresh insight into both the phenomena and the concept of personal honor. Before beginning our account of honor's reach, however, three cautionary comments are in order.

First, the English *word* "honor" or "honour" (and its cognates) is not always used, even in areas of life where the *concept* of (personal) honor has vital application. Much in the following chapters is devoted to describing how contemporary humans in fact *do* use the concept of personal honor even when they may not explicitly employ the term "honor" to describe what they are doing. Sometimes deeds and practices do speak more loudly than words, and what they say, I think, is that personal honor is considerably more widespread than the term "honor."

Second, description of actual use is not enough. There is also widespread *potential* application of the concept. Hence sometimes in the following chapters I will recommend use of the concept of personal honor for the purpose of gaining greater understanding of contemporary lives even if this concept is not one we would ordinarily think of using for ourselves. I hope to show that although honor is already a concept we actually use in some areas of life, its potential reach is even greater.

Third, in exploring how honor is and can be a ubiquitous concept for us, I don't mean to imply that I am an insider to the practices I depict — no one *could* have intimate experience of all areas of human life into which honor reaches. I am no warrior, no serious athlete, no politician (though a citizen like you), not a professional lawyer but an academic, and so on. Some may mistrust the observations of outsiders, and for good reason, especially when those outsiders begin to recommend employment of concepts not in current use by insiders. Nevertheless, I hope that my observations and recommendations are firmly grounded in the accounts of reliable insiders. Of course, I may be mistaken, and I remain open to correction by insightful insiders. But I would be quite surprised to find that honor is any *less* widespread than I depict.

The point about insiders and outsiders is worth amplifying, as it impacts the entire Part II; I will illustrate it with the topic of the next chapter, warriors and war. For better or worse, I have never experienced war first-hand, whether as warrior or victim; I have no military experience, and have never visited, much less lived in, a war zone. For many this lack of personal experience will taint and perhaps disqualify everything I say: How can someone who hasn't been in war — seen warriors in battle, much less been a warrior battling — hope to understand what honor means to a warrior? Of course I can't, in the sense of living a warrior's honor myself. But I do think an outsider can gain some insight into the concept of warrior honor. My defense is three-fold: in general, outsiders to conceptual practices can gain considerable understanding of insider significance; there is a large insider literature, consisting of reports by participants and observers alike, that permits considerable access into insider perspectives; and sometimes outsiders can see certain conceptual features better than insiders.

On the first point, I regard understanding as a matter of degree and depth, not all-or-nothing. Even insiders to a conceptual practice (by which I mean those who employ a concept in its primary sense in, to and through their own experience) have varying degrees of understanding, and perhaps various kinds and scopes of comprehension. Some insiders will use a concept well, others poorly; some will have greater or smaller zones of imprecision and vagueness in their usage; some will be able to articulate the applications and content of the concept better than others; and some will be able to explain to others the ramifications of the concept in relation to other concepts. Outsiders will display a similar range of understanding. But doesn't outsiders' lack of first-hand experience mean they can never grasp the concept fully, particularly if the concept is rich and nuanced? Perhaps inevitably in practice they will miss some nuances of the concept or mistake some of its implications, but not necessarily, for any given error is corrigible in principle — perhaps by insiders who take the trouble of correcting an outsider's ignorance, naiveté, or sheer foolishness.

On the second point, there is a vast abundance, almost a surfeit, of accounts that touch on the honor of warriors, though all have their limitations, and most their deficiencies. To begin with, warriors themselves have provided — in their memoirs, autobiographies, letters and the like — intimate and detailed accounts, chiefly defenses, of their honor.[1] There are of course reasons to discount or distrust such accounts — they are often self-serving, conceptually unsophisticated and unreflective — but they are not without value to an outsider seeking understanding.[2] Further, warriors have long lived symbiotically with poets, those who from Homer onward have honored (and occasionally undermined) warriors by giving glorious voice to their exploits and values. Of course, the story is inevitably more complex, since poets have their own lives to lead, needing to justify their own existence as more than a parasite upon the body politic; poetic values may at times conflict with warrior ones; not all poets find war glorious; and there is always martial suspicion of poets who lack first-hand wartime experience. But poets, sensitive to all life through the medium of their own lives, often do discern important elements of a warrior's world, however, heightened and distorted.

---

[1] Cf. for example Keegan & Holmes, 1985; Shulstad, 1986; Sorley, 1998; Stockdale, 1984, 1993, 1995.

[2] Marshall, 1947, is exceptionally useful precisely because it is a study of warriors by a warrior for the potential use of future warriors.

And poets, of course, are not the only ones writing of warriors: journalists,[3] historians,[4] biographers,[5] social scientists,[6] even philosophers[7] have sought to illuminate aspects of the warrior's life. From all such sources an outsider may learn a lot about the honor of warriors, however partial, incomplete and inaccurate the accounts may be.

On the third point, I believe outsiders to a conceptual practice sometimes have better vantage points than insiders. They may not use, or be able to use, the insider concepts so fluently in practice, and they will often miss subtle nuances. But outsiders do have certain advantages. The very effortless intuition of an insider may hinder reflection, particularly upon a practice's deeper features — why worry about what comes so spontaneously? Possessing a concept is no guarantee that one can explicate, or even understand, that concept's structure, connections with other concepts, or worth. Concepts so intricately enmeshed in a particular culture may not be compared and contrasted with, or analyzed against, concepts from other cultures. So there is room for outsiders, certainly for those explicating the intricacies of a particular honor group, but also for a philosopher exploring broader human cultural themes. Such a philosopher may well discern necessary conceptual notes imperceptible to an insider.

In the end, even though an outsider's grasp of a warrior's life, or that of an athlete, or professional, is limited by lack of personal experience, and only partially redeemed by others' accounts, there may be novel insights to be gained from taking a philosopher's point of view. Since the topic at hand is so important to human existence, and since any understanding of anyone's existence is partial, it seems that we should welcome insight from any quarter. But the disclaimer remains: none of what follows is an insider account — *caveat lector*!

A short road map of Part II may guide the reader. I begin with a consideration of warrior honor (Chapter 6), arguably honor's most ancient and potent context. Warrior groups are essential honor groups, though not all deadly fighters are honorable warriors. Next I look at competitive sports (Chapter 7), and find strong reasons to regard sportsmanship as

---

[3] Cf. Ignatieff, 1997.

[4] Cf. Braudy, 2003; Fussell, 1989; Keegan, 1978; Keegan and Holmes, 1985; Keen, 1965; Kitchen, 1968; Shay, 1994;

[5] Cf. Sorley, 1998;

[6] Cf. Best, 1982; Haas, 1990; Kagan, 1995; Milne, 1934.

[7] The philosophical literature on the morality of war is extensive; representative works are Clark, 1988; Cohen, 1989; Holmes, 1989; Johnson, 1984; Melzer, 1975; Paskins and Dockrill, 1979; Sherman, 2007; Walzer, 1977. There is also a large literature on military ethics, which treats of the moral aspects of soldiering, and persistently conflates honor and morality: cf. Axinn, 1989; Elfstrom and Fotion, 1986; Fotion, 1990; French, 2003 ; Gabriel, 1982; Galligan, 1979; Hartle, 1989; McGrath and Anderson, 1993; Gray, 1959, provides a philosophically fertile account of his experience as a WWII warrior.

honor, a perspective that illuminates the topic more clearly than customary approaches. I then explore honor in politics (Chapter 8) — not the honor of politicians or polities (though I believe honor is not absent there also), but the honor of citizens: construing patriotism as citizen honor provides a distinctive solution to the controversy over the morality of patriotism. Next I look at the Academy (Chapter 9), and consider not only student, but also faculty and administrative (at least potential) honor groups. Many of the conflicts internal to contemporary Academe are put in a new light when seen from honor's standpoint. Finally, I explore professions more broadly (Chapter 10), with the law as a case of special interest, showing how many things become clearer when professions are viewed as honor groups.

Chapter 6

THE HONOR OF WARRIORS

War and honor are very deeply entangled — so deeply, they appear inseparable. It is not just that honor has its historical origins and paradigmatic significance in fighting wars, as well as its most glorified and horrific contemporary instances, but that the very concept of honor seems rooted in war-making and that these martial roots apparently condition honor's meaning everywhere else. But among those who agree that honor and war are inseparable, there is a great divide: those who prize the honor of warriors see only its pale reflection elsewhere, thinking nothing else can measure up; while those who deplore war and violence deprecate honor's vestiges elsewhere, believing all honor is stained with warrior blood. Others have more mixed reactions, both admiring and worrying about warrior honor even while wishing it weren't necessary or efficacious. In this chapter I cannot hope to explore, much less disentangle, all the many interweaving threads of honor and war. My aims are more modest: to explore one central meaning of personal honor as it applies to those who fight honorably in war. I seek to understand, however partially, the personal honor of *warriors*, in a special sense, and how this honor may be judged, without passing judgment myself. In doing so, I hope to chart a middle course between the fans and foes of warrior honor and perhaps account for some of the mixed reactions warriors incite.

I. Limits of Inquiry

My inquiry into warrior honor is limited, in four ways.

First, honor impinges upon actors in war in many ways. In particular, various kinds of human groups, and not just states, go to war for many reasons, including reasons of honor.[1] But I shall be concerned with the honor of

---

[1] Reasons of honor even at the national level are often more potent than the usual "causes of

warriors, not with the honor of those who send warriors to war.

Second, exploits in war bring many military honors, both achieved and conferred, and civilians may also honor the virtues as well as the exploits of warriors. But my concern is not with these "external" kinds of honor but with the "internal" personal honor of warriors — regardless of justifications for the wars they fight and regardless of how the fighters are regarded by superiors or by non-warriors "back home."[2]

Third, traditional theories of "just war" divide into two parts, *jus ad bellum,* the justice of going to war, and *jus in bello,* the justice in war. But neither compartment contains my subject: not the going to war of the former, and not the (presumed) universal norms of justice of both former and latter. Honor in war is not the same as morality in war, and the honor code of a warrior is not coextensive with the universal "laws of war" so beloved by moral peacemakers — or so I shall argue.

Fourth, my account of a warrior is abstract and ideal; it certainly does not apply equally well to all fighters in violent conflicts past and present; it is particularly problematic in an age of collapsed states, free-lance violence, piracy, and international terrorism. But in my view not all fighters are honorable fighters, and it is worth making that distinction clear even if it is not accepted universally by all who fight. Even those who deprecate war could well agree with this conditional: if there is to be fighting, better that warriors fight it.[3]

II. WAR AND WARRIORS

War[4] is notoriously difficult to capture in a single sense; very often descriptions have a disciplinary bias (for example, sociologists always mention

war" treatments admit. Thucydides lists it as one of the three causes of the Peloponnesian War, but most modern historians and social scientists favor "interests" over anything suggestive of honor. Of course interest and honor are not mutually exclusive. But I think Pamela Stirling is at least partly right in discerning that "Coalition forces invaded Iraq not because Saddam Hussein was a threat but because his existence was perceived to be a living insult to the honour of the US" (Stirling, 2004, 5). Similar points could be made about most wars; cf. Van Creveld, 1991, Chapter VI, "Why War is Fought."

[2] To borrow my earlier distinctions: I am here concerned with personal (and therefore to some extent commitment and trust) honor, not with conferred, recognition or positional honor.

[3] Geoffrey Best seeks to put honor in service not of states but "a wider field of humanity" than "ultranationalism" (Best, 1982, 76), but even nationalistic honor would be better than what we have in many places today, as Michael Ignatieff so clearly notes: "The Red Cross acknowledges that a warrior's honor is a slender hope, but it may be all there is to separate war from savagery. And a corollary hope is that men can be trained to fight with honor" (Ignatieff, 1997, 157).

[4] I am concerned here solely with war in the literal sense, and put aside metaphorical "wars" against such things as domestic crime and other social ills (e.g. "wars" on poverty, drugs, drunk driving, illiteracy and the like), individual battles of all kinds (personal vendettas or domestic violence), non-violent competitions (sports, business, even the "battle of the bands"), and all

"societies," political scientists "states"), and all depictions seem stipulative and restrictive, with invariable counter-examples and borderline cases. All wars do involve lethal armed violence by groups of humans against other groups of humans, but not all such violence is war. Gassing civilians, ethnic cleansing, terrorist bombings are not acts of war but mere slaughter, whether regarded as "senseless" or as all-too-sensible from certain abhorrent points of view. Moreover, war is not necessarily only a function of nation-states; wars were fought before the latter's invention, and they are still fought today by groups that are not nation-states and may not even aspire to become nation-states.[5] Hence wars are not necessarily fought by armies, those armed and organized arms of the state (the pun is intentional). Finally, calling a violent group conflict a "war" is politically contentious, for one person's war is another's insurrection or rebellion; "war" implies a certain equality and legitimacy or local sovereignty of the contending parties, and one or another side may be unwilling to concede even that to their enemy.

Rather than seeking a characterization of war sensitive to everyone's usage, I will proceed in a different fashion, by defining "war" and "warrior" from a certain standpoint, that of an honorable fighter. This will give these terms more precise, but also narrower, and normative, meaning. Such restriction may seem perversely narrow or arbitrary, even though I think it squares fairly well with much historical usage. Nevertheless, my purpose is to focus on honorable fighting and fighters as meriting special consideration. If this focus omits what the reader wants to call "war" and "warrior," then she may substitute "honorable war" and "honorable warrior," so long as she will grant the consistency if not (as I intend) the redundancy of the terms. Finally, not only will this focus bring clarity to what it is to be a warrior (as an honorable fighter), but it may also constitute a kind of recommendation to those engaged in fighting today, by appealing to their sense of themselves as (potentially) fighters with principles.

The kernel of my focus on war, then, is this: *war is just what warriors fight* (and it is what they fight insofar as they *are* warriors). If the killers are not warriors, then their conflict is not war but something else: mere (!) slaughter, butchery, savagery, massacre, assassination, terror, extermination, wanton killing, or murder. Likewise, if someone is not prepared to fight a war, then that person is not a warrior. Warriors fight wars — that is what it is to be a warrior — and wars are what warriors fight. The elements of this view of war are encapsulated in the following claims:

human struggles against non-human entities (invasive or threatening species).

[5] Hence a key provision of *jus ad bellum* — that a just war must be authorized by legitimate authority, which typically means a state sovereign — is typically lacking in insurrections, rebellions, incursions, intifadas, jihads, and the many other forms of contemporary group violence.

1   To fight is for one group of humans to employ lethal violent force at will against another group of humans (the enemy) who resist in kind. To fight, therefore, is to be liable to the enemy's use of lethal violent force.

2   (Only) warrior groups fight wars.

3   Warrior groups fight (only) wars.[6]

4   (Only) warriors belong to warrior groups.

5   Hence wars involve groups of warriors fighting against one another.

6   Each warrior group essentially has a code of honor, shared by all members, concerning (primarily) the appropriate use of lethal violent force.

7   Warriors are therefore honorable killers, whose killings are constrained by their code of honor.

8   Different warrior groups may, but need not, have different codes of honor.

9   Those who employ lethal force unconstrained by a code of honor are not warriors but mere killers, and their violent actions aren't acts of war.

10   Honorable killers aren't necessarily morally blameless, nor do they necessarily lack, or deserve, moral or other kinds of praise (glory, honor).

11   Warrior honor is not necessarily gendered.

The remainder of this chapter will explicate these claims.

III. Warriors

What is a warrior? Nature follows function, and function follows context. So what is a warrior's context? Clearly it is a fighter's context: being a member of a human group employing lethal violent force at will against another group of humans who resist in kind. It is important to see that this context is not one of killing (or seeking to kill) defenseless others but rather of killing other fighters who pose genuine threats to one's own life and limb. To fight is to be liable to the enemy's use of lethal violent force.[7] Moreover, there are no external limits to the kinds and extent of violence employed in fighting; there is no outside power constraining behavior, no referee enforcing rules, in fact no rules at all save what the fighters impose upon themselves. Fighting knows no sovereign; violence is used precisely because there are no imposed

---

[6] Warriors engaged in peacekeeping, policing, parading and the like are not acting as warriors. Nor are those who support fighters in war but do not fight themselves. (I owe these points to Bernard Chachula, personal communication.)

[7] Van Creveld, 1991, rightly emphasizes this point; cf. Chapter VI, "Why War is Fought." Of course, "to be liable" doesn't mean to expose oneself foolishly, needlessly, or carelessly, much less to welcome lethal violence. It means only not to flinch from the real risk of violent death and to willingly put oneself "in harm's way."

limits upon the imposition of each fighting group's will, only the limits of the enemy's resistance to one's own power, plus the internal constraints of one's own principles, if any. These, then, are the central and interdependent facts of every fighter's life, what he[8] must constantly prepare for in thought and deed: the willingness to kill and the liability be killed at will. In fighting, fighters put lives at risk — others' lives and their own — through their willful use of violent force.[9]

What is required to function well in such a dangerous context?[10] First, and most obviously, a fighter needs fighting skills — physical prowess to be sure, and knowledge of available arms and their capabilities, but also the practical knowledge of how to use those arms to fight, including knowledge of enemy strengths and weaknesses. He also needs self-knowledge just as much as knowledge of his enemy. Further, he needs qualities of temperament such as courage, endurance, determination and self-control; he has to have the mind and heart as well as the physique of a fighter. And not least, he must possess the will to fight — not necessarily a love of violence or joy in combat but an overriding resoluteness to fight when required that includes a certain self-abnegation, a willingness to risk and even surrender his life in fighting.

But there is a further set of qualities necessary to functioning well as a fighter. Fighting is deadly business, but it is not solitary business. Fighters fight in groups against groups; they fight together against others who fight together against them. Fighters therefore need the other-regarding virtues that enable them to be effective members of a fighting group and thereby enable the group to be an effective fighting unit. These fighting groups[11]

---

[8] I will refer to fighters and warriors with masculine pronouns, in light of the fact that historically nearly all of them have been males; but the connections of gender and war will be more carefully examined below (Section IX).

[9] Note that a warrior's context, as I have described it, does not mention why fighting occurs. There are three cases here: (i) the reasons groups have for fighting; (ii) why members of those groups fight at all; and (iii) why they fight as they do. My focus excludes the first, because why groups fight is (somewhat) independent of how and why fighters participate in that fight — not entirely independent, of course, for the cause may condition the fighting not only by placing restrictions on killing but also in motivating fighters to join a fighting group and join in the fray. Nevertheless, there is some independence; one can fight an unjust war justly, and a just war unjustly. I will consider later the special cases of (ii) and (iii) as they apply to warriors: why and how warriors fight as they do (particularly Section VII).

[10] One may call these qualities "virtues" or "excellences" — Aristotle's αρεται — so long as the moral overtones are erased, or simply "desirable qualities" (desirable, that is, from the standpoint of a warrior).

[11] As I use the terms, "fighting group" and "warrior group" are not co-extensive with "army," which is an organ of a state. Armies are fighting groups, but they are not the only kinds. Likewise "soldiers" are members of armies, but they are warriors only if they also share a code of honor; this latter is what makes an army, or a part of an army, into a warrior group. Certain features prevalent in and perhaps even necessary to armies — hierarchical command structure, strict obedience, uniforms, group discipline — are contingent for warrior groups. Finally, armies are formed and armed by states in the interest of effective or successful fighting, not of honorable fighting.

differ widely in their size and structure: from tribes, war parties and squads to phalanxes, hordes and armies. But all require their members' commitment both to the group and to its members. Such commitments may be obtained in various ways: through coercion or threat, the authority of command or of exemplary leadership, self-interest (wages and promises of plunder), loyalty to a cause (nation, tribe, religion, ideal), the personal choice of the fighter — or a sense of honor.

This, then, is the context and required character of a fighter. But not all fighters are warriors. Warriors are fighters who belong to fighting groups that are also *honor groups*. Honor groups have two features relevant to our purposes here: (i) They are united by an honor code that all members of the honor group accept, acknowledge, and apply in their lives. The code is common to the members, and recognition of this commonality constitutes them as a community. Failure to live up to this code occasions a deep sense of guilt in a member's own eyes. (ii) Their members mutually recognize one other as sharing this common code of honor, attempting to live up to it, and judging one's own and others' lives in its terms and light. Failure to live up to the code occasions a deep sense of shame in (a member's view of) the eyes of others.

Now the personal qualities needed to live as a member of an honor group go beyond those needed by any fighter. Blind obedience to commanding officers may make effective fighters in certain groups, but such fighters are not (yet) honorable fighters; they are more like robots following another's program — replaceable hardware for commanders' software.[12] In contrast, honorable fighters or warriors must be able to understand and follow a code of honor, must be able to recognize its application and avoidance in themselves and others, and must be dedicated to honor (i.e. must choose to follow it of their own free will). Honor's dignity rests on ultimate individual responsibility.[13]

---

[12] This is one reason why some have thought honor belongs only to the leaders of an army; only officers are thought to have the autonomy of will and action honor requires, while mere soldiers are their implements and hence incapable of honor (or dishonor): soldiers are the "arms" of armies, mere "cannon-fodder," acting only as commanded by superiors. But this is a provincial and historically limited view of warrior honor. Other fighting groups can extend honor to soldiers as well as to officers, by equipping them with honorable expectations, dispositions, and ranges of action. There are many advantages and disadvantages to both narrow and wide scope of honor in a fighting group, which I cannot consider here, but I will offer one rhetorical question: Can a democratic society afford to secure its defense with a military in which only officers can be honorable?

[13] Two cases: (i) A warrior's code of honor may require obedience only to "lawful" commands (where "lawful" may be explicated in terms of the "laws of war," international agreements, the "general sentiment of humanity," or moral or religious principles). Here choice between following orders and following only lawful commands may be excruciating at times, but the honorable way seems clear if hard to follow. (ii) Some warrior codes of honor may require following orders without hesitation or question, even if one's independent judgment might dictate otherwise;

But further, warriors must be loyal and truthful. Loyalty is the heart of "one for all and all for one;" it is loyalty not only to the honor code but also to the honor group, a personal commitment unto death to the other members of the fighting group, a willingness to defend their lives with his life, a warrior's solidarity.[14] Truthfulness enables "one for all" to become "all for one." It is integrity of word and deed, not just speaking the truth — though giving true information to the right persons at the proper time may be crucial — but also truly doing what one says one will do, carrying out one's acknowledged responsibilities and obligations, being a person who can be trusted, whose words as well as actions are reliable and not simply predictable. Note that both loyalty and truthfulness are independent of any causes, ideals, goals or other groups for which an honor group may fight: the primary allegiance is to the honor group, and only secondarily to something outside that group.

Such, then, is a warrior in our special, but by no means idiosyncratic, sense: an honorable fighter, bound (though also, he would doubtless say, freed) by voluntary commitment to a group of fellow honorable fighters, united with them in sharing a common code of honor, and mutually recognizing one another as reliable unto death in this sharing.

IV. Good Warriors

A warrior is not necessarily a good warrior, and this in two ways. First, a warrior may fall short of the honor code — may commit acts contrary to his group's honor code or omit acts required by that code. An ideal warrior exemplifies his code of honor at all times, on and off the battlefield, in all ways; and a good warrior lives up to this ideal, more or less. Indeed, a good warrior exemplifies honor by displaying such virtues as loyalty, courage and self-control not only in fighting and killing but also, and perhaps ultimately, in dying — for a fighter, an honorable death is a death in battle, a death that comes in and through fighting honorably. But fighting honorably is not enough. Good warriors must also fight well and effectively, and so they must have whatever it takes to fight well and effectively. Earlier (in Section III) we

---

here the honor rule of "follow orders" trumps the rule of "obey only lawful commands." Such warriors will look just like those blindly obedient fighters just mentioned. But being obedient as a matter of honor is profoundly different from being blindly obedient out of fear, coercion or insensibility. For an honorable person, reasons of honor are freely adopted, and they dignify or ennoble — and make responsible — even when they dictate the very same actions enforced by brute compulsion or mechanical habit.

[14] Loyalty is fostered in many ways. There are of course bonds of blood, heritage, culture, language, class, history, religion and ideology, as well as more particular common goals. But there are also ties of friendship forged in common experiences, and, most importantly in our context, the connections of honor: sharing a common honor code and mutually recognizing one's peers in honor (who likewise recognize oneself).

mentioned the qualities needed by any fighter: (i) physical abilities for the kinds of fighting required;[15] (ii) psychological qualities for persevering in the face of adversity and prevailing against an enemy; (iii) practical virtues such as self-control, courage, loyalty (to others in the honor group), trustworthiness and integrity (truthfulness, consistency of word and deed). A good warrior possesses all these qualities to a high degree, and indeed serves as an exemplar or model to others of their excellent employment. The first two sorts of quality are clear enough, but a few comments about the third sort are needed to prevent misunderstanding.

The practical virtues of a good warrior are sometimes regarded as the pre-eminent practical virtues for humans, and sometimes they are even regarded as moral virtues. Both views are mistaken. Being a virtuous warrior is not necessarily being a virtuous person in all contexts, nor is it the same as being a morally virtuous person. On the first point, these practical virtues are those needed to succeed at one particular kind of human activity — war — and are not necessarily pre-eminent or even useful in other activities, where other, perhaps even contrary, virtues will be required. For example, care for the weak, sensitivity to others' feelings, fairness, and other practical virtues may be needed in peacetime as well as, or instead of, the warrior virtues. Courage may well be needed universally, but a warrior's courage may be inadequate where something other than fighting is required. In short, warrior virtues, like most virtues,[16] are context-dependent, and they may not export well. Indeed, some of them, unless generalized or altered, may be not virtues at all but vices in other circumstances: e.g. if loyalty remains loyalty only to one's honor group of warriors, it threatens not only commitments to other groups but also fair and equal regard of all.

On the second point, the practical virtues of an honor group are not necessarily moral virtues. Morality is as elusive as war, but surely central features of morality include universal scope and equal respect for all. A moral requirement binds everyone and considers everyone equally; a moral virtue is a virtue for everyone, and for everyone equally. But warrior respect and virtue are more restricted and partial. For example, though warriors respect both enemy warriors and non-warriors, they do not respect them in the same way — warriors do not treat non-warriors as equals,[17] and may regard them

---

[15] These will vary across times and places, depending especially upon available military technology. What Achilles chiefly required for combat (physical strength, foot speed, agility) differs somewhat from what a fighter pilot requires (acute visual discrimination and lightning reflexes). Still, where the combat is face-to-face, the qualities will be remarkably similar across different technologies.

[16] Perhaps fully moral virtues are independent of context. But perhaps not. Cf. MacIntyre, 1988.

[17] Though, paradoxically, they may treat non-warriors as warriors, as when fighting non-warrior fighters (cf. Section VI below).

as less worthy or noble than warriors — and though good warriors are highly prized in times of war, they may be ill-suited and the opposite of useful in times of peace.

V. WARRIOR CODES OF HONOR

The core of a warrior's code of honor concerns legitimate and illegitimate use of lethal violent force: against whom, when and how may such force be honorably used — and how may it not? Here we consider five central features of a warrior's code of honor (clearly there are many others).

(a) Two crucial distinctions must be made among enemies: first between enemy fighters and enemy non-fighters (combatants v. non-combatants or "civilians"), and second between enemy fighters who are warriors and those who are not warriors. These distinctions generate three categories of enemy: warrior fighters, non-warrior fighters, and non-fighters. All enemies pose threats, but only enemy fighters are "dangerous men" who pose directly lethal threats to warriors (cf. Walzer, 1977). Non-fighters may contribute greatly, even essentially, to a war effort, but they are lethal threats only indirectly, through the fighters they support. The initial point of a warrior's honor is that only enemy fighters may be killed at will. It is a matter of honor that a warrior does not kill those who do not directly seek to kill him. Non-fighters are not killers, even though they may wish, seek and help to have enemy warriors killed, and so they must be dealt with differently from enemy fighters. In effect, a warrior gives different kinds of respect to fighters and to non-fighters (and in the former category, to warriors and to non-warriors). He respects fighters by fighting them (using lethal violence against killers), and he respects non-fighters by not fighting them (refraining from using lethal violence against non-killers). The rules for proper, respectful, honorable treatment of fighters and non-fighters vary considerably from honor group to honor group; only some outlines can be sketched here.

(i) Rules for fighting enemy warriors are premised on warrior equality: warriors are equal in honor; whether friend or foe, they are all honorable and deserve honorable respect. The fundamental rule is a principle of reciprocity, a kind of Golden Rule of War: a warrior is permitted any action against an enemy warrior that the enemy warrior is permitted against him. Of course more specific rules of permissibility will vary widely, e.g. concerning use of stealth, deception, distance weaponry and the like. Likewise there are tricky issues of capture, surrender and captivity (cf. (e) below). But all such rules of honor recognize the enemy warrior as a person of honor himself, such that it simply would not be proper (i.e. honorable) to do certain things in certain ways or times or places to him.[18]

(ii) Rules for treating non-fighting enemies at the minimum prohibit indiscriminate killing. Such enemies are the "innocent" non-fighters who not only do not directly threaten a warrior with lethal force but also lack a warrior's honor; even if it is within a warrior's power, it would be "beneath" him to line up defenseless civilians and shoot them. Quite likely non-lethal personal violence will be prohibited as well (rape, beatings, torture). But there are wide variations in what else may be done to non-warriors. Some codes of honor will respect civilian property as well as person, while others will permit seizure, confiscation, even looting. Civil liberties will likely be severely curtailed, though the populace need not be enslaved. A warrior need not feel compassion for non-fighting enemies, but he must at least feel compunction, the sense that an honorable warrior doesn't kill or violate such as these in ways such as these. Of course there are complications, particularly if non-fighters practice certain forms of resistance, such as assisting, supplying and concealing enemy fighters, but here the principle would seem to be that by becoming complicit with such fighters, the non-fighter inherits some or all of the liabilities of treatment possessed by the fighters (categories (i) and (iii)).

(iii) Rules for dealing with enemy fighters who aren't warriors are the most difficult. The category includes all enemies who do pose a lethal threat (not only to warriors!) but who don't fight honorably. They are not the same as common criminals, furthering private ends; such ordinary killers should be caught, tried and punished for murder according to law. But non-warrior fighters are in a different category: they fight on an enemy's side, for an enemy cause, but kill indiscriminately, not like a warrior. I shall treat these in a separate section below (Section VI).

(b) It is also a matter of honor how the warrior treats his fellow warriors, friendly members of the same honor group, his honorable "comrades," "mates" or "buddies." Here it is essential to be loyal and trustworthy, reliable in word and deed, not simply because these qualities make for a more efficient fighting unit, though they may well do so, but essentially because honor requires it. Reliability or trustworthiness at all times (at least regarding other members of the honor group) is a key provision of any honor code, but especially in circumstances of war. Fighting a war means placing one's life in others' hands, and theirs in yours: all can be for one only if one is reliably for all, and conversely.

(c) Honor shines forth *in extremis*, in two ways: (i) Often greater warrior recognition honor accrues to those who risk more in killing. Facing an enemy

---

[18] Often warriors on both sides will share a common sense of what is permitted, but this is not necessary. What is necessary is that both share a sense that whatever one side permits for its warriors it also permits for enemy warriors.

warrior in one-on-one combat is honored, but greater still is single-handedly taking on a whole group. Firing across no-man's land while risking return fire is courageous, while sniping from a concealed secure position is less so. (ii) The honorable warrior can be relied upon by his friends in fighting, because he values his honor, and therefore them, more than his own life; he is willing to die as well as to kill for his honor, and this includes a willingness to sacrifice his life for his comrades in arms, if that's what it takes to defend them against a common enemy.

(d) Typically the honor code includes provisions regarding means and methods of killing, concerning what is desirable, what is acceptable, and what is unacceptable. Such provisions will be highly culture-relative, dependent especially upon the current state of military technology. In one age, an honorable warrior only (or preferentially) engages in face-to-face combat with other warriors using only hand weapons (swords, knives, clubs), scorning distance weapons (arrows, spears) as unacceptable for a true warrior. In another time, an honorable warrior may use mechanical distance weapons (rifles, artillery) but not chemical or biological ones. Some groups may consider sniping or mining dishonorable; others may regard them as honorable (or at least not dishonorable). Such rules concern also off-battlefield means: may hostages be taken, may captives be tortured, may civilians be subjected to military law?

(e) What about surrender and captivity? An honor code may disallow surrender, and it may take no prisoners, so that all (honorable) fighting will be to the death. But other codes may make provision both for honorable surrender and for honorable capture, and that requires rules for the treatment of prisoners of war. Captive warriors must be treated differently than fighting ones; they cannot be killed at will. Moreover, typically they cannot be tortured or punished corporally; such treatment is thought contrary to the respect required, for even though a captive is humbled, he is still a warrior and should not be humiliated. Still, captive warriors are necessarily enslaved to some extent — at least until the hostilities are over, or ransom or prisoner exchange made — and it is difficult for captive and captor alike to preserve honor under such conditions.[19] It is a further matter whether escape is an option, especially when different sides may interpret the relevant rules differently. Always, though, there is a sense of reciprocity embedded in an honor code, such that in acting honorably towards honorable others one wills (and expects) to be similarly treated were the positions or roles reversed.

The rules of conduct outside of war are peripheral to a warrior's code of honor, though some codes may contain such rules. For example, being an "officer and a gentleman" binds together both battlefield bearing and peacetime politeness, but it is the former that matters qua warrior. Of

---

[19] Recognition of this fact may be one reason why some honor codes forbid surrender.

course warriors may be unable to confine their fighting to wars — they may be susceptible to barroom brawls, domestic violence, road rage and other forms of individual violence — and some such extrabellum violence may even be expected or at least permitted according to their particular code of honor. But that is not what constitutes them as warriors; it is not the central part of their code of honor. Being a warrior centrally means fighting other warriors.

VI. Fighting Non-Warrior Fighters

Still, warriors will sometimes find themselves confronted by enemy fighters who are not warriors.[20] What should a warrior do, what can a warrior honorably do, against enemy fighters who not only don't share his particular code of honor but lack any code of honor altogether? There are two main cases.

The first is that of a *sheer killer*,[21] who lacks a warrior's reasons for discriminating between warriors and non-warriors and so might be called an *indiscriminate killer*, though of course such a killer may well discriminate on grounds such as the relatively vulnerability of potential victims — but this is not a principle of warrior honor. It might appear that an honorable killer is at a competitive disadvantage against a sheer killer, who will often use means and tactics that are out of bounds for warriors, so there will considerable pressure to "fight fire with fire," not to "fight with one hand tied behind one's back." But to employ the same means as the sheer killer is to fight dishonorably, and that is ruled out for a true warrior, for whom retaining honor means more than victory or life itself — better to lose honorably than to win dishonorably. A warrior's actions are self-determined, not determined by an unscrupulous other. It seems, then, that a warrior will treat enemy sheer killers as he would treat enemy warriors, though without expecting similar treatment in kind.

But even while insisting upon the paramount importance of honor, a warrior is not doomed to lose the fight. There are, in fact, good *fighting* reasons to remain honorable, for honorable fighters have many global advantages unavailable to non-honorable fighters. Since members of honor groups are internally motivated by honor, their bravery is distinct from the bravado of someone whose self-confidence rests only on their power to destroy another. Further, warriors can often maintain their *esprit de corps* and discipline more readily in difficult times, while sheer killers face debilitating dissonance between the presumed value of their cause and the ghastly means they employ on its behalf. Finally, warriors generally enjoy wider support from

---

[20] This seems increasingly the case in today's "asymmetrical" wars.
[21] NB: This is a technical term.

non-warriors at home than sheer killers, and they may well win even grudging respect from enemies (after all, they respect enemy warriors and non-warriors alike, and the implicit reciprocity contained in this treatment may well be admired and copied by the enemy). To surrender those global advantages for merely tactical or temporary gain is usually quite a bad bargain.

There is a further class of non-warrior enemy fighters even more problematic than sheer killers, in part because they more closely resemble warriors. These are fighters who are persuaded, indoctrinated, or deluded into thinking that the transcendent greatness or sanctity of their cause licenses, even encourages or requires, them to silence (kill, subdue, convert) *all* enemies, whether fighters or not. These are *fanatical fighters.*[22] Here the fanatic seems to mimic the honor of the warrior, for both kill on principle, discriminately, and are absolutely loyal to their respective groups. Yet there are crucial differences: Fanatics do discriminate — only enemies are to be killed — but they do not discriminate *among enemies,* as warriors do. They pose an equally severe threat to enemy warriors and non-warriors alike. Second, whereas a fanatic can only defeat an enemy by eliminating all opposition, a warrior can do so simply by defeating its fighters, without the need to kill or convert all enemies.

Fanatical fighters' unshakable conviction of the absolute rightness of their cause might seem to make them an implacable fighting force. But even when facing a fanatical enemy, an honorable fighter will not sink to his enemy's level; a warrior is willing to die for his honor just as much as a fanatic is for his beliefs, but not in the same way. A fanatic surrenders himself to a cause or principle that transcends even allegiance to his fighting group; his cause transcends his honor (or perhaps, he might say, his cause *is* his honor). A warrior, on the contrary, will not sacrifice his honor for his cause. Thus he will not demonize fanatical enemies but will fight against them as if they were warriors, though once again without expectation of similar treatment in reply (in fact, even with the assurance that similar treatment will *not* be forthcoming). Once again an honorable fighter has some advantages over a fanatical fighter, although not necessarily courage and *esprit.* But warriors are much more likely than fanatics to attract voluntary support of neutrals, and their principles and objectives can withstand rational critique better than those of a fanatic. Even so, fighting a fanatical enemy in an honorable way may be the ultimate test of a warrior's commitment to honor, with the twin temptations either to treat the enemy without respect, as sub-human, or to become like the fanatic in seeking victory no matter the cost. Giving into either temptation, however, means surrendering one's own honor, and this is something a warrior will not do.

---

[22] Again, this is a technical term.

VII. Why Become a Warrior?

Some think there could only be bad reasons — false, self-deceived, hypocritical rationalizations — for becoming a warrior, on the grounds that all killing is morally wrong or that all wars are unjust, or at any rate that modern wars cannot be fought justly. I do not have space here to argue against these claims, though I think all are false. I want instead to bracket such global questions about the justice or morality of the killing warriors do in order to explore the question of why it is that persons become warriors willing to fight and die.

There are many consequentialist reasons. Some persons "down on their luck" may see no better livelihood; some may seek the spoils of victory (in some ages, plunder and ransom); others treasure the non-material rewards warriors often receive from society (admiration, recognition [fear *or* fame!], honors, "glory"). Some may admire the power warriors have and exercise, not merely on the battlefield but in peacetime as well, and others may enjoy the dangerous lifestyle of a warrior for its sense of adventure and living *in extremis*. Some may even find the exciting danger of war compelling.[23] Some may feel the pressures of family or society to pursue a military career (even if one doesn't like to fight). Some perhaps are coerced or threatened into joining. But such reasons seem superficial and almost irrelevant to joining an honor group. There must be reasons more intimately connected with honor itself.

And indeed there are. One is that even non-warriors may admire the honorable qualities of warriors, their very qualities of fighting honorably. Without necessarily ascribing morally exemplary qualities to warriors, one may nonetheless feel the attractiveness of their lives. Warriors do "great" deeds, pushing certain human capabilities to their limits. They display admirable restraint and self-control in their use of lethal violence, when the passions of so many rage without limit. They are paradigmatically courageous, putting their very lives on the line for some greater good. They focus on their vocation in ways ordinary folk often can only admire, and their discipline and perseverance in pursuit of goals are attractive to many. They transcend themselves not only in their results but also in their actions, transmuting not only their reputations but also their souls into the higher stuff of honor.

There are also reasons of camaraderie. Undergoing hardships together — and there are few if any hardships greater than combat — can forge deep and enduring bonds of friendship. War "buddies" are one's deepest friends, not because they are likeable but because they are loyal to the limit.

---

[23] Cf. Van Creveld, 1991, who believes war's danger is "among the principal attractions, one would almost say its raison d'être" (164).

One may be enticed into joining a warrior group out of a dim sense of the deep desirability of such friendship.

But perhaps the most important reason becomes apparent only from the standpoint of honor itself: one wants to be a warrior in order to be honorable, to gain because one deserves the respect (including self-respect) of warriors. Of course, if one is not a warrior one may not think a warrior's respect important, may even think such respect otiose if one has no taste for a warrior's occupation or code of honor. Nevertheless, there is a universal human motivation that is at work in all systems of honor. We deeply want others to think well of ourselves. We want them not only to notice us, to take account of us, but to count us for something, to think favorably of us, to like and admire us, ultimately to respect us. Moreover, we desire this favorable regard from others the more we regard those others favorably. Honor groups are precisely like that, where each member respects and esteems the others in light of the same honor code, as honorable persons. In such a group, ideally at any rate, others respect one precisely on the same grounds as one respects those others (and oneself!). There is therefore a deep mutuality of favorable recognition that is self-reinforcing; one wants to belong to a society of honor the more one belongs to such a society, the more one has committed one's life to such a group of honorable others. So whatever initially attracts one to the society of warriors, it is likely to be honor itself that keeps one there in the end. Honor serves as the deepest reason for wanting to be a warrior — from the standpoint of being a warrior.

VIII. Judging Warriors

Warriors may, but need not, be judged positively. Warriors often are praised and even glorified as social heroes, saviors of states, defenders of the faith, protectors of the weak, and so on. They may be given, or may seize, pre-eminent social status in the wider society, becoming its leaders or tyrants. In short, they may gain all sorts of conferred and positional honors. But not necessarily. The honor of warriors in terms of social role and status is distinct from their personal honor as warriors. So it is possible that negative judgments can, and sometimes should, be made from other points of view.[24]

From within different warrior groups with different honor codes, there may be disapproval of acts that violate *their* code, but also perhaps approval

---

[24] There is of course a warrior's own point of view, and even here the judgment may be negative: a warrior may fall short of his own code, judged dishonorable by himself (convicted by a guilty conscience of shameful behavior). But honor's self-evaluation, even when rigorously applied, is a limited point of view. Other judgments emerge from principles and points of view differing from the warrior's own code of honor, and these are the ones in which I am interested here.

insofar as the warrior behaves honorably according to his own code, and this approval may take two forms: first, recognition of virtues and values in the warrior's code analogous to their own ("he fought well even if that's not what *we* would do under the circumstances"); second, recognition of someone as a person of honor, being committed to some kind of honor system, however misguided ("he is an honorable person, even if his code is askew and his allegiance misplaced"). Warriors' judgments upon their own kind therefore may be mixed, for honor is relative in the contents of its code and allegiances to its group even if honor is universal among warriors.

From a position outside warrior culture, whether friend or foe, again the judgments are mixed. There may, for example, be admiration for the warrior's code and behavior according to that code, an admiration compatible with a deep desire that war be abolished: "His killing is understandable, indeed admirable, under the deplorable circumstances."[25] Commitment to peacetime values may cut in a different direction, however, leading to deprecation of war-making and conceding only a kind of grudging acknowledgment to warriors: "Even if killing is necessary at times to preserve greater values, it still remains repugnant; we should invest in non-violent peacemaking; there are better lives to lead than being warriors." But non-warrior values may also go further in condemning all killing, seeing warriors as misguided at best, foolhardy, obtuse, or arrogant at worse. Clearly the honor of warriors need not be honored in all quarters.

What judgments issue from a universal moral point of view?[26] Here everything depends upon the content of the warrior code of honor. Many codes of honor, even when cloaked in moralistic language, are *amoral* — i.e. they neither necessarily contain nor are constrained by, principles of morality. Allegiance to the group is an honor code's fundamental premise, and this loyalty may cloak the group's unfair power, status or history, or subservience to corrupt and tyrannical rulers. Such allegiance may therefore trample moral commitment to all. Members of such a group may fight honorably according to their own code of honor, but that group and code are in the service of immoral ends. "They fight well, even honorably, but their cause is profoundly unjust (or they fight in unjust ways); they should realize their injustice and cease fighting in those ways. Their honor is no shield from moral blame and potential prosecution as war criminals."

But, contrarily, there is nothing to prevent honor codes from containing or deferring to moral principles, though the depth of an honor group's

---

[25] Warriors themselves, particularly those who have freely chosen to defend their group in times of need, may feel likewise: it is right and proper to praise the virtues of warriors, but would that warriors were not needed!

[26] Again, warriors themselves as well others may make such judgments, and warriors may make them even about themselves, however painfully.

commitment to morality may vary. So a warrior group may incorporate principles of morality, such as the international "laws of war" or traditional principles of *jus ad bellum* and *jus in bello*, into their honor code, and seek to live up to that code in a morally blameless way, in which case judgments of "good warrior" and "morally good person" may not diverge. This may emerge most poignantly when warriors are called upon by their society to fight an unjust war or to fight it unjustly; here, paradoxically, a morally honorable warrior may preserve his honor only by not fighting.

So however much a warrior's honor raises him above sheer indiscriminate killers or fanatical fighters, it does not place him blameless beyond possible criticism, particularly from a moral point of view. Honorable warriors, whose honor shines spotlessly bright, may still be morally tarnished if their cause is unjust. But a warrior whose honor is *moral honor* (cf. Chapter 4) may avoid such tarnish.

IX. Gender and War[27]

Warriors have always been overwhelmingly male, and warring seems inextricable from masculinity and manhood. But is war necessarily an affair of men, and are "real men" necessarily (potential) warriors? If so, and if this gendering of war derives from, relies upon, and furthers the oppression of women, there may be an additional important moral reason for discounting or deriding the honor of warriors: it is irremediably sexist. Here it is useful to distinguish the following questions:

1 Has war in fact always been gendered? The historical record is unambiguous. Myths of Amazons notwithstanding — they are *only* myths — warriors have always been overwhelmingly male, just as they are overwhelmingly male today, in nearly all cultures. It is as close to an anthropological universal as one gets: war is a nearly exclusively male domain.[28]

2 Why has war been such a male preserve? Here I will rely upon Joshua

---

[27] This section may seem peripheral to the main line of argument, yet the topic has a larger purpose as well as intrinsic interest. Later, in Chapter 11. vii, I will argue that honor isn't necessarily patriarchal or gendered, and the honor of warriors is a central test case.

[28] Cf. Goldstein, 2001, Chapter 1: Over 97 percent of the estimated 23 million soldiers today are male, and 99.9 percent of all combat forces are male; with very few exceptions this disparity has held historically and across all societies. "As far as the available evidence goes, no society exclusively populated or controlled by women, nor one in which women were the primary fighters, has ever existed." (19) Further, ". . . war exists in virtually all cultures, and the potential for war can suddenly come to the fore even in a relatively peaceful society." (34) Braudy goes even further in holding that "all violence can thus justify itself as being connected to some issue of male honor" (Braudy, 2003, 53).

Goldstein's remarkable study, *War and Gender,* which surveys twenty social-scientific hypotheses to explain why men but not women fight. The best explanation, he believes, is that small but statistically significant male v. female biological differences (average size, strength, roughness of play) become reinforced by society as gender markers (the "cultural molding of tough, brave men, who feminize their enemies to encode domination"). In short, warriors are mostly made, not born.

3   Could war be gendered otherwise, or even not at all? Goldstein thinks the evidence shows that, given the varying distribution of qualities conducive to fighting (size, strength,stamina), the ability to fight is not confined to men.[29] Granted, men on average do inherit more fighting skills than women, but clearly many women have enough of these skills to be successful in fighting, and some women have more than most men.[30] So women are not incapable of fighting, and it is ridiculous to suggest that women are incapable of honor — they are equally capable as men of loyalty, trustworthiness, commitment to an honor group and an honor code. If fighting and honor ability were all that mattered, then women could well be warriors, even if not many have actually been warriors.[31]

4   Is male gendering of war a bad thing? Goldstein argues that it is, both for women and for men. Women are often victims of violence during wartime, and they also suffer oppression at the hands of men running the peacetime structures required by the "war system." But men are also oppressed by the war system, most obviously in dying disproportionately from fighting but also in being reared to become "'tough' men who can shut down emotionally in order to endure extreme pain (physical and psychological)," which damages men emotionally while enforcing their manhood. "Thus manhood, an artificial status that must be won individually, is typically constructed around a culture's need for brave

---

[29] Goldstein debunks such myths as that there is a distinctive genetic code for war (present only in males) and that sexual hormones explain propensity to fighting. (Chapter 3.)

[30] Goldstein says the evidence shows that (some) women have performed as well as (most) men in all military roles; in particular, women's strength is adequate to many combat situations (127), especially where technology undercuts the importance of brute muscle power.

[31] I thus take issue with those who conflate historical association, however common, with necessary connection. Consider, for example, the equation of "is" with "has traditionally been" in the following passage: "Honor is a masculine concept. It has traditionally regulated relations among men, summed up the prevailing ideals of manliness, and marked the boundaries of masculine comportment. Its codes sprang from the social and political arrangements of male-dominated warrior societies in which the possession of honor, together with its wealth and its perquisites, was essential for elite status" (Nye, 1993, vii). In my view honor is not necessarily a masculine concept, just as it is not the special possession of warriors. (Nye is further mistaken in thinking that "honor has flourished as nowhere else" in modern France (viii) and that "the high-water mark of modern honor" was the second decade of the twentieth century, because he confuses one noteworthy example of honor, with its distinctive honor code and conception of honor, with the broader concept of honor, permitting many different instantiations.)

and disciplined fighters" (Goldstein, 2001, 283). Further, having warriors around contributes to the likelihood if not the inevitability of war; the war system has a vested interest in blocking more pacific ways of settling differences and protecting interests. So male gendering of war is bad not only because it is sexist but because it harms both males and females. Better to dismantle the entire war system.

But what if the war system cannot or should not be dismantled? Goldstein presumes (hopes? dreams?) that war is a dispensable evil, and that one may eliminate sexism and war with one stroke. But what if this presumption is false and war is inevitable or (regrettably) for the best, all things considered? For the former, what if there will always be free riders on any peaceful scheme who will seek to gain their ends by violence against which non-violent resistance is ultimately futile, so that fighting may be the only way to block their violent efforts and to preserve important values?[32] If so, war may be a necessary evil, and if necessary, better that it should be fought by warriors than by mere killers or fanatical fighters. Alternatively, what if fighting, while not strictly necessary, is nevertheless the best (least bad) means of securing positive values against aggressors in the long run? If so, then war may be the least undesirable form of fighting. So in either case, whether war is necessary or expedient, it would be well to have warriors, all things considered.

Still, if there need to be warriors, why should they only be males? One view is that the human costs thereby are cut in half — only males are psychologically harmed by being conditioned to become warriors, though all share in war's great and chaotic suffering. On this view, sexism is a cheaper price to pay than making males and females alike bear the burdens of becoming warriors.

But those who view sexism as a greater evil than war, or an evil at least as great, and a dispensable evil at that, might go a different direction: Keep a necessary or expedient war system, but purge its sexist gendering. Let (some) women be warriors and permit them to share the burden of fighting, which requires that they suffer the cultural practices that will make them as tough and brave as men similarly conditioned; then they would be equally capable as men of becoming honorable killers liable to honorable deaths. Some might fear that military morale or "the male psyche" would be damaged,[33] others that male–female difference would disappear and sexual attraction

---

[32] Arguably, non-violent means can be much more successful against violence than usually supposed — to borrow a quip, it is not that non-violence has been tried and found wanting but that it has not been wanted and so not tried. Cf. Sharp, 1973, 1985.

[33] "It [women's participation in combat] tramples the male ego. When you get right down to it, you've got to protect the manliness of war" (General William Westmoreland in 1980, quoted by Goldstein, 2001, 283).

lost,[34] and that these consequences would be worse than the current system. On these views sexism is the price societies must pay to defend themselves. But if a non-sexist society is worth having, and if it can only be preserved by warriors, it will require that at least some females as well as some males become equipped to fight honorably.

X. Conclusion

Honor and war *do* go together, though not all lethal fighting is honorable. War is probably honor's original home (though not its only current home) as well as perhaps its most important manifestation. A sense of personal honor is what sets warriors apart from mere fighters and killers; it contributes to some of the nobler features of war and mitigates some of its harsher aspects, by requiring dangerous, self-sacrificing deeds and by prohibiting indiscriminate killing and other forms of disrespect for friend and foe alike. But honor is no cloak of immunity from all kinds of criticism. Honorable warriors can do reprehensible as well as praiseworthy things even in just wars — reprehensible not merely because they fall short of their own codes of honor but because those very codes do not coincide with moral principles. Warriors can find themselves fighting morally dubious wars in morally troublesome ways. So while it is better for fighters to be honorable than not, it would be better still if fighters were honorable warriors who were in the right.

---

[34] "Had war not existed, separating the sexes and making them attractive to each other, then probably it would have to be invented" (Van Creveld, 1991, 189).

Chapter 7

SPORTSMANSHIP AS HONOR[1]

Everyone agrees that sportsmanship[2] is vitally important in sport, and nearly all can readily recognize cases of good and bad sportsmanship. Contrast, for example, Cornell's forfeiture of an apparent last-second football victory over Dartmouth in 1940 because of an inadvertent fifth down, with Colorado's refusal to forfeit a win over Missouri in 1990 under similar conditions.[3] Or contrast Lindsay Morton in 2000 providing a tennis racquet in a championship game to an opponent who broke a string — and who then beat Morton with the borrowed racquet — with Kevin Whipple and Eric Butorac, who settled their 2003 national singles championship match by flipping a coin instead of by playing tennis, so that they could be fresh together as a team later in the day for the doubles championship. Or consider Sean Avery, left wing for the New York Rangers hockey team, and his inspired — or demented — new way of blocking the goalie by directly facing, shadowing and obstructing his vision. "That's not hockey," said the New Jersey Devils goalie Martin Brodeur, and the National Hockey League agreed, promulgating overnight a new explicit rule prohibiting such conduct — the "Sean Avery rule." Such examples could be multiplied endlessly across all sports.

But agreement ends with widespread recognition of good and bad sportsmanship, particularly when it comes to the essential matters: What exactly *is* sportsmanship, and why is good sportsmanship important? In this chapter, I aim to take a fresh look at these intertwined issues by viewing sportsmanship from the vantage point of honor. Much that is otherwise murky about sportsmanship becomes clearer when seen from this standpoint, even if

---

[1] This chapter somewhat revises Sessions, 2004, without changing its fundamental thrust.

[2] The term "sportsmanship" may have negative gender connotations for some, but I intend no offense. There seems to be no viable alternative ("sportspersonship" is grotesque, "sports(wo)manship" is no better, and "sporting sense" is inaccurate). I certainly want to include female as well as male athletes of all classes in my discussion, and I ask the reader not to confuse my usage with other meanings.

[3] I owe this example to Mike Walsh.

not everything in everyone's conception of sportsmanship thereby receives illumination.[4]

I restrict my attention to *organized competitive sports,* in distinction from (a) other kinds of competitions (economic, social, intellectual, etc.), (b) games that are not competitive (cooperative and solitary games), and (c) competitive games that are not formally organized (lacking stated rules, officials, governing bodies, and the like).[5] Doubtless sportsmanship exists in cooperative as well as in competitive contexts, but the latter is the harder case, and more illuminating. It is harder because sportsmanship appears to be, and often is, in tension with a central point of competitions: winning. It is more illuminating because it shows how a sense of honor may exist among even fierce antagonists.

To engage in a competitive sport is necessarily to play to win. Indeed, in the immortal words associated with Vince Lombardi, "winning isn't everything; it's the only thing."[6] Moreover, winning's importance is magnified in many sports by the lure of winning's rewards: fame and kudos, of course, but also fortunes. Plus there are pressures exerted on those who play by those who do not: coaches, fans, sponsors, dependants, gamblers — all have a stake in the outcome of sports that does not necessarily pay much attention to sportsmanship. Even so, nearly everyone in and out of sports recognizes that winning *isn't* the only thing: not all's fair in love and war and sports. One should play to win but one should also play fairly; one should abide by the letter of the law of the game, but also by its spirit; one should respect the game by being a good sport, win *or* lose. So even though the attractiveness of sportsmanship may at times seem overmatched by the blandishments of victory, most competitors continue to want to be good sports. But why does sportsmanship matter? And what is sportsmanship such that it does matter?

---

[4] I will not attempt to say just how important sportsmanship is in relation to competing values. I merely present an account of what gives sportsmanship a large portion of whatever importance it has: Sportsmanship is at least as important as an athlete's honor.

[5] This usage contrasts with James Keating's influential but also much criticized distinction between "athletics," competitive games, and "sport," cooperative pleasant amusement or diversion (Keating, 1964); Keating's "athletics" is my "sports," and I shall not treat of "sport" in his sense. More fundamentally, I think taking sportsmanship as a moral category is a major mistake that has misled many. For other criticism of Keating, cf. Fraleigh, 1984, and Arnold, 1997.

[6] The quote is radically unclear; in its most obvious meaning it is redundant, though perhaps it could better be construed as "winning isn't the most important thing among many things that matter, it's the only thing that matters;" so construed, it's patently false, and one wonders how many people actually believe it. According to his biographer, the quotation on the wall of Lombardi's locker room traces back through a mediocre John Wayne 1953 movie, *Trouble Along the Way,* where the phrase is uttered by an eleven-year-old girl, back to the "colorful" UCLA football coach, Henry "Red" Sanders. (Cf. Maraniss, 1999, Chapter 21; I am indebted to Tom Burish for this reference). But Lombardi made the phrase famous — or infamous. Such are the vagaries of conferred honor!

I. The Usual Suspects

There have been many attempts to characterize the nature of sportsmanship and thereby to illumine its importance (Rosenberg, 1993). It is instructive to glance at some of these and to recognize their limitations before examining the alternative proposed here. Consider this sample of proposals[7]:

1 Some hold that sportsmanship is fair play and that fair play is a constitutive rule of competitive games; unless a competitor plays fairly, he or she isn't really playing the game at all. This is the so-called "logical incompatibility thesis," the view that competing and cheating are somehow logically inconsistent (cf. Pearson, 1988; Suits, 1967, 1978; with criticism by Lehman, 1988). But this is implausible; fair players and cheaters (up to a point) can still be said to be playing the same game, even though their aims and means diverge. A cheater in soccer aims to win (and may succeed in winning) *a soccer match* and not something else, although his tactics vary crucially from those who aim to play soccer fairly. Further, there are usually rules against cheating, with penalties attached; one doesn't have rules forbidding logical contradictions, nor any penalties besides absurdity and self-defeating pointlessness.

2 Along the same lines, one might adapt a view of Alasdair MacIntyre concerning what he calls "practices":

> By a 'practice' I am going to mean any coherent and complex form of socially established cooperative human activity through which goods internal to that form of activity are realized in the course of trying to achieve those standards of excellence which are appropriate to, and partially definitive of, that form of activity, with the result that human powers to achieve excellence, and human conceptions of the ends and good involved, are systematically extended. Tic-tac-toe is not an example of a practice in this sense, nor is throwing a football with skill; but the game of football is, and so is chess. (MacIntyre, 1984a, 187)

In this view, sports are practices and the principles of fair play are partially constitutive of those practices (cf. Butcher and Schneider, 2001; Arnold, 1997, Chapter 1). Hence to play a sport is to participate in the practice and necessarily to follow its constitutive rules. Sportsmanship once again is considered logically inextricable from sport, this time because competitive games are socially cooperative traditions of human interaction. But also once again this point seems overstated at best:

---

[7] I stress that this is a sample, not a comprehensive survey or a detailed commentary. My aim is to sketch some views of sportsmanship that variously contrast with the honor perspective, in order to illuminate the latter's distinctiveness.

cheaters may break the rules of their sports, but they still play those sports (at least until they are caught in flagrant violation of the rules and dismissed from the game).

3 A modified incompatibility view, one that could also be teased from MacIntyre's statement, is that while good sportsmanship may not be necessary for playing a sport at all, it *is* necessary for playing that sport well or excellently. On this view, a cheat may be skilled — not least in concealing her chicanery — but these are not the skills of the sport. There is something to this view, but it misses the ways in which cheating skills are sport-specific: throwing a spitball undetected is different from holding an opponent undetected; evasion of the balk rule is a fine art cultivated by left-handed pitchers in baseball, and nowhere else. Cheating in a sport is therefore not entirely disjoint from playing that sport, or even from playing it at a very high level.[8]

4 Some account for sportsmanship as personal integrity — being honest, open, and true to yourself (cf. Slusher, 1967). But what happens when someone's principles do not include fair play? Moreover, even when fair play is one's principle, on what does commitment to this principle rest — is it anything more than an arbitrary existential choice that could be changed at will? Personal commitment may be necessary for sportsmanship, but it is not enough.

5 Many speak of sportsmanship as "respect for the game," a devotion or commitment to a sport that transcends particular triumphs and failures (cf. Butcher and Schneider, 2001). Doubtless most competitors do love the competition independently of the winning (or love the winning in large part because of the competition), but it is not clear how this love extends to "the game" itself, much less what "the game" actually means. It is even murkier why this love should extend beyond the player's playing lifetime: Why should a competitor care about some abstraction — a constellation of rules of play and principles of fair play — or some future instances of that abstraction that he or she will not participate in or even be around to enjoy?

6 Some hold that sportsmanship is necessary for games to endure as ongoing competitions; without widespread sportsmanship, rule-governed competitions would degenerate into all-out struggles not unlike love and war. There is some truth here, but clearly sports can survive indefinitely with a modicum of cheating, both recognized and hidden; free riders we will always have with us. The deeper question is why a present competitor should care about the continuation of the competition;

---

[8] Though not at the highest possible level? Is winning without cheating higher than winning by cheating? Is beating a cheat without cheating higher than winning fairly against a fair competitor? It all depends on what one means by "higher": more skillful or more excellent?

why not just care about the sport only so long as one is able to compete in it?

7   Some hold that the principles of fair play preserve and promote *equality* among competitors — a "level playing field"— thereby stimulating them to stretch their talents to the utmost; equal conditions are necessary for excellent competition (McIntosh, 1979). Again this is an exaggeration; those with truly great talent may rise to new heights of excellence precisely when the odds are stacked against them. Moreover, equality is clearly not sufficient for excellence: mediocre competitors may be evenly matched, and well-matched competitors may not bring out the best in one another, much less in the game as a whole.

8   Perhaps the most widespread view is that sportsmanship is simply a matter of applied ethics — universal moral principles and virtues applied to sports (Arnold, 1997; Fraleigh, 1984; Gough, 1997; Lumpkin *et al.*, 1999; McIntosh, 1979; among many others). Russell Gough expresses the prevailing view this way: "Sportsmanship is a matter of being good (character) and doing right (action) in sports" (Gough, 1997, 21). It seems that almost any moral principle or virtue may be applied to sports: fair play is justice in sport; camaraderie is altruism in sport; competitiveness is courage in sport; and so on. But this view strikes me as moral overkill — seeking the ultimate and conclusive reasons of morality as the only alternatives to discreditable reasons of self-interest.[9] No doubt bad sports are usually not morally admirable, even if the rules they violate are morally neutral, but that doesn't mean that morality is the only or best vantage point for viewing sportsmanship. Not every normative judgment of right and wrong, good and bad, virtuous and vicious, need be a *moral* one, and sportsmanship may be something other than morality applied to sport.

II. Sportsmanship as Personal Honor

All of these views of sportsmanship have some plausibility. Some, however, are shallow, while others are too broad. All are incomplete. I suggest that we can gain a better handle on sportsmanship by regarding it as a matter of personal honor among competitors in a given sport (the basic honor group). The rules and principles of sportsmanship aren't constitutive of the game but rather of (part of) that group's honor code — a set of principles held in common as matters of honor by all members of the honor group, in a bond of mutual recognition. To make this suggestion cogent, we need to recall

---

[9] Fraleigh e.g. holds that only "morally mature" action-guides are ultimate (Fraleigh, 1984, 193–4).

certain points from our earlier discussion (in Part I) of different concepts of honor.

First, *conferred* and *recognition honor.* Conferred honor is the regard of someone given to someone on some attributed basis (or the token of this regard — gifts, rewards, attention, and the like). Recognition honor is public appreciation of genuine excellence that rests not on an attributed basis but on something objectively excellent. Of course, it may be difficult to discern in practice whether something is conferred or recognized, and the esteem, plaudits and tokens may be much the same in both; but the underlying principle is quite different. Conferred honor is a gift from others, resting finally on their view of the honoree; it is basically reputation in their eyes. Recognition honor, on the other hand, is not a gift but something owed; the honoree's excellence controls the honorer's public recognition. Still, both conferred and recognition honor are external, requiring the notice and acts of others. Both kinds of honors are widespread in any social group, and not least in competitive sports, with its innumerable trophies, prizes, medals, pins, ribbons, awards, titles, certificates, ceremonies, banquets, and the like. There are even awards for sportsmanship,[10] but these honors should not be confused with the personal honor that sportsmanship is based upon; and truly fair-minded competitors don't play fairly in order to be recognized as "Sportsman of the year"!

Second, *positional honor.* This is a matter of being, having or doing something that positions one "above" others in a social group, whether in terms of status or of achievement. People with positional honor are society's "winners," and positional honor is what winners in competitive sports receive — victory in competition, records set, standards established — and it is also often what they strive to achieve, quite apart from any conferred or recognition honors; the activity of winning may matter more to the winner than being recognized as a winner (recognized by outsiders anyway; recognition by other competitors is closer to the bone).

Third, and most salient, there is *personal honor.* Recall that having *an effective sense of honor* means adhering firmly to the honor code of some honor group, understanding what that honor code requires, prohibits and permits, being able to act according to the code, being intrinsically motivated to do so, and effectively willing it. Moreover, this commitment goes deep; someone with an effective sense of honor regards her honor as one of the more important

---

[10] Cf. the home page of the Institute for International Sport at www.internationalsport.com for a plethora of links to numerous agencies rewarding sportsmanship. One would like to think that sportsmanship awards are given only to those who act without an eye toward receiving such awards; otherwise they would undermine the quality of character they seek to promote, by giving it the wrong kind of motivation. As we shall see, the kind of honor that good "sportspersons" treasure is personal honor, and its most fundamental reward is respectful mutual recognition by like-minded others, which doesn't require formal awards.

features of herself, deeply connected to her sense of self.

But even though personal honor connects deeply with an individual's sense of identity and worth, nonetheless such honor is intelligible only in terms of the social backdrop; it is commitment not only to a *code* but also to a *community*, the *honor group*. Recall that members of an honor group (i) are *honor-capable*, i.e. have the capacity to act honorably and to be honorable; (ii) have the same *sense of honor*, i.e. understand and are effectively committed to the same *honor code*,[11] and (iii) *mutually recognize* one another as members of the same honor group. Membership in an honor group is not automatic or conferred; it must be earned through voluntary adherence to a practice with a tradition. Honor requires effort and talent to achieve, even when it looks effortless. Further, belonging to an honor group means adhering to an honor code that is socially shared and publicly supported (at least within the honor group; cf. Solomon, 1992, 221). Finally, an honor group is a society of *equals in honor* — all members have the same standards of honor to uphold, all are presumed equally capable of upholding them, and all are deemed equally honorable until proven otherwise.

It is worth repeating that loyalty to an honor community is not just commitment to an abstract set of principles (the code); rather, it is public involvement with the actual individuals comprising that honor group — recognizing in myriad public ways that they belong to the same honor community as oneself, even as one recognizes that they likewise so recognize oneself. Honor is verifiable and constantly verified, in all the myriad actions and interactions of the members of the honor group. Of course it is possible to seek to acquire personal honor for other purposes (e.g. conferred honors), though motivations may change as one internalizes the honor code. And it is also possible to appear to act honorably, so far as public detection can reach, while remaining personally dishonorable.[12] The point is, rather, that public behavior normally displays to others not merely actions in conformity with the honor code but also the intentions, beliefs, and motivations that lie behind it. An honor group can rely upon its members only if each member's commitment to the honor code and to the honor group goes deeper than some utilitarian calculation about the results of so committing oneself. The credit of trust honor that is extended from one honor group member to another presumes this deeper commitment, and so the creditor presumes

---

[11] An honor code includes all norms of conduct that are held as matters of honor in some particular honor group, whether or not these norms are explicitly codified. Not all norms of an honor group are matters of honor.

[12] There are at least two ways this can occur: the usual case, where there is a secret act of dishonor that continues to fester so long as one remains committed to honor; and, perhaps the more interesting case, where personal honor is regarded privately merely as a means to some further end, to be discarded if and when the two come into conflict, even if such conflict never occurs.

that he can (usually) detect such commitment in others. Personal honor is public honor even if it is not reducible to observable deeds.

Personal honor involves *mutual respect* of other members of the honor group: such respect values all members of the group, including oneself, qua group member,[13] and differs from *esteem,* which values someone for talents or achievements apart from group membership. Such respect is deeply treasured, in part because personal honor is not an inherited or conferred status but a personal achievement; it may be gained, lost, and, sometimes, regained through actions and inactions. One acquires personal honor by acquiring those habits of heart and mind that dispose one thoroughly and intuitively to follow the honor code of one's honor group. Honorable character is learned through honorable actions, and it is expressed through such actions.

An honorable person can be counted on both to follow the honor group's code (commitment honor) and also to remain steadfastly loyal to other honor group members (trust honor) — and to do both without hesitation, question or even much reflection. An honorable person can be relied on by others to act in solidarity *with* and *for* (the members of) the honor group. She can be trusted to act honorably, and she is worth trusting because of her honor.

Once again we must emphasize that personal honor is not necessarily moral (cf. Chapter 4 above). The honor code of an honor group may command or prohibit acts that are morally indifferent (e.g. dress codes, or the rules of hospitality) or even contrary to morality (e.g. the honor codes of street gangs and the Mafia). Further, honor is relative; different honor groups have different honor codes, and honor codes change over time. But it is possible for an honor code to be morally acceptable, when it contains or is constrained by moral principles.

The application of this picture of personal honor to competitive sports is straightforward. It is natural to see sporting competitors, individuals or teams, as belonging to a larger honor group that transcends team loyalties. Sportsmanship is part or all of that group's *honor code of competition:*[14] these are the rules or principles (not all of them explicit or even capable of being made explicit) that govern the behavior of those who participate in and recognize others as participating in the competition. On this view, good sports

---

[13] Recall that this is not quite moral respect — valuing individual persons qua individuals rather than qua members of some group. But it is not thereby incompatible with moral respect, for one may respect the same person in various ways.

[14] Note that there could well be more to a sports honor code than rules for competition: perhaps there could also be rules for public and private discussion of others in the sport, or rules for treating non-competitors in various contexts (e.g. speaking to the media, signing autographs, coaching beginners), or rules of off-field dress and decorum. But these would not be, strictly speaking, rules of sportsmanship. Note also that there could well be non-honor communal norms that (should) govern competitions. The upshot is that "code of competition" and "sports honor code" greatly overlap but are not quite co-extensive.

are personally honorable in competition; they are honorable competitors. They are motivated by a desire to compete (and, yes, to win) according to their group's code of sportsmanship; their effective sense of sportsmanship is their sporting code of honor.

Moreover, sportsmanship matters to honorable competitors in the way that honor matters: deeply. Commitment to the game is a natural byproduct of commitment to other members of the honor community who compete in playing that game; commitment to abstractions such as "the game" follows from and mutually reinforces commitment to actual entities — one's competitors, particular other persons. To be sure, honorable competitors are attracted by the intrinsic delights of fair play as a context for developing and extending their athleticism — and they are not adverse to the rewards of competitive success — but they are also drawn to the social joys of a community of honor: respecting and being respected by those competitors who play fairly according to the same rules and in the same spirit. Their solidarity with fellow competitors goes beyond mutual use as means for achieving personal goals and satisfying individual interests; it is a loyalty that is constantly manifested both on and off the field. Commitment to common principles of sportsmanship is linked with loyalty to other members of the group of competitors.

III. Two Complications

Two points require further clarification — one about the relation of honor to morality, the other about the membership of an honor group.

On the first point, it may appear that viewing honor as sportsmanship relativizes morality. Indeed, some may think my views demote morality from a "transhistorical" point of view with a set of "rational" (objective, universal, overriding) principles to a situated community's contingent common consent about norms and values (cf. Burke and Roberts, 1997, with criticism by Dixon, 2001). But I intend no such relativizing or demotion of morality; appearances to the contrary are due, I suspect, to thinking that sportsmanship and morality coincide. Such coincidence is precisely what I am denying. Whether morality is objective and absolute is not at issue, for sportsmanship is simply not the same thing as morality in sports. No doubt there are moral principles applicable to sports, or anyway to the people who participate in sports, but those moral principles are not the whole, nor even the epicenter, of sportsmanship.

Since personal honor is not the same as morality, it follows that sportsmanship as honor is not the same as sportsmanship as morality. Of course, the rules of sportsmanship *may* be moral, but they need not be; they may also be non-moral, amoral or even immoral. Sportsmanship is therefore relative to social context in ways that (putative) objective morality seeks to avoid. But no member of any honor group — sports groups included — is *confined* to that group's honor perspective or unavoidably *bound* to its morally contingent rules. Questions about practices regarded as honorable within some honor group may be raised from various perspectives: from self-interest, personal commitments, other honor groups, and the wider society, to be sure, but also from the standpoint of an arguably objective morality. Such concerns may provoke changes in the honor code — or perhaps its complete rejection (bullfighting?). But in the end, where the perspectives of honor and morality diverge, the individual person remains free to commit herself to either perspective, and there is no guarantee that morality will prevail. Honor is corrigible by morality, but it is not always so corrected.

On the second point, who, precisely, belongs to, or constitutes, the honor group for sports? There is no single honor group for all sports, because the various honor codes in various sports differ in their specifics, though there may be considerable overlap in generalities. But who constitutes the honor group within a given sport? By any measure, actual current players form the core of a sport's honor group, and it is their mutual recognition of one another's honorability that sustains, and in a sense constitutes, the honor code of the group. But MacIntyre is right that sports are "practices" in his sense, and practices have traditions — histories and prospects. So former players, and future ones as well, are also members, at least potential ones. Further, those who care to assist, regulate and study the sport (coaches, officials, commentators) may also be viewed as members of the honor group, particularly if they have previously been competitors and have had time to ponder and reflect upon the honor code — they may become the wise women and men who deserve to be consulted, heard and followed when difficult cases arise; they are the sages of sport. But what about spectators, who also claim to love the game? Here admiration of fair and excellent play all too frequently yields to taunts and chants of "we're number one"— i.e. interested spectators of the game become partisan fans concerned with winning regardless of sportsmanship, at which point they definitely do not belong to the honor group.[15]

At a finer level of analysis, we can see that not even all competitors in a given sport are members of exactly the same honor group. In every sport there are levels of competition, with age and gender (and sometimes race and class) also splintering the sport into different communities of competition. In the narrowest sense, one's honor group consists only of peer players. Nomar Garciaparra and a little-league shortstop are in some sense members of the same honor group of all baseball players, but they are leagues apart

---

[15] That is, they don't belong to the sports honor group. They might well belong to another (quasi-)honor group with different standards: e.g. soccer hooligans. (I owe this point to an anonymous reader of the original article.)

not only in levels of skill but also in their senses of honor (at least in its fine details and applications). We might also speculate that there can be different and variously overlapping honor groups within the same game at the same level. How soccer is played at a national level in different parts of the world varies not only in style and strategy but also, for example, in what constitutes a fair tackle within the rules of FIFA. But no matter how variegated the honor communities within a sport, it is inconceivable that the rules, or sense, of sportsmanship should be so finely ground as to include only members of one's own team, much less oneself alone!

IV. Implications

Viewing sportsmanship as personal honor brings into clearer focus a number of aspects of sportsmanship that are not well explained by other conceptions; here are ten of them:

(a) Sportsmanship as honor explains a crucial part of the anxiety competitors feel when they are about to meet a completely unknown player or team: the worry is not just over their opponent's talent, intensity and desire, and hence over the outcome of the pending competition, but even more seriously over their opponent's character: Is she a good sport, are they sportsmen, or will she or they play dirty and cheat, turning a joyous contest of skill into a grim struggle for survival? Honor thrives not in anonymous crowds but in groups small enough to become acquainted with one another's character, so that mutual recognition of honorable behavior can occur. To be assured of the honorable character of an opponent is not to be assured of winning or losing; it is to be assured that one will be treated fairly, neither humiliated in defeat nor despised in victory, and this is a very important assurance indeed.

(b) It explains the primal motivation of those most committed and dedicated to a sport — not necessarily at a given time, but over a lifetime. Few if any of the best and most admired career players in a sport play solely or most deeply because of the extrinsic rewards of money, prizes and fame, though the attractions of these conferred or recognition honors is perhaps never absent; but neither do they strive solely for the positional honors of achievement and status, of winning and being "at the top" of a sport. They have, to be sure, an intense "love of the game," in the sense of sheer intrinsic enjoyment of their own mastery of the intricacies of competitive exertion; everyone loves what he or she is good at doing, and an excellent player exults in his excellence (though careful in his celebration not to denigrate the competition?). But also, and vitally, they are driven to gain and hold the respect of their peers, and this respect is forthcoming, or at least merited, only for those who are good enough to seriously play the game according to the spirit of fair play as defined by the group's sense of sportsmanship — its honor code. Sportsmanship and dedication to a sport go together most deeply not out of love of some abstraction called "the game," but out of a deep desire to belong as a fully equal member to an honorable group whose behavior and very identity center on that sport.

(c) It gives a richer account of the importance of striving for excellence in sport: Excellence is not just a useful or even necessary means to the end of winning, nor is it simply an intrinsically enjoyable achievement, nor only a combination of both; it is also what one's peers admire and pursue themselves, what one admires in them, and what they admire in oneself. There is an ineluctable social dimension to the pursuit of excellence in sports.[16]

(d) It explains the wide variation in what counts as sportsmanship in different sports. Just as honor groups vary widely in their honor codes, so different sports have their different standards: intentionally causing injury to another is differently viewed in boxing and wrestling; acceptable ways of psyching out an opponent vary from baseball to tennis; deception varies in basketball and football; grandstanding is differently regarded in track and soccer; and so on. Moreover, it also explains how standards of sportsmanship may change over time within one tradition of sport — consider the rich history of end-zone celebrations in American football or in international rugby. But even though honor codes may vary, it is still a matter of honor to abide by the code of the honor group to which one belongs. When in Rome do as the Romans do, and more particularly, when you are a gladiator in Rome do as the Roman gladiators do.

(e) It explains the empirical findings of Andy Rudd that while participation in competitive sports may build what he calls "social character" (such values as teamwork, loyalty, and self-sacrifice), it does not enhance what he calls "moral character" (honesty, justice, responsibility) (Rudd, 1998). This is precisely what one would expect if sportsmanship is pegged to a sense of honor that is not necessarily, or not fully, a moral one but is rather tied to a particular honor group's morally contingent code; but it is counter-evidence to the view that sportsmanship is inherently moral or simply an application of moral principles — why should good sports be so *selectively* moral?

(f) It can help explain the faint but lingering odor of upper-class elitism and snobbery that some detect in the notion of sportsmanship (Young, 1984), and it can also explain why this elitism (epitomized in a certain class-based distinction between "amateur" and "professional") is inessential to sportsmanship. What truly matters in sportsmanship as honor is that one's peers respect one as an equal competitor, not that one does or doesn't earn one's

---

[16] Peter Arnold emphasizes sportsmanship as social union (in addition to providing pleasure and serving as a vehicle of altruism) without mentioning honor as a feature of this union, except glancingly in a footnote about the tennis player Mats Wilander (Arnold, 1997, 64n4).

livelihood from the competition. One's peers may be gentleman amateurs of the old school, but maybe not. Of course, this view ignores the reality of power politics in the governing bodies of sports, which have all kinds of vested interests in controlling the official rules of the sport. But while sportsmanship, like all other normative notions, can be hijacked by interests of class, race, commerce, and nation, this is not its essence.

(g) A corollary is that honor can help us better understand the historical context out of which a sense of sportsmanship arose. Sportsmanship, like honor, seems to be an originally aristocratic and elitist notion that has been somewhat democratized, or at least more widely disseminated. But traces of the past remain in the present, as in the enduring importance of peer respect, even when the peer group alters by admitting talent from "lower" classes.

(h) While the perspective of honor is most useful in explaining the lure of sportsmanship in refereed competitions such as tennis or football, it can also help explain at least part of the motivation for sportsmanship in self-policing sports such as golf. Serious golfers (not hackers) deeply desire to belong to the honor group of peer golfers, and violating the rules of golf, even when one could do so without detection, stains one's honor and clouds one's membership. That is why there are so many examples of golfers, even in competitions where large amounts of money ride on every shot, calling penalty strokes on themselves for unobserved infractions. It is not just that they would be penalized or embarrassed should others observe an unreported violation of the rules (i.e. they are not simply concerned for the stigma that being caught would produce on their reputations, nor even for what it might cost them in victory; those are conferred and positional honors, respectively). Rather, their personal honor matters to them: They truly want to be honorable, just as they want to be recognized as being honorable by members of the honor group of golfers.

(i) It can explain some of the perceived deterioration in sportsmanship in contemporary sports. Sportsmanship is threatened from many sides today, chiefly by the high financial stakes of winning and losing: who can fail to be tempted to cheat when there is so much money riding on victory? But there are other factors, and one of them involves honor. Size matters to honor — the size of the honor group cannot be too large, or it loses the capacity for mutual recognition so crucial to honor. As the group enlarges, there comes a point where one cannot reliably check upon the character of others through their observed or reported behavior — they are literally strangers — and so one cannot rely upon their honor. Similarly, I conjecture, as a sport enlarges, one will inevitably encounter *competitive strangers* — not simply competitors of unknown talents and achievements but persons whose senses of honor are unknown. When this happens, one cannot depend upon the stranger's sense of fair play — it may differ from one's own, or even be absent altogether — and this weakens one's own disposition to play fairly with the stranger.[17]

(j) Finally, it can also explain the clash of different regional standards within a single sport. More than mere variant "styles" of play, these standards are different views about what is permissible and impermissible in the sport, like ice hockey as played in North America vs. Eastern Europe a few decades ago. Such clashes may be due to different honor codes maintained by different local honor groups. Their resolution, if any, may involve changes by one or another group to adopt the code of the other, or it may require agreement on some basis other than honor (so that the differing groups might continue to view the other's behavior as legal but still somehow dishonorable). Teams may continue to compete without a shared code of honor, but they are likely to do so with the thought that their opponents are bad sports, unfair, or even dishonorable.

V. Conclusion

There are, of course, limitations to this view of sportsmanship as personal honor. All of the other views noted earlier (Section I) have some contribution to make toward understanding sportsmanship; honor is certainly not the only point of view on sportsmanship, even if it is, as I believe, the best overall. Beyond that, some may feel that honor is too serious a matter — a matter of "real life" or even of life and death — to apply to sports, though this would be challenged by those who live sporting lives, for whom sport *is* life. Others may think that moral reasons for playing fairly are superior to reasons of honor: what most deeply underwrites sportsmanship, they hold, is not the respect of one's honorable peers but moral principle — it wouldn't be (morally) *right* to lie and cheat and play unfairly. (But even if they are different, honor and morality need not be antagonists; honor could still be important even if it doesn't always track morality.) Still others may find it odd that athletes today typically do not think of sportsmanship in terms of personal honor — but is this perspicacity about oneself or conceptual ignorance (partaking in a more general cultural blindness)? Finally, some may claim that sportsmanship as honor is only an extended analogy, not a literal characterization; and with this claim I am in considerable sympathy, though I think the analogy is quite extensive indeed.

---

[17] Perhaps something different from though analogous to honor can take over when the competitive group grows too large — rules aimed at enhancing fair play, enforced by officials on and off the field, or even positive laws adjudicated by the state. Perhaps also athletes could develop a corresponding sense of fair play and commitment to these rules. (I owe this suggestion to an anonymous referee.) But I think this external substitute for internal honor is likely to be less effective and stable in promoting fair play than a true sense of honor.

All things considered, then, there is great promise in viewing sportsmanship as honor, not least because it reveals important and often unnoticed
similarities among the great human institutions and endeavors where honor
is found. Sportsmanship is, I believe, but one important outcropping of
the massive bedrock of honor that runs throughout human life in all times
and places. Honor is found not simply in love and war, nor in hospitality
and feuds, nor in social class and religion; most emphatically, honor is not
confined to distant ("tribal," "warrior" or "traditional") societies. Honor lives
also in the strenuous games our contemporaries play with and against one
another. Honor in sport is sportsmanship.

Chapter 8

___

PATRIOTISM AS HONOR

Patriotism is a many-splendored thing — or maybe not so splendorous. It has been praised to the heavens, recommended warmly or warily, deplored generically or specifically, and condemned categorically or with qualifications. But perhaps it is more in need of understanding than of praise or blame. In this chapter, I seek to illuminate the political scene from an angle unusual in political philosophy today, that of honor. Much becomes clearer when we view patriotism as a species of personal honor.

First we should focus our light: We are concerned with personal honor, not conferred, recognition, positional, commitment or trust honor, though the realm of politics has endless examples of all these peripheral forms of honor. And we are concerned with personal honor in politics — though not with all of personal political honor, which we may divide roughly into three kinds:[1]

1   *The honor of politicians.* This is what most people first think of when they hear the words "political honor." Or rather, what they think of is the *lack* of honor, the often-flagrant *dis*honor displayed by many political leaders: adultery, lying, cheating, stealing, bribery, fraud, graft, nepotism, scheming, sleaze, dishonesty, corruption — unprincipled behavior and lack of integrity. But there are also the lapses of officials — "public servants" however personally virtuous who nonetheless fail to serve the public good — sometimes by serving instead the private interests of their leaders or their party out of misguided loyalty, and sometimes by serving instead their own personal interests also out of inappropriate allegiance. The honor of leaders and officials is interesting on its own, and I conjecture that an approach taking seriously their respective honor

___

[1] Cf. Philp, 2007, for a fine discussion of "political conduct" under three headings: (i) rulers; (ii) servants, followers, and officials, and (iii) subjects, citizens, and institutions. I will attend to some aspects of the last group. I have also learned much from Dobel, 1999, who focuses on the integrity of public officials, although my concerns here lie elsewhere.

groups and honor codes would be insightful, although considerable attention would have to be given to politicians' lust for conferred and status honor. But that is not my concern here.

2   *The honor of polities.* Though less frequently than in previous centuries, one still hears about the honor of countries, nations and states — political groups of all sorts and sizes. Wars are still waged on behalf of national honor, even when other reasons are officially broadcast, and many public acts and policies are designed to retrieve or enhance such honor.[2] One might also consider a polity's institutions as instancing a kind of corporate honor — benign or corrupt — independently of the agents who work within those institutions. The regard or respect tendered one country by other countries is often a major policy consideration, whether out of "a decent respect to the opinions of mankind" as in the Declaration of Independence or out of more pragmatic considerations. Moreover it matters greatly what kind of polity is in question, for different institutions and structures view their own honor, and that of others, differently. Here again an analysis of this kind of political honor, both in and between states, would be worthwhile, but also again my present concern lies elsewhere.

3   *The honor of citizens.* Here we will focus our attention primarily upon the citizens of liberal democracies, but our discussion is relevant to those in other polities. What does it mean to speak of the honor of citizens? I suggest that we view their patriotism, the patriotism of the members of a "body politic," as a species of personal honor. Of course, each citizen's sense of personal honor is likely to include more than patriotism; after all, citizens are people too. Nonetheless the analogy is illuminating. Here the honor group is the whole country, with every citizen a member, and the honor code includes shared normative principles that guide citizen behavior toward insiders (fellow citizens) and outsiders (aliens). This code may be explicit, as in a written constitution or pledge of allegiance, or it may be implicit in public rituals and symbols, or engrained in traditions, stories and institutions, but it is presumably shared by all citizens — and only by them. In order to give flesh to this skeletal account, we need to take a closer look at patriotism and some of the supposed moral issues frequently discussed in connection with patriotism.

---

[2] Cf. O'Neill, 1999, for an illuminating game-theoretical analysis of international honor and war, although I think game theory is ill equipped to deal with the concept of personal honor.

I. PATRIOTISM

Patriotism is simply love of country. But no love is simple, and this one is complex to a fault. There are complications about the love, about whose love it is, and about what is loved.[3] Igor Primoratz explains that this love is ". . . motivated in part by the fact that it is one's country, and expressed in a special concern for its welfare and that of compatriots" (Primoratz, 2002, 11). Stephen Nathanson says the elements of his preferred "moderate patriotism" are a special affection for one's own country, a desire that it prosper and flourish, a special *but non-exclusive* concern for it, support of *morally constrained* pursuit of national goals, and *a conditional* support of its policies.[4] Simon Keller, who thinks patriotism "not a virtue and probably a vice" (Keller, 2007, 92), holds that patriotism is a dangerous form of loyalty, and "loyalty is the attitude and associated pattern of conduct that is constituted by an individual's taking [not taking] something's side, and doing so with a certain sort of motive: namely, a motive that is partly emotional in nature, involves a response to the thing itself, and makes essential reference to a special relationship that the individual takes to exist between herself and the thing to which she is loyal" (Keller, 2007, 21).

All seem to agree that there is something "egocentric" about patriotism: it is always love of "*my*" country, not love of countries in general or love of country in the abstract (the idea of a country) (cf. Primoratz, 2002, 10). But at the same time my love is "for" something I regard as valuable in certain respects I regard highly: it is always a love for some traits, achievements or qualities I believe, qua patriot, that the country possesses (*ibid.*) and that I esteem or treasure. Further, patriotic love involves loyalty — to my country, of course, but also loyalty to the other members of my country as well as loyalty (commitment, in my terms) to the valuable characteristics my country supposedly exemplifies.

Beyond these features, there is considerable disagreement, or at least difference of emphasis. Some, like Keller, focus on the psychological motivation of the patriot — the affections or sentiments or dispositions and their connection — or rather disconnection, as Keller asserts — to beliefs and evidence. Others, like Kleinig, stress more the behavior or conduct generated by the motives (Kleinig, 2008). Still others dwell on the rituals, sentiments, and symbols that energize and concretize the motives and channel the behavior. Most construe patriotism as a dyadic relation of citizen to country,

---

[3] Cf. Callan, 2006, for further complexities of love and country.

[4] Nathanson, 1993, 34. Presumably "patriotism" that was not "moderate" would eliminate the phrases I have italicized; in his chapter in Primoratz, 2002, 114, Nathanson adds to these points a sense of personal identification with one's own country, and a willingness to make sacrifices for it or to protect it.

but some think there is normally a third term, and hence a triadic relation: I am loyal to my country *above, or even as opposed to, other countries.* In this view, partiality to one's own country is suffused with indifference or convulsed with antagonism towards other countries.[5] One's own country is deemed superior to other countries, and this supposed superiority meshes with the often profound loyalty demanded by and given to one's country: my country is not just good; it is better, so its demands can be proportionately greater. Finally, patriotic love is entangled with respect: Dishonoring a country is (felt as) disrespecting its citizens, and a citizen's love of country manifests itself in myriad ways as respect for those who are loyal to his country, i.e. ideally, all other fellow-citizens.

In discussing patriotism, terminological perils abound. The patriarchal overtones of "patria" ("fatherland") need not detain us. "Motherland" or "homeland" equally assimilates patriotism to family and lineage, to "birth and blood" (Carnovan, 2000, 424) — a deep and natural though misleading connection. John Schaar stresses another ingredient in "homeland": "At its core, patriotism means love of one's home place, and of the familiar things and scenes associated with the homeplace" — in short, territoriality (Schaar, 1981, 287; cf. Schaar, 2002). George Bernard Shaw expresses a more cynical view: Patriotism is your conviction that this country is superior to all other countries because you were born in it. But I am concerned with polities that are not (necessarily) based on familial, familiar or first person connections.

"Nationalism," though sometimes regarded as synonymous with "patriotism," tends to carry too much cultural and ethnic baggage: a "nation" is one's native land, one's place of birth, and cultural associations (ethnic, linguistic, racial) as well as (genetic) kinship may be presumed to accrue, by birthright, only to "natives." Love of country need not be the same as love of nation, though there is a political meaning to "nation" (roughly as "nation-state") that comes close to the meaning of patriotism I have in mind, save for the unhealthy connotations of nationalism, "patriotism's bloody brother" (quoted in Schaar, 1981, p. 285). Patriotic gore indeed! (McCabe, 1997) Finally, George Kateb holds that 'country' is an abstraction, "a figment of the imagination," not something concrete like "a discernible collection of discernible individuals" or territory or place (Kateb, 2000, 907). But Kateb merely heightens the ambiguity of "country" in "my country" — different for different people.

The perils of the preceding paragraphs are, of course, not merely linguistic. The strength of patriotic fervor may easily fuse, or confuse, these different

---

[5] Cf. Kateb, who says patriotism is "a jealous and exclusive loyalty" that needs enemies (Kateb, 2000, 908–13). Certainly some forms of patriotism fit this bill, and not just the last refuges of scoundrels.

meanings. In practice, therefore, patriotism cannot easily be separated from its semantic siblings. Still, I do wish to focus on the political sphere as (at least conceptually) distinct from the cultural, geographical and biological spheres. So patriotism is love of *country*,[6] complexly motivated and behaviorally tied. But I do want to insist on one final point: patriotism, however construed, is dangerously potent. It generates profound feelings and extraordinary actions — it can lead people to kill and die for their country, and to do so in hordes. The power of patriotism is undeniable, however we construe or evaluate it.

II. Patriotism as Personal Honor

Given the features of patriotism just highlighted, it is perhaps surprising that few have construed it in terms of personal honor. For it seems apparent that the concept of personal honor captures most of the major features of patriotism in an illuminating way: the egocentricity of loyalty to "my" country; the high valuation of my country; the lurking invidious comparison with other countries; the entanglement of self-respect and other-respect with love of country; perhaps even the profound power of patriotic feeling. Let me expand on each of these points.

(a) *Egocentricity*: A genuine patriot loves "her" country, whether or not she was born there or belongs to the dominant ethnic or linguistic or racial group (a patriot need not be a nationalist). This means, first, that she is loyal to other members of her country in a way she is not loyal to members of other countries.[7] Second, she embraces the (supposedly) valuable characteristics of her country, an embrace shared by other citizens — by any fellow citizen *as such* — and in doing so she embraces *them*: loyalty to other citizens is reinforced by common loyalty to shared principles, norms, and values, and these reinforcing loyalties are mutually recognized, a further cementing connection. But third, this set of loyalties is particular, not universal; it is not loyalty to persons as such, nor to all human beings, it is primarily loyalty to this or that *particular* group of human persons (and secondarily to the values, history, culture, and geography they share, which only adds to the properties that are *not* shared by all).

---

[6] But always keep in mind that country is neither state nor nation, much less ethnic or religious or cultural group.

[7] This does not mean she necessarily behaves badly toward aliens or foreigners; that will depend upon whether her country's principles are intolerant, xenophobic, jingoistic, racist, etc., and if so whether she follows her country in these respects. It is also possible for a country's principles to embrace tolerance, hospitality, even universal respect — though a patriot who embraces these principles does so in a different way than a cosmopolitan simply interested in morality as such: her acceptance of these principles is conditional upon her patriotic loyalties, not direct obedience to an unconditional and universally binding categorical imperative.

These are all features of honor groups; indeed, honor groups are *constituted* by such loyalties (to members) and commitments (to a shared honor code). These loyalties and commitments are necessarily particular, limited to some persons and some principles and not to all. Further, and perhaps surprisingly, honor groups are *voluntary* in ways similar to countries, though not to nations. Honor groups need not be constituted by criteria that necessarily exclude some or many, such as birthplace, race, language, etc. (though doubtless many have been so constituted); many are qualified though perhaps few are called or chosen. What matters for membership in an honor group is capacity for personal honor, just as what matters for patriotism is capacity for citizenship, and arguably these capacities are very widely possessed in both cases, and not exclusive to an elite group of superior beings (that just happens to correspond to the set of actual members!).

(b) *Valuation:* In loving their country, patriots value their compatriots, their country, and the norms they hold in common, just as members of honor groups value their fellow members, their honor group, and the honor code they share. Perhaps it might be thought that patriotic fervor runs higher than honor-group loyalty, but this is only contingently true, if true at all — patriotism can run just as hot and cold as honor, and for the same reasons: personal and group experiences good and bad, private interests coinciding with or running contrary to common goods, other loyalties reinforcing or conflicting, and so on. Likewise the way in which the group and its members are valued are similar: the value of both country and honor group is held partly on evidence and partly on faith. A patriot has some but not conclusive evidence for the goodness (if not the superiority) of her country and the patriotism of her countrymen, just as a member of an honor group respects his fellow members as honorable partly because of favorable experience. But there is also a deeper reason: a patriot is bound by patriotic duty to treat fellow citizens as patriots, even when there is no common experience, just as members of honor groups are bound as a matter of honor to treat one another as honorable[8] in advance of experience.

There is this difference: a country's value, according to a patriot, lies not only in its normative principles, though these may lie at the heart of some patriotisms (cf. constitutional and covenant patriotisms, below), but also in such properties as its excellent geography, splendid history, noble traditions, brilliant culture, etc. Of course such properties might give rise to norms — e.g. to promote and defend these things — but they need not carry implications for action. An honor code, however, is oriented to action, not just in prescriptions and prohibitions but also in ideals for living.[9] But

---

[8] Not as if honorable: There should be no conditionality, no provisionality, no hesitancy in such treatment.

[9] Although in ideals the norms concern not acting but being or living, still the orientation is

this difference diminishes when patriotism is distinguished from nationalism: where the presumed valuable properties of one's country are political
and not cultural, they *do* bear on human action both directly and indirectly.
The political principles that concern patriots are normative just as honor
principles are normative. So the kind, degree and basis for valuation are very
similar. Once again patriotism resembles a sense of personal honor, with the
body politic occupying the role of the honor group.

(c) *Comparison:* Not all would agree that patriotism must involve (favorable) comparison of my country with other countries, but few would deny
that much actual patriotism does involve such comparative evaluation,
especially when patriots are called to the defense of their country, or when
my country is disrespected by other countries; the extreme loyalty unto death
countries routinely require if not inspire can hardly exist without a sense of
the country's (extreme) importance. Another way to put this point is that
patriotism is an exclusive and jealous loyalty, a loyalty that normally claims
priority over other loyalties and seeks to limit their scope. Of course this claim
is defeasible, but it is often quite compelling.[10] Honor is like that as well.
Honor groups inflate their importance, and honorable members are often
drawn to seemingly hyperbolic claims: "my honor matters more than my life
itself; I couldn't live without my honor." Likewise, honor groups often pride
themselves in comparison with outsiders: those without a sense of honor
are "beneath contempt," and even members of different honor groups may
be regarded as having a lesser sense of honor, or even no honor at all. Just
as countries adopt an air of superiority to cultivate extraordinary patriotic
loyalty, so honor groups adopt a sense of elitism to bolster personal honor
with status or achievement honor.

(d) *Respect:* Patriotism is often depicted as a brutish instinct, slavish pack
mentality, the submergence of individual autonomy and dignity into an
overwhelming collectivity. There is some truth to this view, but it is an exaggeration. Patriotism can be, instead, the epitome of individual self-respect.
Self-respect has many sources, but one of them is others' respect for oneself.
It is hard to muster self-respect in the absence of respect by others — harder
still in the presence of their contempt. So rooted, self-respect ties one to
others, to the group of others whose respect matters to oneself. When one
is a citizen, the respect of fellow citizens matters — or should matter, if one
takes citizenship at all seriously. When respected others are disrespected,
one's own self-respect is challenged or damaged. That is why disrespect of

how character potentiates action and how living honorably involves acting well.

[10] Cf. E. M. Forster's classic quip: "I hate the idea of causes, and if I had to choose between
betraying my country and betraying my friend, I hope I should have the guts to betray my country"
— though the whiff of scandal in the final phrase shows that loyalty to country is normally assumed
to take precedence over friendship, as well as to involve a greater courage.

one's country often prompts violent patriotic reaction. Again, honor is like that. Many sociologists and anthropologists have linked "cultures of honor" to testy tempers, sensitivity to insult, and violent retaliation (cf. e.g. Aase, ed., 2002; Miller, 1990, 1993; Patterson, 1982; Peristiany, ed., 1965; Peristiany and Pitt-Rivers, eds. 1992). While I do not think honor groups necessarily are violent (cf. Chapter 12), it is true that sensitivity to insult is a form of concern for others' respect, upon which self-respect hinges. Honor groups can seem to exist for little else than promoting and maintaining respect, mutual respect for others and self. This is an especially tempting model, or analogy, for national honor (though the personal honor of rulers is often the issue for real-politik), but it is also helpful in understanding patriotic honor.

(e) *Power:* Patriotism is a potent motive, driving people to ceaseless exertion limited only by death. Its power is admired, even worshipped,[11] but also decried. But it cannot be denied. The source of its power is unclear, but may be similar to that of honor. Personal honor also moves people to perform extraordinary acts even to the point of surrendering (or taking) life itself. Why? One vital root is the importance of others' regard of oneself. We are social beings not only during the long dependency of infancy and childhood, but throughout our lives. Our relationships to others matter to us throughout our days. The nature and quality of those relationships essentially depend on others' regard for us. Of course we learn to value the regard of some more than that of others. In particular, we want to be well regarded by those we regard highly. This is precisely what honor groups provide — and indeed require. Loyalty to other members of the group is reinforced not just by allegiance to common principles (the same honor code) but also by the regard of those others: their respect, qua honorable, not only matches but also catches the respect we have for them and for ourselves in an honor group. Such respect can make life seem worth living, and also worth surrendering. Similarly patriotism rides upon a country's regard — the regard of fellow members of the body politic — to create a powerful social motive. We do not wish to be regarded as disloyal by compatriots, because their regard matters to us: because *they* matter to us. Patriotism is so powerful because we deeply want to belong to a group that deeply wants us to belong.

[11] I mean this almost literally. Patriotism can come very close to religious worship: concern "for God and country" [not to mention Yale] can sometimes seem a single passion, however clearly the objects of that passion may be distinguished. Certainly religious and patriotic passions need not differ greatly in motive force, and may prompt the same strenuous actions.

III. The Morality of Patriotism

Is patriotism morally admirable or morally reprehensible? A conversation on this issue goes back at least to the Greeks and is epitomized in the iconic phrase "My country, right or wrong."[12] Looking at the issue from the standpoint of honor can shed some light on the debate. I will argue that patriotism as such is *a*moral, neither morally right nor morally wrong in all cases, but that particular instances of patriotism can be morally acceptable, morally worthy, perhaps even morally required, while other instances can be morally mistaken, impermissible, even shockingly reprehensible. The primary moral terms in the debate are misapplied directly to patriotism as such.

Patriotism is thought to be morally dubious, in light of several overlapping distinctions (cf. McCabe, 1997):

- *Universal/particular:* Moral principles are thought to be universal in at least two ways: They are rules that obligate everyone — every person capable of understanding these rules and guiding her life accordingly is a moral agent — and they also apply to everyone — every person is a moral patient (there may be other moral patients, perhaps all sentient beings). But patriotism is essentially particularistic because it is egocentric: it is love of *this* country because it is *my* country, and that implicitly excludes other countries and their lovers (as such). The obligations of a patriot as such extend only to compatriots, not to all except insofar as his country's code obliges him to treat aliens in certain ways. Moral and patriotic loyalties seem on a collision course.
- *Impartiality/partiality:* Morality is impartial, considering the interests of all and weighing equal interests equally, caring for all and not just for some, and caring for equal needs equally no matter whose they are. Like the law, morality is no "respecter of persons" in the sense of not giving greater respect to some persons over others; morality equally respects everyone the same. But patriotism is emphatically partial: partial to one's country and fellow countrymen, partial to its and their interests, respecting compatriots over (and sometimes instead of) aliens.
- *Inclusivity/exclusivity:* Morality erects no barriers of care or respect among people; all are included in the moral community, the kingdom of ends. But patriotism draws a line between insiders and outsiders; by including some it excludes others. Indeed, without such exclusion, patriotism couldn't exist; without special and exclusive loyalties to one's own country there would be no countries and hence no patriots.

Various attempts have been made to resolve these issues. One approach

---

[12] Would that it occurred more often as a question!

is realpolitik: Patriotism is a real-world sentiment that quite often cannot be checked, or even touched, by moral considerations. Another is incompatibilism, the view that patriotism is inevitably morally wrong — indeed, "typically a grave moral error" (Kateb, 2000, 901; cf. McCabe, 1997). A third is cosmopolitanism, extending back to at least the Stoics and exemplified by Martha Nussbaum, who wants to replace or strongly condition love of (a particular) country with allegiance to "the worldwide community of human beings" (Nussbaum, 1996, 14; cf. Turner, 2002). Loyalty is universalized, and love of a country becomes love of all countries, or at least of no country over all others.

A fourth attempt marries patriotism and morality by conceiving of morality as grounded in particular communities and resting on the particular loyalties they engender. Alexander Oldenquist and Alasdair MacIntyre are leading proponents. Oldenquist holds that particular loyalties ground our "social worlds" and cannot be reduced to impersonal morality or self-interest. In effect, all morality is tribal morality, or a nested set of such loyalties (Oldenquist, 1982, in Primoratz, ed., 2002, p. 31). "As a matter of historical and sociological fact, moral virtues for good citizenship are marginally effective and harder to produce in the first place; it is primarily group loyalties — group egoism and tribal morality — that have produced the caring and commitment that keep our social worlds going" (*ibid.*, 40). MacIntyre's influential Lindley Lecture, "Is Patriotism a Virtue?," effectively stands moral critique of particular loyalties on its head, arguing that loyalty to particular communities is a precondition of having a morality (MacIntyre, 1984; in Primoratz, ed., 2002, 48; cf. criticism in Dombrowski, 1992, among others).

A fifth effort seeks to moralize patriotism by fencing in particular loyalties with universal principles, as in Nathanson's "moderate patriotism," Schaar's "covenanted patriotism," Anderson's Rawlsian "patriotic liberalism," Müller's "constitutional patriotism," or Viroli's "patriotism of liberty" (Viroli, 1995, 17). For Nathanson, moderate patriotism is particular loyalty subject to universal moral constraints. Not all countries may merit loyalty, and not every action by one's country should be supported; but some may, and some should (Nathanson, 1988/89, in Primoratz, 2002, 100). For Anderson, national identity in a liberal democracy is based on a shared conception of justice (Anderson, 2003). For Schaar, "We are a nation formed by a covenant, by dedication to a set of principles and by our exchange of promises to uphold and advance certain commitments among ourselves and throughout the world," and the "dialectic of devotion" involved in such "covenanted patriotism" makes moral principle a partner with lesser loyalties (Schaar, 1981; in Primoratz, ed., 2002, 239 and 244). For Müller, constitutional patriotism is "the idea that political attachment ought to center on the norms, the values and, more indirectly, the procedures of a liberal democratic constitution" (Müller, 2007, 1; cf. also Ingram, 1996, reprinted in Primoratz, ed., 2002;

Shabani, 2002; Markell, 2000; and Habermas, 2001, among many other writings).

All these attempts seem misguided when viewed through the lens of honor, though, perhaps surprisingly, realpolitik comes closest to recognizing the nature of patriotism as seen from this perspective. Most approaches err, I believe, either by trying to assimilate patriotism to morality, by hedging it in with moral conditions, by grounding morality in particular loyalties, or by trying to condemn patriotism as inherently incompatible with morality. Instead, I think, patriotism is essentially amoral but accidentally moral or immoral — patriotism as such is neither morally right nor wrong, though its instantiations may be either or neither. In this regard patriotism is just like honor. While a group's honor code may indeed contain moral provisions or conditions of application, this is not necessary. The respect given and owed within honor groups is not necessarily a moral respect (it may not be extended to non-members). Moral assessment and criticism may indeed be applied to honor groups and honor codes, but, as the advocates of realpolitik realize, such moral discourse may well fall on deaf ears.

So matters of patriotism, like matters of honor, are not *as such* matters of morality.[13] Still, this does not mean that morality is irrelevant to patriotism. On the contrary. People are not merely patriots (just as they are not merely persons of honor); most are also open to the appeal of more universal, impartial, inclusive principles, and various effects may ensue. Some may find morality compelling and their patriotic (or honor) commitments morally unworthy, and thus give up the latter, perhaps to join instead something like Nussbaum's "cosmopolitanism" — and hope that others will join them, though they are people without a country. Some may find the power-plays of practical politics compelling and discard morality as useless and unworldly, though they should not delude themselves that moral considerations are *necessarily* impractical — it is the thinking morality impractical that makes it so, not the morality itself. Still others may seek to moralize their patriotism, to combine morality and patriotism, in various ways and proportions, resulting perhaps in something like Nathanson's "moderate" patriotism — but recognizing that the moral constraints on patriotic loyalty are not essential to patriotism and so they may be eroded in stressful times.[14]

---

[13] Contrary to such as McCabe, who make morality essential to patriotism: by "patriotism," he means "the doctrine that co-nationality is a morally significant relationship" (McCabe, 1997, 203, emphasis added). Patriotic bonds are normally quite significant, but my point is that this significance need not be a moral one, nor need it be regarded as such.

[14] James Gaffney claims that patriotism was once a virtue ("civic generosity") but now is "more often than not" a vice ("characteristic arrogance") (Gaffney, 1993, 146). I would say it is not that patriotism per se has changed but that different instantiations of patriotism may be judged morally quite differently.

IV. PROBLEMS

All in all, therefore, viewing patriotism from the standpoint of personal honor does shed light on a problematic concept. Yet problems remain; I shall attend to five of them.

First, some may think the concept of personal honor is inapplicable to political groups simply in virtue of size. Honor groups function through mutual recognition of members; the size of the group matters because without face-to-face interaction it is hard to generate this mutual recognition. It seems that countries are simply too large and diverse to permit the face-to-face contact vital to honor groups; citizens are mostly strangers to one another, not honorable comrades. This is a serious concern, and to the extent to which citizens are unknown, anonymous and even unrecognizable to one another, the foundations of *personal* honor cannot be laid, and patriotism must be seen in different terms. I think this charge has merit — a sense of personal honor *is* attenuated by increasing size — yet it is mitigated by a number of considerations.

(a) There are various ways that even in a large and diverse country citizens can recognize one another, though these ways are potentially dangerous because they often involve cultural matters. Even if race, ethnicity, and religion are excluded, the common cultural insignia of recognition may be morally insignificant (interest in certain sports; flag lapel pins) or morally hazardous (linguistic accents). It is entirely too easy to conflate patriotism and other values. Still, these other values often go proxy for patriotism.

(b) Public symbols (flags), rituals (Independence Day events) and institutions (mostly state-sponsored but also pastimes, secular shrines, museums) can provide occasions for mutual recognition. Acquaintance and interaction with these forms permits a culturally diverse people to share a minimal common experience.

(c) Explicit sets of principles, like declarations of independence or constitutions, can focus patriotic pride. While honor groups typically rely heavily on unwritten "codes," presuming that a person of honor should be able not only to govern herself by honor but also to discern honor's requirements for herself, it seems that the larger the group the more need there is to make explicit the group's code. These expressions cannot capture all the code contains, but they do allow a common focus for people from even widely divergent backgrounds.

(d) Common procedures or experiences, like voting, paying taxes, or serving on juries provide some solidarity. Granted, these civic exercises may not actually involve all, but to the degree there is unwillingness to participate in them there is a corresponding weakening of the patriotic spirit.

(e) Public education provides not only common experiences but also common knowledge: traditions, principles, civic understanding. Once again this bonding can be attenuated. Private schools and home schooling fragment both knowledge and experience to varying extents.

(f) Patriotic passions are aroused in international competitions, particularly sports (James' "moral equivalent of war"). Much depends upon the extent to which the population identifies with a given athlete or team, and broad representation of the population on sports teams is preferable to minority participation. There are dangers, of course, in a country's priding itself on Olympic medals while ignoring the weightier matters of justice, equality, and decency.

All in all, therefore, patriotism can achieve some measure of the mutual recognition required by honor groups. But the constant danger is that a country will substitute more-easily discerned insignia of culture, race, and religion for the true criteria of patriotic loyalty — a matter of character, not of appearance. Character is inherently more difficult to discern than surface features, and the anonymity of crowds makes it more difficult still.

Earlier (in Section III), I argued that viewing patriotism as honor helps to resolve the conflict over whether honor is moral or immoral, a virtue or a vice. Viewed as honor, patriotism is neither; it is amoral. Does this mean, then, that we have simply avoided dealing with crucial moral issues — not unlike realpolitik, which often just ignores, not answers, morality's claims? Not necessarily. One might indeed leave one's patriotism unexamined and unchallenged, just as one might similarly treat one's honor. But one might also examine, challenge and seek to alter both. Being patriotic need not dull one's moral sense, and when country and morality diverge, a person who is both patriotic and moral has a variety of opportunities: either to recall one's country to its forgotten moral compass or to seek to change the implicit or explicit code that authorizes immoral conduct. Neither path is easy, and either may prove practically impossible or require saintly exertion. Still, being a patriot or a member of an honor group does not necessarily foreclose moral inquiry about one's group or one's membership.

Is patriotism inextricably linked to nationalism, its "bloody brother"? Earlier (in Section I) we noted the terminological problem and claimed that though they may be semantic siblings nonetheless patriotism and nationalism can be distinguished. But that is not good enough if there are no actual instances of patriotism that are not nationalistic in origin, character and operation. The worry is that without the patriotically extraneous bonds of culture, ethnicity, race, religion and the like, the kind of loyalty patriotism requires will not be generated. This commitment is very strong indeed, strong enough to move people to offer life and limb on its behalf. I concede that nationalistic appeals to blood and soil, to race and religion, to culture and ethos, are very powerful indeed, and that they are all too ready-to-hand for an unscrupulous politician (Samuel Johnson's "scoundrel" who makes this false "patriotism" his last refuge). Still, the efforts of those who seek a "moderate," "covenanted" or "constitutional" patriotism — and think they see their efforts bearing fruit in certain Western democracies — indicate that the scoundrels need not triumph.

Simon Keller has propounded a different kind of argument to show that patriotism is immoral (or "probably a vice," as he rather cautiously puts it). In Keller's view, patriotism inevitably or usually (Keller hedges his bets) leads to bad faith. According to him, patriotism involves belief in the goodness of one's country — in order to make it worthy of loyalty — that inevitably or usually outstrips evidence that one's country is not special, superior or more worthy than any other country and requires a patriot to conceal this over-belief from herself. ". . . [P]atriotism is a kind of love for country that makes reference to, or latches onto, aspects of a country that are taken to merit pride or approval or affection or reverence. Without that, you do not have patriotism." (Keller, 2007, 67) Like a football (soccer) fan who is fanatical about her team, derides referees who make calls against her heroes, worships her players above those from other teams, and the like, a patriot is committed to thinking well of his country beyond the evidence — or even despite or against it — and also to concealing the lack of evidential support for his beliefs from himself. The patriot's true motive for belief in country is necessarily hidden from him; he is disposed to bad faith even if not actually in bad faith (Keller, 2007, 76). Keller qualifies his conclusion by saying that his argument provides only a "presumptive" case (p. 83), but it is clear he thinks the presumption is quite strong.

I don't think Keller's case is at all compelling. In his view a patriot has to be loyal beyond all rationally warranted belief, i.e. beyond all the available evidence. But then he has to rule out "moderate" (or "constitutional," etc.) patriots as not really patriots. Moderate patriots, as construed by Nathanson, are loyal to their country, but not willing to surrender moral critique; they would be willing to fight and die in their country's just wars, but not in all wars; they would root for their country's team without believing it never commits fouls, its heroes are superior to those on other teams, etc. In short, moderate patriots are fans who are not fanatical, while Keller requires "real" patriots to be fanatics. I believe patriots *can* be clear-eyed loyalists who do not necessarily succumb to bad faith.[15]

Finally, viewing patriotism as honor gives a rather thin account of the political sphere. There is much more to political life, to what Mark Philp calls "Political Conduct," than patriotism (Philp, 2007). Granted. There are

---

[15] Curiously, the overall conclusion to Keller's book — that loyalty is a complicated aspect of human psychology (p. 219) and not morally pure — could be used against his strictures on patriotism: not all patriotic loyalty is, or need be, morally vicious. In short, patriotic loyalties are diverse from the standpoint of moral assessment.

also institutional structure and process, official roles and responsibilities, the character of rulers and followers, and much else. Viewing patriotism as honor doesn't illumine everything. Still, I believe, it does illumine something central to political conduct. Without patriotic loyalty, countries survive (and do not thrive) only by use of coercion, threat or bribery, a tenuous project for the long term. Understanding patriotism, then, is clearly of the first importance for political theory. My claim is that such understanding can be advanced by means of the concept of personal honor.

V. Benefits

Assuming that the limits of this kind of account of patriotism as honor are understood, let me end by briefly noting two benefits of thinking this way. First, it enables us to explain why patriotism is morally hazardous — because, like honor, patriotism is not fundamentally a moral notion at all. I reiterate that I don't mean that patriotism is fundamentally or normally immoral. The country to which a patriot is loyal may have a constitution, polity, and policies reasonably consistent with morality, and may on occasion seek or require extraordinary commitment to its causes without violating moral strictures, all things considered. But equally, a country may be thoroughly corrupted and even depraved in principle or practice, such that patriotic loyalty is morally impermissible. There are no guarantees that countries will be morally worthy (or unworthy), and loyalty to those countries is at equal risk. Patriotic citizens may be morally obliged to put their country to moral examination, with no guarantee of passing the test, and they can of course work to make their country measure up morally as they see it. But they may fail on both accounts. Finally, citizens can love their country even in resistance; they can be patriotic in seeking to thwart, mitigate and alter even fundamental elements in their country's code. Indeed it might be the highest reach of patriotism not to die for one's country "right or wrong" but to give one's life to help one's country live up to morally permissible or obligatory principles — to make the code of one's country conform to the morality of everyone.

Second, understanding patriotism as honor helps to explain a feature of patriotism universally noticed, whether in reverence or in terror: the *strength* of patriotic fervor. Patriotic loyalty is like religious devotion in its capacity to arouse deep-seated passions and to motivate extraordinary outpourings of self-sacrificial action. Patriotism stirs many souls to (often literally) self-effacing actions they would not contemplate simply from the standpoint of self-interest. I think the concept of honor helps us to understand this power. Recall that members of honor groups are not just committed to abstract principles, the honor code; they are also loyal to concrete persons, their fellow members, whose respect they treasure (and reciprocate) as coincident with their own self-respect. Patriotism is like that, a commitment to a country's "code" (to its constitution, its guiding principles, its fundamental traditions and institutions), but also loyalty to other citizens, whose respect one seeks in seeking civic self-respect. Patriots feel they "couldn't hold their head up" among fellow citizens should they be — or be perceived to be — disloyal to one another and to their common country. Since the roots of our concern for others' regard run deep and wide, it is no surprise that patriotism, like honor, can not only incite intense feelings of identification but also move people to sacrifice self in devotion both to cause and to community — to this community, to *my* country. Patriotism, like honor, can thereby constitute my self, and therein lies its power.

Chapter 9

ACADEMIC HONOR

Honor's place in contemporary academe is puzzling, in several ways.[1] An initially striking puzzle will turn out to be superficial, but it needs to be solved before the deeper issues can be raised and a more positive portrait of academic honor sketched.

I. The Superficial Puzzle

The superficial puzzle has three parts: honors galore, plenteous study of others' honor, and silence about one's own honor. Its solution will require using our distinctions among different concepts of honor.

First, the academy is replete with "honors," all presumably conferred for intellectual accomplishment: prizes, awards, scholarships, fellowships, lectureships, citations, recognitions, *festschriften*, jubilees, memorials, endowments, celebrations, grants, and their many permutations. It is clear that academics delight in pursuing the accomplishments that bring such honors:[2] grades earn "laude" on the transcript; articles and books receive the approbation of one's peers; research is both underwritten by grants and often undertaken for their sake; endowed professorships honor a benefactor and pay the bills but also honor the distinguished faculty; conferences honor someone's work by paying it the notice of critical attention; collections of articles are published "in honor of" someone whose scholarly life has attracted attention; rankings of departments, programs and institutions are compiled and almost fanatically

---

[1] I use "academe," "the academy" and "academic" to refer primarily to contemporary American post-secondary institutions of teaching and/or research; but there will be considerable application to post-secondary education elsewhere, and perhaps even to primary and secondary institutions as well.

[2] Academics are also susceptible to other, non-academic forms of honor: media attention, wider fame, fortune, influence, and the like. But my concern here is with honor specific to academe, so far as it is distinct from other forms.

113

pursued, as are citation lists in various fields; and so on. Moreover, academe seems obsessed with comparative honors: "best student in a class (or school or generation)," "best scholar in her field," "teacher of the year," "top national liberal arts college." One can almost picture academics frantically clambering over one another to get to the top of various hills of honor and peaks of prestige. Clearly honor in some forms is immensely important to academe.

At the same time, many scholars have devoted entire careers to the study of honor in a wide variety of societies, both past and present, around the world. In brief compass we can mention only a few shelves in a vast scholarly library:[3] there is, of course, the very extensive anthropological literature, not just about "Mediterranean honor," including the Biblical world, but ethnographic studies of cultures around the globe. There is an equally large sociological literature about various "deviant" groups in contemporary society, such as street gangs, pirates, gypsies, thieves, and outcasts. As we might expect, there are many studies of military honor. Classicists have long recognized the importance of honor and related notions in heroic and classical Greece and ancient Rome. Medieval and Renaissance scholars have likewise paid considerable attention to honor, as have researchers of other parts and periods of the world, from Latin America to the Middle East, from China to Japan. American historians have been acutely aware of the importance of honor in the American past — not just the ante-bellum South but also the American founders. Likewise literary critics have noted honor's prominence in writings and writers from various cultures.

This list could be extended indefinitely, and would itself be a proper object of academic attention — one could imagine a lengthy series of monographs on honor as a theme in various secondary literatures ("The Concept of Honor as an Analytic Tool in Literary Criticism," etc.). But what is distinctive about such a list, and what constitutes the third part of our puzzle, is that all this scholarship is about the Great Other. Honor is explored — endlessly, patiently, thoroughly, carefully, critically, respectfully — only so long as it is *someone else's honor*, the honor observed in other cultures, past societies, deviant sub-groups, and distant authors. The scholars describing this observance of honor do not themselves belong to those honor groups, however much they may ingratiate themselves for purposes of research. Contemporary academic examination of honor never seems self-reflexive.[4] Indeed, for most academics, honor is a moral pariah, not an idea to be taken seriously

---

[3] Cf. the Introduction, footnote 1, for representative references. Many, many more could be listed.

[4] There are apparent exceptions. Academics do occasionally write about collegiate "honor systems" (though honor here usually gets truncated to honest attribution in student exams and papers), research ethics, and administrative integrity. But even when academics are studying the ethics of academics, "honor" is mentioned only in passing, not as a central theme or concern of the community, and certainly not as a matter of personal concern to the author.

in one's own community or personal life. Many academics would share Carol Gilligan's disdain for "cultures that value or valorize heroism, honor, war, and competition — the culture of warriors, the economy of capitalism."[5]

A minor but revealing part of this pattern of academic neglect of honor in the academy is philosophy's silence on the topic. Philosophy is a discipline that (among other aims) seeks to wrestle with values as such, and when philosophers fail even to consider a value others prize, this is a signal that the value doesn't seem viable in the society the philosopher represents. If honor is not addressed philosophically in the academy, therefore, it is likely because honor is not taken seriously as a norm either in the academy or in the wider society. Philosophy's silence about honor is particularly striking in light of the resurgence of interest in the last several decades of so-called "virtue ethics," where the moral life is viewed in terms not of rules or results but of qualities of character, habits of mind and heart, dispositions to do and feel.[6] Philosophers and their fellow travelers have written extensively in recent years about plenty of particular virtues, but honor, traditionally regarded as a major virtue, has received almost no attention. To be sure, anglophone philosophers have written about honor in the history of philosophy, in the US military, and, all too rarely, about collegiate "honor systems." But there has been *no* serious normative examination of the concept of honor as such. It seems that philosophers, like other academics, are not interested in honor as a living value anywhere in our society, much less in the academy itself.

So there is our superficial puzzle: Honor clearly matters to the academy, where honors proliferate and where honor (i.e. the honor of others) is extensively studied. But there is little self-study of honor *in* the academy. How are we to explain this puzzle? Distinguishing among our six concepts of honor will help.

The multitude of explicit honors in academe consists of *conferred, recognition,* and *positional honor.* This is precisely what we should expect of a society that, in general, confers status on the basis of achievement recognized by established authorities, or accomplishment according to "objective" standards, i.e. the standards of high-status others. Honors are given to those who are taken by the relevant authorities to excel in intellectual attainments, whether as individuals (students, teachers, researchers) or as groups (departments, programs, institutions). Here the academy is clearly self-aware, almost painfully so: students obsess about grades and class rankings, faculty fret about course evaluations and appointments, researchers agonize about grants and publications, and administrators anguish over institutional reputations. All are constantly at work reviewing, evaluating and "assessing" one another, occasionally themselves, and, though rarely, the criteria

---

[5] From the *Boston Globe* in 1996, quoted in Sommers, 2000, p. 72.
[6] Cf. the references in Chapter 1, footnotes 4–9.

of assessment. Moreover, they are concerned not only to seek and gain the myriad conferred and recognition honors, but also, as good academics, to explore and understand what it takes to get these honors and what they mean in terms of position in academe: top student, best teacher, respected researcher, elite institution. Nevertheless, in all this concern for conferred, recognition and positional honors, academics are no different — no better and no worse — than others; they are simply human. Academic honors may have different bases and tokens than elsewhere in society, but the kinds of honors are the same.

Commitment and trust honor play less prominent but still vital roles in academe. Students are (usually) loyal to their peers, often to a fault by placing social commitments above intellectual ones, or loyalty to fraternity above allegiance to law. Faculty are (mostly) devoted to their students, and students to their teachers and mentors; faculty honor their employment contracts, often by working not "to rule" but far beyond the letter of any legal agreement; they trust their colleagues, on the whole; and they are also often committed to principles — intellectual principles, to be sure, of inquiry, argument and subject-matter, but also moral and/or political ones. Administrators are (normally) deeply committed to the people and institutions they manage, seeking to advance the common good instead of pursuing personal advantage. Nearly all in academe are committed in some manner or other to some wider community — to their local institutions, their academic disciplines or professions, their town or area, perhaps even some international group. But in all of their trust and commitment, academics again are nothing special. Most people in most societies do as much, and as well, honoring not only agreements, principles and individuals but also groups and institutions to which they variously adhere. Commitment and trust honor in academe are not much different from commitment and trust honor in other sectors of society, even though the particular objects of trust and commitment may differ.

II. The Deeper Puzzle

The deeper puzzle at the heart of the superficial puzzle of academic honor concerns *personal honor*. It is clear that academics don't study or talk much about personal honor in the academy among themselves, even while they pursue conferred, recognition, and positional honors and while they intensively analyze others' personal honor. But why this particular silence? Various hypotheses suggest themselves: (1) Perhaps the concept of personal honor simply doesn't apply to contemporary academic communities; it is indeed a concept only for others, for other kinds of social group. (2) The concept does apply to academic communities, but academics have good reasons for not speaking about their own honor: perhaps there is an inherent taboo in all honor groups about self-examination of their own honor; or the academy is so *dis*honorable that only an embarrassed silence is appropriate; or personal honor as such is mistakenly identified with one or more of its noxious instantiations elsewhere, and so overlooked in its potentially more attractive exemplifications closer to home. (3) The concept applies, but academics are somehow blinded to its presence by their very form of communal life, aided by this form's collusion with self-interest. They are silent because they are conveniently oblivious to personal honor as a living value, even if it *is* such a value for them. I will discuss each alternative in turn, and argue that none of them provides adequate reason for remaining silent about personal honor in the contemporary academy.[7]

1   It would be convenient for academics if they could seal off academe from the concept of personal honor, for then they would not have to answer to its demands. This could be accomplished in several ways. By focusing on societies distant in time or place, or on marginal and deviant groups in contemporary society, one can fixate on morally dubious features from which one can easily dissociate oneself: honor killings, duels, snobbery, patriarchy, feuds, violence, enslavement, and the like. If this is honor, then surely it is absent from the kind and gentle academy! Alternatively, one can hold that personal honor requires a certain kind of social context found only in "primitive" or "traditional" societies — ones that are hierarchical, heroic or warlike — but absent in modern mass egalitarian societies.[8] Or, one can link honor tightly, even necessarily, to warrior "bands of brothers," with their traditional gender biases and violent tendencies, and seek to disassociate the academy from all that aggressive male bonding. Finally, one can reduce personal honor to conferred, recognition or positional honor, and effectively say that intellectual achievement and recognition are all there is to honor in academe — there simply is no room for (the concept of) personal honor in the academy.

But none of these attempts succeeds. Focus on particular other societies or subgroups is worthwhile and fascinating, but highlighting differences from one's own society may blind one to similarities. Not all honor groups share the qualities (e.g. violence, sexism, snobbery) that one finds odious in some honor groups. There are doubtless social conditions for personal honor, but no one has shown that these conditions

---

[7] Doug Campbell (personal communication) suggests another possible reason: perhaps academics talk about integrity, honesty, civility and the like, thinking that these concepts cover anything worth discussing that falls under the concept of personal honor. If so, they are mistaken, for honor is distinct from and irreducible to these other concepts — and distinct in ways that are worth exploring — as I shall argue in Chapter 12, Section V. Doubtless there are other possible reasons as well.

[8] Cf. Berger, 1970.

restrict personal honor to "primitive" or benighted or feudal or warrior contexts. It remains possible, even credible, that there are honor groups with a *moral* honor code, and that such honor groups may exist even within academe. Finally, when the concept of personal honor is clearly distinguished from other concepts of honor, it remains an open question whether personal honor exists in academe and whether it should be established or promoted. So academic study and discussion of personal honor in academe is not precluded on the grounds that the concept is somehow inapplicable. We need to look and see.

2a   In many traditional societies, critical reflection upon and discourse about the constitutive norms of the group is taboo — and even to speak of taboos (or of this taboo) is taboo, with silence about an unspoken norm an inherent part of the norm. Perhaps this silence is thought necessary to protect the norm; perhaps it is dimly felt that to speak about the fundamental values of the group, much less to criticize them, is to call them into question and to put oneself outside the group. Might discussing honor be similarly taboo in any genuine honor group? Could it be that simply studying and speaking about honor — as opposed to acting and living honorably — shows that one has moved beyond the bounds of honor and can no longer be counted as honorable? Strangely enough, could it be that the academy's silence about personal honor is itself evidence that the academy is an honor group?

This story is implausible. Academics are doubtless committed to many values and principles, but surely one of them is that nothing should escape intellectual scrutiny. Even more, only values capable of withstanding — and indeed welcoming — such scrutiny are worth allegiance in any person or institution embracing Socrates' maxim that "the unexamined life is not worth living." So if personal honor can't be studied or spoken of, then it cannot be part of academe. Doubtless there may be good reasons why certain forms of honor — say the honor of Bill Bonanno, the self-described "retired" Mafia leader, who defines honor by "respect," which is "an acknowledgment of power and place, yours and someone else's" (Bonanno, 2000, xvi) — might be unable to withstand critical scrutiny and so can be held, if at all, only as unexamined principles. Placing a taboo on speaking of such honor might well help to preserve that kind of honor group. But there is no reason to think that personal honor *as such* requires a taboo of silence, and there is every reason to think that if personal honor were present in academe then it couldn't be taboo to examine it. So if academics don't speak of their own personal honor, it cannot be due to some taboo forbidding such speech.[9]

---

[9] There is a further possibility, suggested to me by Ed Craun (personal communication): Perhaps

2b In fact, not everyone *is* silent about honor in academe, at least by implication. Some critics of academe[10] employ concepts of reproach that border on dishonor, and certainly they have many and broad academic targets: rampant cheating among students; plagiarism among scholars; stolen, fudged, and misrepresented data among researchers; subservience of open inquiry to commercial gain; dishonest claims and misguided aims among administrators; grants and benefactions diverted to uses contrary to the intentions of donors; malicious personal innuendo masquerading as "scholarship;" political correctness; lying, cheating, stealing from institutions in the cause of personal advancement or careerism; and so on. It would take a very large book to chronicle "The Shame of Academe," where "shame" reflects widespread dishonor. But while there is ample grist for this mill, it does not grind nearly all academic grain. To call such practices "dishonorable" presumes a backdrop community and standards of honor — an academic honor group and an academic honor code. But if academe is, or contains, honor groups and codes, why are *these* not recognized and examined as such? Why is there attention only to deviance and disobedience? Surely there is also — and at least as much — adherence and obedience? Silence about personal honor is not explained by embarrassment over personal dishonor, even if its incidence is high and wide.

2c Perhaps, then, academics have other reasons to think that honor shouldn't be mentioned in academe. Perhaps they think "honor" has archaic, obsolescent or even unsavory connotations, so that it would be better to think about, and govern, one's behavior in other terms and categories. Perhaps personal honor as such has negative value, so far as academics are concerned. Perhaps they are pursuing some ideology — e.g. feminism, socialism, liberalism, egalitarianism — that brands "honor" with the stigmata of male chauvinism, elitism, racism, homophobia, and general oppression. Perhaps they are postmodernists throwing off the shackles of categories of all kinds. Perhaps they are seeking to make academe into a kinder, gentler, more cooperative society, and they wish to disassociate their cause from the competitive and aggressive run of honor groups.

    Such reasons explain academic silence about academic honor

speaking of one's own personal honor is taboo because it would be a forbidden, i.e. dishonorable, form of boasting — just as the truly humble person doesn't discuss his humility, so the truly honorable person doesn't discuss her honor. Perhaps so, but still this point only rules out certain ways of talking about one's own honor, not all forms of speech (e.g. self-criticism) and not for everyone (others' honor). It remains unclear why academics do not discuss personal honor in non-boastful ways. If there are taboos here, why should they be so unselective?

[10] Cf. M Anderson, 1992; Bennett, 2003; Readings, 1996; Robin, 1995; Sykes, 1988; Wilshire, 1990. Granted, not all of these critics are themselves academics, but some are. The dishonorable practices they criticize are in any case not invisible to academics, and some have the courage to speak truth to their own institutions.

essentially by saying: Academics don't value personal honor. But this explanation is inadequate. First off, not valuing a value is no reason not to study it; many have spent their scholarly lives exploring while rejecting and condemning all manner of vices and disvalues. Second, even if honor is to be rejected, it may still be present in academe; one's ideals for the academy shouldn't blind one to the realities of the academy. But third, personal honor is rarely, if ever, rejected as such; the rejection is almost invariably aimed at one or another of its contingent instances. Carol Gilligan, for example, does not want to be a warrior, conflates a warrior's honor with honor per se, and concludes that she doesn't want to belong to any honor group. Others think that honor groups are necessarily elitist (or sexist or snobbish, etc.), reject elitism (etc.), and conclude by rejecting honor. These are patently invalid inferences, confusing certain historical instantiations of personal honor (no matter how vivid or common) with personal honor as such (in my terms, confusing some conception of personal honor with the concept of personal honor). So perhaps some of the silence of academics about personal honor in the academy is due to having bad or mistaken reasons for rejecting honor as a value for themselves.

3   But perhaps there is a further reason for silence: perhaps academics are somehow constitutionally blind to personal honor, so that they wouldn't notice it even if they were swimming in it. How could this be? What could possibly produce such blindness, if not the ignorance or mistaken beliefs canvassed above? Surely academics are bright and observant people, trained to notice anything that befalls the human lot, no matter how recondite or how familiar? Perhaps. Nevertheless, there is reason to suspect that contemporary academics, like the rest of their society, are in the grips of a myth so strong that it clouds or even precludes recognition of certain kinds of social facts and values. The myth I have in mind is *individualism*.[11] I will focus on four interrelated features of this Hydra-headed creature of modernity.

First, individualism metaphysically locates the "real" or "true" self in an "inner" core that transcends all social roles and relations and is free to choose or reject any of them at will. This is Kantian autonomy hypostatized; in its extreme, Sartrean version, the self is completely empty, pure freedom without any nature or essence at all; the self makes itself, and chooses all properties of the self (or all of the significant ones). Here individual freedom reigns supreme — at the limit the individual self is a creator ex nihilo of all meaning, including the meaning of itself. Social roles and relations exist only by benefit of individual consent and

---

[11] Note that this is a technical term and doesn't coincide with everyone's understanding of individualism. It is defined in context by the four features.

construction. Our place in a social group doesn't define us — unless we choose to accept its labels. Second, individualism centers all value in such autonomous individuals: individual selves are "ends in themselves," valuable for their own sakes quite apart from any value they might have for other selves. Things that are not selves have only the value or disvalue individual selves confer upon them. In particular, social groups and relations matter only to the extent individuals choose to allow them to matter. Third, individualism locates individuality in properties that individuals have on their own that make them different and independent from others — hence "uniqueness" is prized above commonality, dependence and connectedness. Individualism fears the specter of collectivism, the menace of the mob, the inauthenticity of the common herd. Fourth, individualism sets the fundamental project for human life: to make of oneself what one wants. This translates in the work environment into "careerism," the task of fashioning a career for oneself, using the tools and opportunities others offer to pursue self-enhancement and emolument as one pleases; one's commitment ultimately is to self, not to others (unless, of course, one chooses to commit to them).

This myth is crudely sketched, but its potency should not be underestimated. Protean in form, it penetrates all aspects of contemporary American society, from politics to religion, from entertainment to news (often a negligible distance!), from work to play. Perhaps surprisingly, academics are particularly susceptible to its blandishments — precisely, and ironically, because of certain features of their social roles.

Undergraduates find themselves away from home, often for the first time, with little to no adult supervision and time on their hands, and they are urged to choose friends, fashions, a major, a career — a whole identity of their own making (or so it seems). If their school has an "honor system" at all, or only administrative penalties for blatant cheating, there may be little reinforcement of community. Honor systems forbidding plagiarism but lacking an "informer rule" (requiring students to report peer honor violations) and with minimal student control have the perhaps unwitting effect of enforcing individualism: each individual is made responsible (by others!) for his or her own work, so that all student academic achievements might be more clearly recognized as individual ones.

Teachers are lords of their own classrooms, deciding what is to be taught, when and how it is to be taught, and how it is to be evaluated. Many scholars, particularly in the humanities, pursue the particular topics and conclusions they choose, and their publications are solo efforts, however much the assistance of others is acknowledged. Scientific researchers do collaborate, often elaborately so, but jealously guard their individual priorities of discovery, perquisites of achievement, and prerogatives of position. Many, perhaps most, faculty are freer than most in our society to schedule their daily and weekly lives as they see fit — not that they are less busy than workers in other organizations, but no one tells them when to do what they need to do (apart from the exigencies of deadlines, classes and meetings, which are resented all the more as they are the intrusive exceptions to a self-scheduled life). Further, scholars and researchers are deeply committed to their disciplines, and as they achieve stature in their academic specialty they often become somewhat detached from their local institutional contexts; they are valued in the disciplinary market, and as market players value themselves, not for their local roles and relations but for their marketable qualities that seemingly belong to themselves alone, as individuals.

Administrators are less free than students and faculty to schedule their own lives — indeed, administrative academic life greatly resembles managerial life in other sectors of society in its press of other-generated meetings, memos, problems, and issues. But individualism rears its head in administration precisely when it comes to decision-making time. Academic institutions profess collegiality and collective judgment, but administrators believe in their heart of hearts that such decisions eventually land on the desk of a single individual. Managers have many contacts and, if successful, numerous friendly associates, but they are, and must view themselves as, lonely individuals in their official capacity if they are to have any real administrative responsibility.

So it is no wonder that academics see themselves as individuals — not as members of social groups or institutions, playing roles defined by the constitutive rules of those groups. Even though post-modern academic ideology often claims to transcend individuality, the social reality of the academic life leads academics to overlook their own social existence — to see academic communities merely as aggregations of a large number of individuals. From such a perspective, therefore, honor will be largely invisible — or visible only as individual virtues of honesty, courage and integrity. But personal honor, although it requires individual trust of others and commitment to principles, is ineluctably social, since the individual is honorable only within some honor group, a group consti- tuted by a publicly shared sense of honor, held in common and mutually recognized; an honorable self cannot be self-defined or self-created, for it is constrained by the sense of honor shared by all. Thus it is that through the myopic lens of individualism, personal honor in academe may not be seen for what it is — and may not even be seen at all.

Finally, the myth of individualism creates and colludes with individual self-interest. I do not think that academics, on the whole, are any more or less selfish than other humans, who have their own self-interests to look after. But academics are intellectuals, and intellectuals are particularly prone to rationalizations — often elaborate and persuasive reason mongering — that conceals while furthering self-indulgence. Students may hide their irresponsible hedonism behind the cloak of self-exploration and social bonding; teachers may claim their self-serving schedules and course offerings are chiefly for the benefit of students; researchers may assert their research programs advance the field and not their own careers; and administrators may cloak their professional advancement and lust for status as altruistic service to the institution. As Kant said, we can never be certain our motives are free of the "dear self" (Kant, *Grundlegung*, Section II; cf. Frankfurt, 2000). The dear academic self may have — and provide — strong incentive for averting its gaze from personal honor, in fear of self-condemnation, or at least fear of expanding the horizon of concern and obligation beyond oneself. How convenient for the academic dear self, one might say, if it didn't have to worry about personal honor.

Still, none of these reasons for ignoring personal honor is convincing; none provides a good or sufficient reason for thinking that the concept of personal honor doesn't apply in academe. For all we have said, personal honor may be present but unnoticed, not unnoticed because absent.

III. Personal Honor in the Academy

I turn now to constructing a positive case both for thinking that personal honor does indeed exist, in special ways, within the academy, and for thinking that such honor might be not only worth noticing but also worth promoting. Viewing the academy from the standpoint of personal honor will bring to light some often overlooked features. Academic communities do form honor groups with honor codes, I believe, but these various groups have somewhat different, though overlapping, functions and aims, and so quite naturally their honor codes differ. In fact, some of the persistent tensions within academe can be viewed as conflicts among different honor groups and their respective codes. If this positive case has any merit, then academics would do well to break their silence and notice what they have ignored — to think again, and harder, about personal honor in the academy. I will divide my treatment into three parts, one each for students, faculty, and administrators. In each part I will first present mistaken views of personal honor in that context, then a somewhat idealized portrait of what personal honor should look like there, and finally an estimation of how and whether this ideal can be actualized under contemporary conditions.

Students: It is a tempting mistake to confine student honor to formal honor systems,[12] and to shrink the latter to juridical systems of classroom honesty. On this constricted view, honor is reduced to following certain rules of academic life designed to ensure that submitted work is a student's own. "Don't lie, cheat, or steal in any work you submit for a grade," goes the basic rule. Motives for following such a legalistic code boil down to the penalties attached to getting caught for cheating — grade reduction, failure, suspension, expulsion — and students become expert in weighing the rewards of cheating against the severity and probability of potential penalties. But such a legalistic system is not really an *honor* system at all, and its "honor" label is merely vestigial. The code is at best only a fragment of a possible honor code, or of a former honor code; the students don't constitute an honor group; and they follow the rules of academic honesty not as a matter of honor but out of self-interest.

Full-blooded honor "systems" (or structures) have many potential advantages to students: the benefits of ensuring others will not cheat, the ease of an atmosphere of trust (v. suspicion), the depth of well-earned respect both given and received as a communal bond, and the like. But what is required for an "honor system" to be truly a structure of *personal honor*?

First off, the membership boundaries of the *honor group* should be fairly clear: Does it include all and only students? Or are there perhaps separate groups for different schools, or for undergraduate, graduate and professional students? Are faculty, administrators, staff also members of the honor group, expected to abide fully by the same code and procedures of honor, or do they play at best ancillary roles — or no roles at all?

Second, the *academic code of honor* needs to be established — not necessarily, nor even desirably, as a set of explicit rules, with a complicated bureaucracy and formal procedures, but rather as a set of informal yet understood expectations about what should and shouldn't be done in order to remain a member of the honor group. Details of codes will differ, depending on local conditions and traditions, but the following guidelines apply.

The code must focus primarily on maintaining *academic integrity* — the integrity of the academic learner, the academic learning process, and the academic community. At its core, this integrity requires students to be

---

[12] There are other kinds of student associations that might also be considered honor groups: academic honor societies such as Phi Beta Kappa, honors programs and other assistance for talented students, and fraternal social organizations. The first are chiefly concerned with conferred, recognition and positional (status) honors. The second provide various financial rewards and special academic opportunities for selected students; such programs are chiefly recruiting devices for attracting academic talent, though they do carry conferred, recognition and positional honors. The third are local groups, often residential, that have written and unwritten codes of conduct, and can often be considered honor groups. The former two are not concerned with personal honor in practice (e.g. the character component of PBK is routinely ignored; only grades matter), and I will treat the latter, which is concerned with personal honor, in tension with the more prominent academic "honor systems."

truthful[13] and honest about the sources of their academic work, written and oral. This means taking credit only for work that is one's own — and for all of it. Plagiarism (unacknowledged "borrowing" of others' work) is of course forbidden, but so are other failures to acknowledge assistance received. Unacknowledged assistance given may also be prohibited, as both giver and receiver need to be openly honest about their aid. Honesty in academic work would be required for honorability in learning even if it were not needed for assessing achievement, giving grades, and awarding degrees and other honors. A person who is dishonest in learning has failed to learn — failed to learn the subject, failed to learn in a way appropriate to the subject and required by the teacher, and failed to learn what learning truly is. Such a person has effectively if not formally removed himself from academe. He cannot be trusted by others in the academic honor group — and perhaps by members of any honor group.

It should be obvious that academic integrity is a communal as well as an individual matter. Dishonesty doesn't just harm other individuals (for example, by altering their class rank) but also undermines the trust that forms the basis of the community's central activity — learning — and also the basis of the community itself. The known cheater cannot be trusted to learn and therefore cannot be trusted to remain in a community of learning. Moreover, the known — and tolerated — presence of cheaters arouses more widespread suspicion, which corrodes all matters of honor in the community.

Some honor codes may extend beyond academic integrity, to encompass co-curricular and extracurricular activities (from sports teams, clubs, organizations to informal social life), but such extension risks obscuring and compromising the centrality of academic integrity. Others will have rules about reporting known honor violations ("informer" rules); here the risk is that the academic responsibility teachers desire may conflict with the peer loyalties of students.

Third, the code needs be *fully owned* by the members of the honor group: it can't be a set of rules established, imposed and enforced by others (faculty, administrators, trustees). Ownership implies both effective control of the system and intrinsic motivation to adhere to the system. Only members of the honor group should be eligible to decide the rules, to adjudicate and enforce them, and to initiate and educate new members into the group. Ownership doesn't necessarily mean that all members are equally involved in such decisions and judgments, for they may delegate these matters to a few;

---

[13] Note that truthfulness here doesn't mean believing everything one says to be true — one may only be giving the teacher what she thinks is true while withholding one's own assent. But it does mean acknowledging what one believes are the true sources of what one says. It would take a chapter on its own to explore the varieties of truthfulness and the ways in which each is involved in academic honor — and a book to do the same for truthfulness in other honor contexts.

but all are responsible for the system, and without their willing allegiance and support it cannot survive as a system of personal honor. Students have got to want to be honorable — want to belong to an honor group, subscribe to its code, and be mutually recognized as such by other members.

Fourth, just as there are *rewards* to those who are honorable (conferred and political honors, to be sure, but more importantly the trust and loyalty of honorable others, and a sense of self-worth), so there must be *penalties* attached to dishonor, and mechanisms for detecting and adjudicating violations of honor. The ultimate penalty, of course, is permanent banishment from the honor group; whether this is the sole penalty available, or whether other, lighter penalties should be attached to what are deemed lesser breaches of honor, is up to the group to determine.[14]

Fifth, honor must serve as an *ideal of aspiration* as well as a rule of minimally acceptable conduct. The kind of honor that consists only in never running afoul of the law is too narrow and cramped to sustain an honor group as such. A person with a sense of honor must aspire to be honorable in many things, perhaps in all things, not just the written ones.

Sixth, members of an honor group must find a vital part of their *self-identity* wrapped up in their sense of honor, and they must deem possession of this (sense of) honor to be one of the more important traits, if not the most important trait, anyone can possess; they should prize their own honor, just as they appraise the honor of others. Honor is or becomes a part of their character, and it remains with them long after they graduate, ideally for their entire lives.

Such at any rate is the ideal. How close does it come to being realized in any contemporary American academic environment? Rather than considering particular examples and measuring them against the six criteria, I shall instead mention three formidable obstacles to actualizing the ideal. One is size. Honor groups require mutual recognition among members. As an institution grows in size, such mutual recognition becomes increasingly difficult, and it is perhaps impossible in a Megaversity unless care is taken to form more intimate groups of mutual recognition (e.g. by classes, majors, schools, residence halls, etc.). A second obstacle is lack of ownership. If students feel a school's honor system really belongs to faculty or administrators, and serves only their ends, they either will not embrace its code *as a matter of honor* or else will not embrace it at all. Academic honesty must become a peer-student value for an "honor system" truly to function as a system of honor.

A third obstacle is more insidious. Group norms will always conflict with

---

[14] Harsh as it may appear, an ultimate penalty as the sole penalty (the so-called "single sanction") makes considerable sense: it underlines the seriousness with which the honor group takes its sense of honor and serves an educative function all on its own.

some individual goals and values — cheating may be against the rules, for example, but it may very well advance one's career — and this conflict marks the cost of the norm to individuals. But sometimes group norms conflict with the norms of other groups, with similar costs to individuals who belong to both groups. Thus the codes of different honor groups may conflict, spelling difficulties for students with membership in more than one group. Fraternities and sororities, for example, are arguably established and constituted as honor groups, as witnessed by their frequent use of the language of honor in their founding documents, self-descriptions, statements of purpose, and initiation materials. These organizations at their best promote many worthy ideals, but one invariable value is member-loyalty — solidarity with one's "brothers" or "sisters." Now consider the following scenario (based on a real-life story):

> A freshman student gets drunk at a party, staggers home across a deserted street late at night, and is struck and killed by a speeding vehicle, which drives away unwitnessed. Police spend countless hours tracking down leads, but the trail runs cold until, months later, several obviously distraught students come forward with information that had been gnawing on their consciences. A week after the incident, they had learned that the hit-and-run driver was a member of their fraternity, who had cleverly covered his tracks. Loyalty to their "brother" had prevented them from fulfilling their responsibilities as law-abiding citizens and also from acting honorably as understood by their school's wide-ranging honor system.

This is a dramatic example, yet there are countless daily cases where student loyalties to friends and relations clash with loyalty to the academy: cheating witnessed, unauthorized aid given, cold-test archives preserved and used, etc. The situation is especially poignant, however, where the conflict in loyalties is not between persons and rules but between two groups of persons, each with a different code of honor. It is further heightened when the codes differ but the people are (largely) the same: when the "brothers" are also fellow students.

So there are formidable obstacles to actualizing the ideal of a student system of personal honor. But they are not insuperable. If the ideal of honor is attractive enough to enough people, it can be put into practice. Of course, each actual community of honor must respect local conditions and traditions, and its achievement will require the continual efforts of many across generations — it is much easier to maintain a working honor system than to repair a broken one, much less to reconstitute or even originate one. Finally, ideals are fragile, and rarely if ever fully realized. Yet ideals have an odd way of creating their own conditions of possibility: When they are clearly glimpsed, ideals often inspire persons to put them into practice. Perhaps personal honor can offer such inspiration to students still.

Faculty: How could faculty possibly form an honor group? There is no formal honor system for faculty in any university, only legal contracts, tenure, and school policies. Faculty groups are either administrative or governance units (departments, programs, committees, senates, unions), intellectual associations (study and discussion groups, professional societies, departments and programs again), or social organizations (clubs, teams, parties)— where's personal honor in any of this? Besides, academics pride themselves on their independence[15] — each is a powerful mind thoroughly capable of deciding for itself how to act and what to think — and a collection of independent individuals does not make an honor group. The old decanal saw that managing the faculty is like herding cats is hyperbole, but points up the problem. Granted, faculty might share some values — industriousness, the importance of seeking truth, of being truthful in reporting one's results, and of collegiality (or at least minimal civility) — but surely this is not enough for honor. Besides, and crucially, faculty members simply don't think of themselves and their academic communities in terms of honor. So how can the concept of personal honor apply to faculty?

To discern faculty honor will require taking a different perspective on the academic landscape. There are two steps required. First, the major faculty roles of teaching and research or scholarship must be seen as not just individual pursuits but essentially communal functions, with shared values that make those functions both possible and effective; second, these communities must be viewed as having the distinctive features of honor groups. Whether the concept of personal honor can thereby be made attractive to contemporary faculty I do not know, but the hypothesis at least deserves consideration.

First, consider *teaching* in the academy. Socrates may have needed only the streets of Athens, but his student Plato founded an Academy, and ever since teaching has been largely an academic function, residing in educational institutions.[16] Colleges and universities have traditions, organizations, structure, staff, and funding, none of which can be provided by a single individual. This context of course requires faculty members to teach the subjects they know and to devote themselves to the students in their own classrooms. But the intellectual needs of students are not addressed by a single course, nor indeed by any haphazard set of courses; there must be a coherent program of study, or rather many of them; there must be *curricula*. So faculty are not just individual masters of a particular discipline and subject matter but also colleagues engaged in a common project, the coherent education of young

---

[15] Powerfully reinforced by the myth of individualism mentioned earlier.

[16] There are of course other institutional contexts for teaching: most notably the workplace (apprenticeships, on-the-job training, seminars, consulting), but also in government, arts, religion and other sectors, where knowledge needs to be transmitted, skills honed, and values inculcated; at the limit, one might consider the informal teaching that goes on in the home and indeed in almost any personal relationship. But I will stick to institutions whose purpose is primarily educational.

(and sometimes older) minds. Teaching can seem unutterably solitary or even lonely to someone late at night preparing lectures or grading papers, while at other times it may seem just a one-many relation of a single faculty member to a classroom of students; it is all too easy to lose sight of how these solitary hours and solo efforts are vital moments in a larger enterprise. Faculty teaching ideally lies at the heart of an institution's overarching purpose of educating students, and dovetails with all the secondary functions supporting that primary one, but faculty do not just happen to be co-workers in the same shop. They must also recognize one another as engaged in a common enterprise, sharing the same overarching purpose.

With shared purpose come other things for teachers to share: commitments to one another, to their environing institutions and to certain values. These commitments and values are, or should be, tethered tightly to the aims of education: to be knowledgeable and "keep up" both in one's field and in pedagogy; to prepare for and actually engage one's classes; to discern "where students are" in terms of abilities, information, insight, and interest; to communicate effectively what one knows; to motivate students to learn; to require student work that stimulates and shows their achievement; to have clear standards of quality in academic work, and to evaluate such work fairly and accurately; to provide helpful feedback to students; to use one's power or authority for student benefit and not for merely personal interests; to have regard for students outside the classroom (consistent with one's other responsibilities); and so on.

Is it part of a teacher's loyalties to be committed to the particular people and institutions within which she teaches? Yes, even though this entails what nearly all academics profess to deplore: committees. At least there will be committees if faculty participation in academic governance is taken seriously, as it should be, and if faculty design not only individual courses but also departmental and program requirements, degree requirements, and, ultimately, strategic goals and plans for the institution as a whole.[17]

So teaching in the academy is a communal as well as an intensely individual affair, and an academic teacher is necessarily a member of a community, a faculty *member*. Now, how might this faculty group, with its shared commitments and values, be viewed as an *honor group* with an *honor code*? And what would be gained by doing so? Recall that an honor group requires not only shared values but also mutual recognition — effective allegiance both to the same code and to other members of the group, while realizing that everyone expects everyone to do likewise. So the crucial issues are (i) whether teaching

---

[17] Faculty roles in these will differ, and other constituencies will impinge, or even dominate, at higher levels; but just as students need to "own" their honor system, so faculty need to "own" the educational mission of their school, not simply believing the school is their employer and having a stake in its economic health, but actually having some measure of control.

faculty do subscribe to the same values or code; (ii) whether this code is (like) a code of honor effective in their (professional) lives, and (iii) whether they mutually recognize (i) and (ii) in each other. The short answer to all three queries is that they do. More fully:

Teachers do largely share the commitments I mentioned. These commitments, and not credentials or contracts or titles, are what make them *teachers* and not merely employees or implements of an institution. They are at the heart of what makes teaching a *profession* and not just a job (cf. Chapter 10). But then these commitments are (like) an unwritten but powerful code of honor, adherence to which binds teachers in a community of honor and gives a sense of self-worth. Often society, if it values the role of teaching as it should, will confer other kinds of honors upon teachers (though not often high remuneration!). But the personal honor of a teacher, partially constituting her self-identity, is wrapped up in recognizing herself as a colleague engaged with others in a common function, for common ends, with shared and mutually recognized commitments, thereby deserving and gaining the respect of those worthy others. Teachers, ideally at least, belong to an honor group of fellow teachers, and their sense of honor as teachers is a vital part of their self-regard. Doubtless this is the way most teachers already think of themselves, and it is only a small but important matter to call it what it truly is, to speak publicly of a *teacher's honor*.

Next, consider *research* or *scholarship*[18] in the academy. Sometimes it is as solitary as teaching, and even more abstract — a relation of a researcher not to other persons but to an article or a book, an artifact or an organism, a material or an idea. But it would be wrong to view research as essentially idiosyncratic. One reason, of course, is that most scientific research, especially in the natural sciences, is intensely collaborative, often elaborately so, involving co-investigators by the dozens; most experimental work is done by research *groups*. Second, every scholar, if honest, acknowledges debts and dependencies to many others, from secretaries, technicians and librarians to relatives and friends, but especially to a large group of scholarly peers who provide comments — provocative ideas and trenchant criticisms — that powerfully affect the scholarship. Third, scholars write up their results with an audience in mind, and that audience shapes the *report* of the results: scholarship is the gift of scholars to others, especially to other scholars. Fourth, research is

---

[18] I will use these terms interchangeably and with vague reference: there are many forms of research and scholarship, ranging from "pure" inquiry unfettered by any practical constraints to "applied" research developing theoretical results, and including inquiry into pedagogy that shades off into background class preparation. Nor is all research or scholarship pegged to publication, though inquiry naturally seeks to make itself known to others, especially to peers, in order not only to inform them but also to gain their acknowledgment and approbation. Publication is just a "making public" in this way.

essentially peer-reviewed; without that review it is a private passion.[19]

Fifth, and most important for our purposes, researchers and scholars intentionally accept and abide by a set of norms and values governing their inquiry and publication: these are not so much criteria of *good* scholarship or research as they are constitutive rules for research *as such*. Research, no matter how varied in object, manner, originality, importance and the like, is *research* only because of the values the researcher shares with a community of researchers. Their values include accurate and honest recording and description of data, proper use of instruments, acceptable standards of reasoning, due regard for others' results and appropriate communication of one's own, adequate familiarity with the field, etc. — where "accurate," "proper," "acceptable," "due," "appropriate," and "adequate" are themselves all matters of group determination.[20]

So in research there are indeed shared purposes, shared norms and values, shared commitments to others — all of which constitute researchers as a social group or various such groups.[21] But do scholars and researchers form an *honor* group? Can the norms and values they undoubtedly share be considered an *honor* code? What is gained by looking at them in this light? I think doing so highlights the nature of the scholarly community, helping us to understand such phenomena as the following.

- When scholars or researchers violate this code — by plagiarizing, fabricating data, misrepresenting themselves or others — and are discovered, there is public outcry, even outrage, among other members of the community. It is not just that dependent lines of research have been compromised or that the community's image is tarnished in the wider society, but that a bond of trust has been ruptured within the community, a common code has been violated, a loyalty betrayed. The group wants the violator to be and to feel shamed for this betrayal — to experience not just guilt in his own eyes but loss of respect from, indeed humiliation before, the entire group of his (former?) colleagues. The violator at the minimum loses status in the community of inquiry, and he may well lose his place altogether — exile is the usual

---

[19] I owe this point to Nat Goldberg, a debt that illustrates his point.

[20] Simon Winchester writes of the great scientist (and historian of Chinese science) Joseph Needham: "In professional terms Needham was after all an exceptionally honorable man, a scientist given to following the scientists' code . . . which at every step demands a commitment to honesty and integrity, and which holds as a moral certainty the idea that results can never, ever be fudged, manipulated, or falsified." (Winchester, 2008, 214–15)

[21] Clearly the norms could vary across different groups of scholars, though I conjecture that variations will chiefly be differing local interpretations of the same norms, not different norms, and that they will chiefly be driven by the nature of the subject-matter: compare the goal of accuracy in experimental particle physics to the same goal in translation of a natural language or a philosopher's explication of another's argument.

fate. All this behavior is typical of a community of honor.

- Scholars and researchers make an enormous personal investment of time and energy in their work, with many sacrifices of other interests, but they are encouraged to make that investment, and sustained in their making, by the community of inquiry. That scholarly peers regard one's work as worthwhile, as good work according to community standards, is vital to the ongoing effort. Contrary to the myth of individualism, there are few individuals who are strong-willed enough to sustain a line of inquiry, with all its personal costs, without reflection of its worth from others. Again, this strong sense of seeking community respect is a feature of honor groups.

- Scholars love conferred honors, but want them conferred for the right reasons: scholarly fame should be based upon scholarly accomplishment.[22] That accomplishment should be the scholar's "own work," and not stolen from another, but it must also be "good work" as measured by the standards of the group, not by outsiders.[23] Further, gaining such honors is an important motivating factor for scholars: wanting to do "Nobel-quality work" is wanting to be recognized by one's peers as doing work worthy of receiving a Nobel Prize. The conferred (or recognition) honors are a sign of a valued group's acknowledgment of something worth honoring, namely work instancing the values of research and scholarship. This is the code of scholarly honor.

So researchers, like teachers, arguably belong to communities of honor, whether or not they think of themselves in this light. But do they belong to the *same* honor group(s)? Clearly, teachers and scholars are frequently (and, from some standpoints, ideally) the same people, and teaching and scholarship can be mutually reinforcing, mutually invigorating. Further, teaching and scholarship are not dyadic but triadic relations: among teacher, student and subject matter, on the one hand, and among researcher, audience, and subject matter on the other hand. Perhaps ideally, those two subject matters will coincide, or at least overlap considerably. One might therefore suppose that teaching and research are harmonious because they are "about" the same subject. But this is not necessarily the case: *as teachers and as researchers* they do not approach even the same subject matter in the same ways, for the same ends, and for the same audiences. So I repeat the question: if teachers and scholars belong to honor groups, do they share precisely the *same*

---

[22] Since scholars consider good scholarship to be an excellence, they would insist that these honors are not at all conferred but merely recognized. Scholars, like many others, have a vested interest in conflating conferred and recognition honor.

[23] Note that the reputation of a researcher within the community of research may suffer from too much attention to a wider audience — becoming "too popular" with students or the media marks one as not a "serious scholar."

honor code and the *same* commitments and loyalties to one another? Not entirely, I believe, and seeing how the overlapping honor codes of teachers and scholars partially diverge casts light on some of the deeper tensions in the academy today.

First the overlap: teaching and research *do* share many of the same norms and values. Both seek truth and truthfulness, the accurate description, correct explanation and proper evaluation of an object of study, as well as honestly communicating that information (and the degree of one's warranted assurance) to others. Both prize expertise and virtuosity — certainly with regard to "knowing one's material" but also with regard to how that knowledge is acquired (inquiry) and how it is to be communicated (pedagogy). Both share intellectual values such as clarity, depth and precision of understanding, range of knowledge, insight into complex methods and problems, sheer acuity of mind. Both groups have an implicit hierarchy of status and authority, based on talent, experience and accomplishment, even while there is nominal recognition of peer equality, perhaps expressed in fairly egalitarian behavior and dress. Both seek the respect primarily of their peers — their equals in teaching or research — even while not unmindful of their stake in the wider society's regard (for funding if for nothing else). Both are firmly committed to accuracy, consistency and fairness in evaluating others' work, and (ideally at least) honestly apply the same standards to themselves. Both recognize that intellectual authority is not the same as, nor does it justify, other kinds of power over others; power in the classroom, the library or the laboratory should not be abused, for example, by deliberately making a student "uncomfortable" for the wrong reasons, by tongue-lashing library staff, or by treating laboratory assistants as mere servants.

Next the mutual aid: Teaching requires intellectual capital, and that requires understanding how the intellectual capital is acquired and confirmed, by participating in gaining it — by doing research oneself. Only in this first-hand way can a teacher truly understand the subject matter she imparts to students; second-hand scholarship lacks the living sense of how the knowledge is obtained, its sources and merits as well as its limits and problems. "Keeping up with a field" involves "keeping up *in* a field," and this is part of the honor code of teaching. Likewise research is not only aided by teaching, but some kind of teaching is arguably a part of *its* code. Publication and teaching form a continuum: publication is communicating research results to actual peers; teaching is communicating those results to potential peers. A vital community of research requires infusion of new blood, recruited and trained through teaching. Moreover, researchers sometimes find that their understanding of their subject-matter is improved by the challenge of communicating it to novices and apprentices; doing so brings hidden assumptions to light, challenges murky data and methods, raises worthy questions of all kinds, and suggests new lines of approach.

But overlap and mutual aid are not the whole story. The two codes also diverge, and conflicts may emerge. Of course, as just noted, teaching and research can be mutually fructifying, or at least mutually supportive, and arguably the best practitioners of each practice the other, in varying admixtures. Even so, it is clear that the two commitments can clash in their demands on time, energy and attention — resources spent in teaching, even in class preparation, don't necessarily further one's research; and when research time *is* put to direct pedagogical use, doing research and teaching are distinct and require different attitudes and energies. Likewise pedagogical and research skills are different, and honing them requires different kinds of attention and practice. But the essential tension between teaching and research goes deeper, for it is, I think, largely a difference between two distinct codes — codes that can be viewed as codes of honor.

This difference is highlighted by two contrasts: First, a teacher's primary loyalty is to his or her students, and secondarily to the subject matter, while a researcher's priorities are the reverse. Second, a teacher's commitments to peers are more local, primarily to the community of teachers in the local institution and secondarily to the wider groups and organizations of teachers, while a researcher's commitments are more global, primarily to the community of researchers in her field across institutions and secondarily to the local institution and its mission. Before developing these points, let me make it clear that they are weak generalizations with many exceptions; nevertheless, I think they help us understand some of the tensions facing faculty in academe.

Teachers teach subjects to students, and students take priority over subjects, although of course both are required. Teachers must have command of a body of knowledge and a set of disciplinary skills if they are to guide students in acquiring a similar mastery, or even a smattering of relevant and reliable information; further, a teacher's knowledge relies ultimately on a community of scholars who have developed and ratified that knowledge. But all this content must be imparted to particular students, and that target of instruction takes precedence over its content. Researchers, on the other hand, inquire into subject matters, seeking knowledge initially for its own sake, secondly for the sake of peers (seeking their ratification), and only thirdly for the sake of learners (for their edification).[24]

Second, in part because a teacher's primary commitment is to her students, and because students vary so greatly across institutions (in terms of qualifications and interests), and because institutions vary as greatly as their students (in degree programs, resources, missions, etc.), teachers will be primarily linked to peers in their local institution, with affinities to teachers

---

[24] Of course, there will also usually be other parties of interest: notably funding agencies, employers, business ventures, the media, and the wider public.

elsewhere diminishing as their educational contexts differ.[25] They will co-teach courses, join colleagues in designing and implementing programs for their departments, schools, and university, and gradually over time acquire bonds of loyalty not just to particular people but also to the institution itself as it becomes *their* institution in more than a nominal sense. Teachers become more and more deeply rooted as they remain in one place due to the very nature of teaching.[26] Researchers on the other hand are primarily members of a research community that potentially has global reach; in many cases there will be no one locally who participates in the same research, or perhaps even understands it. Loyalty to this community of inquiry takes the researcher to conferences, makes him correspond with colleagues elsewhere, and generates torrents of papers, poster boards, reviews, articles, notes and volumes addressed primarily to those peers. Researchers are more mobile across institutions; even having spent equal time as teachers in one place, they are necessarily better known and more "marketable" elsewhere, and tenure is less of a tether. Few faculties are raided for their teaching stars.

The divergence of codes and communities may create tensions, or even conflicts, on several levels. An individual who wants to teach and also do research will naturally find she lacks the time to do both as much or as well as she wishes, for teaching and research are potentially infinite tasks — you can always do more class preparation, spend more time with students, read one more book, perform one more experiment. Sometimes just meeting the minimal codes of each is taxing, and producing "good work" according to each can be overwhelming. The stakes are increased by the demands and the lures of tenure, and the understandable desire for a permanent position. Colleges and universities have various stated and unstated criteria for tenure and promotion, and sometimes they send mixed signals: winning a teaching award at some schools can be the kiss of death for a tenure candidate, as it somehow indicates too little interest in scholarship (or perhaps arouses the jealousy of less effective senior colleagues). Contrariwise, spending too much time on scholarship in some schools in hopes of landing a better job elsewhere may lead to neglect of teaching responsibilities at home — and may result in no job offers and an unhappy local tenure.

But these are not just questions of individual career paths and institutional requirements. Sometimes there are also issues of divergent loyalties, clashes of honor codes. Sometimes following the teaching code of primary devotion to one's students hinders following the research code of primary devotion

---

[25] E.g. what teaching involves will differ at a small sectarian liberal arts college, an institute for the arts, and a large public university. There is some solidarity even across such differences, of course, but it is stronger within like-minded and similarly engaged institutions.

[26] Of course, there are many other reasons: tenure provides job security but also makes it harder to move; family and friends establish community connections; the inertia of familiarity takes over; etc. But the nature of teaching anchors these.

to one's subject matter, and vice versa. Sometimes forging and maintaining links to scholarly peers elsewhere comes at the expense of service to one's home institution, and vice versa. Ideally, of course, one teaches what one researches, and researches what one teaches, with mutual invigoration the result. But life in institutions is never so neat: someone has to teach the intro or survey course, and class meetings inconveniently conflict with scholarly deadlines — or is it the other way around? So it may come down to hard choices, and part of the difficulty may be: to which honor group do you owe your primary allegiance? Which honor code matters more?[27]

Administrators: Once again we look for honor in what many consider an unlikely place. Administrators[28] manage the academy, enabling its primary functions of teaching and research, but as administrators they are not members of campus honor systems (that's for students) nor members of teaching or research honor groups (that's for faculty).[29] Administrators are charged, or at least are concerned, with maintaining the positional honor of the school — its reputation among peers, rating groups and "consumers" of its various "products" (one wishes that were only a metaphor!) — and they may identify their own self-worth with the institution's regard among its kin. Honor flows in the opposite direction when administrators honor an institution by being committed to its goals and values and by advancing its mission while preserving civility. And administrators surely receive considerable conferred honors — compensation packages, titles and perks, offices and staff, power imagined and actual. But where is personal honor to be found in any of this conferred, positional, and commitment honor? Does it make any sense to view administrators as such belonging to honor groups with honor codes?

It is tempting, but mistaken, I believe, to look for personal honor among administrators as lodged either within individuals or in professional

---

[27] The insidious academic pecking order that ranks four-year institutions above two-year ones, graduate schools above undergraduate ones, and universities above colleges, is a matter of positional honor (rankings) and related conferred honors (compensation and prestige); in effect it elevates scholarship over teaching, other things equal. Institutions have their own reasons for supporting this pecking order — prestige, funding, attracting "the best" faculty (circularly defined as and by those with the best scholarly reputations)— and their incentives are weighted accordingly. But why should faculty themselves support this order aside from these extrinsic incentives? Do they truly believe, in their heart of hearts, that research is more important than teaching, that the research code always takes precedence over the teaching code, and that they would rather be respected by a community of scholars than by a community of teachers?

[28] I use this term for very disparate groups: the managers of academic institutions, from department heads to deans to presidents and chancellors, but also the governing bodies in whom ultimate corporate (and legal) responsibility is vested. All are responsible in various ways for structuring, maintaining, funding and supporting the functions of teaching and research that constitute the heart of an academic institution.

[29] I realize that some administrators are part-time teachers and researchers, retaining faculty function as well as faculty status while performing administrative duties. But the two functions are distinct, even if performed daily by the same person.

associations, though the latter is closer to the truth. Personal honor, as we have insisted, cannot be solely a matter of individual administrators' rectitude and integrity — e.g. managing funds honestly, people decently, and institutions altruistically. To count as honor, such virtues must be essentially connected to an honor group, and if that group lies outside the administrative role, then it is not *administrative* honor that is in question. Professional associations of administrators are more promising, but all too often they seem little more than sources of useful tips, networking, credentialing, job prospects, and support or consolation — they do not seem to take honor seriously. Nonetheless, I wish to make a case for viewing administrators as potentially belonging to an interesting kind of honor group, a group with both local and more global ties, whether or not it has a formal organization.

Many of the functions of administrators are the same or similar across institutions, the more alike as the institutions are alike. The recruitment, evaluation, and compensation of personnel (particularly faculty); budgeting; planning, strategic and otherwise; the daily detail of governance; funding; generating and managing institutional initiatives; assessment; and so on. About such matters administrators can learn from each other, and perhaps commiserate. These similar functions mean that the roles of administrators are similar, but also, I believe, that their values are likely to be similar, and that there could well be a code, or various codes, of the administrative life, whether or not these are expressed or studied. Doubtless there will be differences in codes depending upon the level and type of role the administrators play (e.g. different for deans of student life and deans of academic affairs, different for provosts, presidents, and trustees). But broad elements in such codes will be widely shared. Any such code would surely include norms and values like the following: concern for the common good, for the well-being of the institution as a whole and not just some of its parts; due regard for the priority of an academy's mission of teaching and research, properly tailored to local realities; dedication to quality in teaching and research; fairness and equity in processes of decision-making and resource-allocation; commitment to consultation and power-sharing; industriousness and willingness to work long hours; and so on. Further, such norms and values will be mutually recognized as shared, and respect will be gained and given by one's administrative peers based upon this shared code. The self-respect of an administrator will depend, in part, upon this respect from other administrators.[30] To fail as an administrator is not only to let one's institution down, and oneself as well, but also, and vitally, to fail those other members of the group engaged in similar work — other administrators. Failure to abide by the norms of administration

---

[30] Clearly there are other sources of respect, especially from segments of the local institution (students, faculty, staff, alumni, parents, etc.). But the regard of other administrators, both locally and in other institutions, is a very powerful incentive.

represents disgrace to the entire group of administrators and therefore shame before them as well as guilt in one's own eyes.

Now all of these features — membership in a group, a shared code, mutual recognition among members, respect and shame — are essential features of personal honor. It therefore seems reasonable to view academic administration in terms of personal honor. Granted this is not how administrators typically view themselves as individuals, nor how their professional associations focus their attention. But I do think most administrators come to realize over time that they have absorbed such a perspective, and I believe it might help to make this perspective explicit. Further, there are some powerful benefits to doing so:

- It could lift the practice of administration, in the eyes of its practitioners and those of the wider society, above what many faculty regard as necessary drudgery, as something less fulfilling and noble than teaching and research, as something to be patronized or barely tolerated, or as just another job. Honor dignifies the work as well as the worker.
- It could help administrators regard themselves as members of a *profession* (an honorable profession), a group with more in common, and more at stake, than merely performing certain functions, working hard, and being paid very well for doing a job.
- It could raise, and help to sustain, the spirits of beleaguered and often isolated administrators who frequently have few immediate colleagues to confide in but who can enjoy an extensive network of peers all able to understand and to sympathize — so long as one does "good work" according to the group's code of honor (cf. Chapter 10).

Of course, honor is not a panacea for all that ails administrators — or students or faculty, for that matter. But viewing the administrative function as the work of an honor group with its own distinctive code of honor, mutual recognition of shared values, and larger purpose than self-aggrandizement or institutional advancement, can give administrators heightened self-respect and a sense of identity, even as it draws them into communal regard. These are not inconsiderable virtues.

IV. CONCLUSION

In this chapter, I have argued that there is more personal honor in the academy, and more potential for it, than academics ordinarily believe. Viewing the academy in terms of personal honor not only illuminates a great deal of the contemporary landscape (e.g. some of the tensions in the academy can be seen as cases of divided loyalties, where students or faculty are torn between two divergent honor codes or honor groups) but can also provide ideals to inspire both individuals and communities. Moreover, honor is a way of establishing community that is a realistic alternative to relying either on internal moral gyroscopes or on explicit rules or policies enforced by quasi-judicial or legal systems. Honor groups have their own problems, to be sure, some of them due to an individualistic age but others peculiar to the nature of honor (e.g. its relativity). But I hope it is clear that personal honor in academe is at once actual, feasible, and quite often desirable.

Chapter 10

PROFESSIONAL HONOR

Professions are important social structures, and they have been elaborately described, analyzed, praised and castigated from a wide variety of perspectives, engendering a vast scholarly literature. Perhaps surprisingly after all this study, the notion of a profession is still contested, even while the list of those groups calling themselves "professions" has ballooned from the earliest trio of divinity, law, and medicine to the several hundreds, perhaps thousands today (cf. Freidson, 2001). At the same time, each of these self-denominated professions has wrestled with identifying, defining, promulgating, inculcating, legislating and enforcing what are deemed to be appropriate "professional" rules or standards — often described as "codes of professional responsibility" or something similar. I believe considerable light can be shed on both these matters — the definition of a profession and the search for appropriate professional rules — from the standpoint of honor, especially personal honor. Although professions do seek conferred and positional honors for their members, they also resemble honor groups, and their professional standards look very much like codes of personal honor. After some general points about professions (Section I), professional honor groups (Section II), and professional codes (Section III), I will consider the legal profession as a case of special interest (Section IV) and close with some moral concerns (Section V).

I. PROFESSIONS

What is a profession? It must be something more than a number of people earning their livelihood by doing similar work expertly and for (very) good pay. But what more? Here are the major criteria proposed by various scholars:

1   A profession is a social group advancing the economic interests of its

members by achieving "market closure," dominating certain kinds of workplace and running erstwhile competitors out of business. (You need a license to practice law or medicine, and getting one is tightly guarded.)[1]

2   It is a fairly autonomous social work group with members who are also importantly autonomous in their daily work. The group organizes, monitors and regulates itself, setting its own standards of membership, competence and dismissal, as well as its own associational structure and workplace conditions, largely free from outside control, and it permits its practitioners wide latitude in applying those standards in their daily work environments. (The various bar associations govern admittance to, and dismissal from, the bar, and lawyers admitted to the bar have wide latitude in how to practice law.)[2]

3   It is the zealous guardian of a body of special systematic knowledge and skill, using such means as mandated specialized formal education, testing, and certification. (Medicine is a science — or an applied science, or at least an art based on science — with elaborate theories of disease, injury, cure and prevention, and it requires lengthy classroom and practical training, as well as special licenses.)[3]

4   It has a certain status or prestige, or its members do. (Professional lawyers occupy higher rungs on the social ladder than do sanitation workers, and not just because of the pay.)[4]

5   It is the guardian of special rituals, not merely of passage into its membership but also of display to the wider society. ("All rise" in court for the entrance of a black-robed judge, and similar deference, if less formal, attends the entrance into the examining room by a white-gowned doctor.)

6   It has (at least ideally) a unique social role or responsibility, providing a special kind of service to the wider community. (The law serves justice and works occasionally *pro bono*; medicine serves health and sometimes volunteers in free clinics; theology serves salvation and often serves up soup kitchens.)[5]

7   It has an internal body of ethics irreducible to general norms more widely applicable and sometimes even at odds with them. (Lawyers in an adversarial system may be expected to do what ordinarily would be regarded as lying.)[6]

8   It cultivates and safeguards a special kind of interpersonal relationship

[1] Cf. Collins in Burrage & Torstendahl, 1990; Larsen, 1977.
[2] Beckman in Burrage & Torstendahl, eds, 1990; Freidson, 2001.
[3] Beckman in Burrage & Torstendahl, 1990; Davis 1999 disputes this claim.
[4] Larsen, 1977.
[5] Bennett, 2001, Chapter 11; Goldman, 1980.
[6] Markovits, 2008; Luban 1988; Simon, 1998.

between professional and client — a "fiduciary" one[7] — with special role-differentiated behavior expected on both sides. (Being a patient is not just being patient, and likewise being a doctor is not just doctoring.)[8]

Further complexity emerges in light of history: what is (or considered to be) a profession changes over time, beginning with medieval craft guilds and evolving via gentlemanly occupations to the numerous trade associations today clamoring for greater social status and, not incidentally, higher pay.[9] Some historians even believe that professions may be a transient phenomenon– "profession" is but "an arbitrary historical usage," bound to Anglo-American culture of the last few centuries and artificially linking "a series of rather random occupations"[10] — but this is still a minority view. Most think professions are distinctive and here to stay, although changing with the times.

Most scholars combine and blend several or all of these criteria, in various ways. Quite naturally, sociologists tend to emphasize criteria (1)–(5), while ethicists stress (6)–(8), sometimes to the exclusion of the other criteria.[11] Here's a sampling of different approaches: Randall Collins (1990) chiefly combines (1) and (4) — "a combination of market closure with high occupational status honour" (p. 36, *in italics* in the original) — with "the ceremonial impressiveness of practitioners" (p. 37), where even educational qualifications have a ritual function (5). Michael Bayles (1989) combines (3) ("extensive training" and "a significant intellectual component") with (6), and thinks (1) and (2) are common but not necessary features. Bernard Barber (1963) downplays (1) and emphasizes the "honorary" rewards of (4), while also including (2) and (6). Eliot Freidson calls a profession "an occupation that controls its own work, organized by a special set of institutions sustained in part by a particular ideology of expertise and service" (Freidson, 1994), thereby combining (2) and (3) with (6) and (7), while slighting (1), (4), (5) and (8). Nathan Hatch (1988) and Bruce Kimball (1992) give prominence to (2), (3) and (6). Daryl Koehn (1994), seeking a basis for professional ethics, finds "the *essence* of a legitimate profession" in (8). Magali Larsen (1977) sees special knowledge and skills (3) as means to market power (1) and social status (4), with morality as an ideological epiphenomenon. Howard Vollmer and Donald Mills (1966) define "profession" in terms of professionalism as including ideology, (6) and (7), plus organization, (2) and (3). Richard Wasserstrom (1975) touches on all eight criteria, as does John Kultgen (1988), who goes quite beyond them in his list of 21 characteristics

---

[7] Elliott, 1972, p. 5.

[8] Sokolowski, 1991; Freidson, 1991.

[9] Cf. Freidson, 1994, Chapter 1; Haber, 1991; Hatch, 1988; Krause, 1996; Larson, 1977.

[10] Veysey, 1988, 17.

[11] Rob Atkinson (personal communication) wryly notes that economists have the most "economical" view — there is only one criterion, the first, economic one.

(13 are "core" and 8 are additional) and J. A. Jackson (1970), who also has 21 "sub-elements," differing slightly from Kultgen's 21 and organized under seven headings; these cut across the eight criteria listed above.

In the end, after all this complexity and lack of consensus (and there's much more!), it is tempting to agree with Eliot Freidson that the concept of profession is "an intrinsically ambiguous, multifaceted folk concept, of which no single definition and no attempt at isolating its essence will ever be genuinely persuasive" (Freidson, 1994, p. 25). I would agree that the ordinary use of "profession" is ambiguous, but I do not think it is equivocal; rather, it seems more a family resemblance or analogical term, with certain central paradigmatic cases including law, medicine and ministry, and with more recent cases stretching the meaning in various directions. If so, then understanding the central cases will help us understand the similar, though differently divergent, peripheral cases.

II. Professional Honor Groups

Rather than discarding this "folk concept" of profession, and without returning to a futile essentialist quest, I think progress in understanding may be made from the standpoint of the concept of personal honor, by viewing at least the central cases of professions as honor groups. To be sure these professional groups do have economic and social functions, resulting in (perhaps even often aiming at) high income, status and other rewards from the wider society. Ironically, these are all forms of honor — but only peripheral ones. More centrally, I believe, core professions may be viewed as honor groups that inculcate and express distinctive forms of personal honor. "What the professions do (and this helps account for much of their excitement and attainment) is to bring into the modern world ideals and standards that are pre-modern — both pre-capitalistic and pre-democratic" (Haber, 1991, ix). Personal honor is at the heart of those "pre-modern" ideals and standards, but though honor is pre-modern in origin, I believe it is also capable of contemporary application and use.

Clearly core professions have many features in common with honor groups: The members are loyal to one another, trusting others as they are trusted, and all are committed to common principles. Professionals view one another as equal members of the profession, and they have special regard for one another, relying upon one another in various ways, especially by crediting their word above that of outsiders.[12] They carefully maintain their image or reputation within the group, reacting strongly to insult (in the form of

---

[12] One might view this as a form of "professional courtesy," but such "courtesy" is not an unmerited gift but what is due as a matter of professional honor.

professional aspersions) by other members, and they are reluctant to insult their peers by questioning their professionalism: giving and receiving insult have serious consequences. The code of the group is a shared, and quite public, commitment, often in the form of swearing an oath, taking a pledge, confessing a creed. The group detects and disciplines errant members, with the supreme penalty exile or banishment (disbarment, defrocking, loss of license).

There are of course problems with viewing professions as honor groups. One is that reality is messier than my depictions both of honor groups and of professions, which seem more like idealizations than descriptions. Partly this mismatch between theory and reality is because my account of personal honor is a normative one, and norms are never actualized fully. An even larger problem is size. Honor groups tend to be relatively small and intimate, so that members can identify and properly regard one another. But modern professions tend to be large, numbering in the thousands or even hundreds of thousands of members. No lawyer will ever know all other lawyers by name or qualifications, though they will know how to check references.

Of course there are mitigations: professionals tend to receive very similar educations, where they are exposed to common norms;[13] they attend common meetings; read the same specialized publications; play golf together. They also tend to identify with subgroups within the larger fold, and this in two ways: (i) They find a specialty, with further training and tools of solidarity; a cardiologist is much more likely to recognize a fellow cardiologist and to be able to appraise her qualifications, than a physician in another specialty. (ii) They cluster in local communities, whether in a small town, a regional courthouse, a hospital, or a law firm.[14] Sometimes the two forms of bonding coalesce, as with the courteous traditional Charleston, South Carolina, general-practice lawyers described by Margaret Tevo (2001). So sometimes a subgroup of a profession will look and act more like an honor group than the profession as a whole.

Still, the question remains: Even if there are significant similarities between professions and honor groups, why view professions *as* honor groups? What do we gain by thinking in this way? Let me suggest several reasons, whose fuller meaning will emerge in sections III and IV.

- This point of view enables us to see professional identity from an internal point of view — the viewpoint of a professional as such — as constituted primarily not by economic or consequentialist concerns but rather by

---

[13] Rob Atkinson (personal communication) notes that this commonality depends on the ability and inclination (or will) of the profession to "control quality," both of which may be lacking.

[14] Cf. Cahill (2000) on Chicago Cook County's civil courts lawyers; Carlin (1966) on New York City law firms; and Landon (1990) on country lawyers; also Nelson, *et al.*, eds., 1992.

commitment to shared values and loyalty to particular persons. The very point of professions, from the standpoint of its members, is to suspend economic and consequentialist calculation, or at least to check its maximizing and totalizing tendencies by enhancing group solidarity. Professional social reality is internally deontological, not teleological.[15]

- The special mutual regard for peers found in professional groups makes eminent sense in terms of honor.[16] This regard is not just recognition of excellence, pursuit of common interests, and sharing similar talents, skills and expertise, but fundamentally a trust in and loyalty to persons one knows in a professional capacity. Professionals share both commitment to a set of norms and special trust in other members of the professional group, both of which go beyond utility.

- The normative status of a professional code is clarified: It is not just an expedient for reassuring the wider society, nor a public relations gimmick to advertise quality and attract business, but a constitutive bond of community. Commitment to a shared public code is a central part of what makes one a professional — not just acting in accordance with these norms but striving to live from them as core values.[17]

- The motivation of practicing professionals qua professionals is also clarified. They are moved by much more than "making a living" and playing a prestigious social role. They of course serve their clients and further important social goals (health, justice, salvation). But they also seek to gain and confirm the highly valued respect of their respected peers. They want to be noticed and well regarded by those peers, just as in an honor group.[18]

- The standpoint of honor frees us from the effort to view professional codes through the lens of a philosophical ethics applying timeless moral universals to particular social contexts and situations. Rather, it allows us to see professional norms as relative to time and place, liable to change and more open to local interpreters than to itinerant philosophers. Professional codes are not the same as codes of ethics, although they may be influenced by ethical concerns.

---

[15] Of course, this internal reality is compatible with economic and consequentialist rationales for the existence of professional groups with such non-consequentialist internal points of view. I am grateful to Rob Atkinson and Ben Eggleston for prodding me on this point.

[16] "[P]rofessionals attend primarily to the good opinion of their peers" (Moore, 1970, 14).

[17] It follows that holding formal professional membership is not sufficient for being a genuine professional, and it means that there may well be some, or many, of the former who are not the latter.

[18] Some may use the honor commitments and loyalties of the profession for ulterior ends, for self-interested or other-interested purposes. But these ulterior ends do not make them professionals. Moreover, being a professional may not always be a good thing — professions, like all honor groups, may need criticism from outside vantage points, especially from the standpoint of morality (cf. Section V below). I owe these and other points to Ben Eggleston.

I don't mean to suggest that professions are nothing but honor groups, nor that other points of view about professions are illegitimate. Nevertheless, viewing professions as honor groups does help us to understand features of professions we might otherwise miss or downplay. Most importantly, it helps us to see professions in a way that I think resonates better with professionals themselves than many of the criteria mentioned in Section I; a profession looks and feels like an honor group to its members, while those other criteria (whether intended descriptively or normatively) seem derived from an outsider perspective.

III. Professional Codes

Many hundreds of occupational and trade groups consider an important part of their effort to be professions, and to be viewed as professions, to involve the formulation and promulgation of what used to be called "codes of ethics" (Heermance, ed., 1924) or even "creeds," but now might be titled "standards," "rules," "principles" or even "laws" of professional responsibility.[19] Most neutrally, these groups seem impelled to find or create, and then to publicize and enforce, norms at least minimally governing the proper daily business of such a group. To some extent the motive is crassly commercial: They believe that customers will be more likely to trust and do business with those they think are guided by such principles — and the temptation is to view this merely as a matter of marketing, concerned with the reality of principled behavior only for the utility of its appearance. To some extent also, by such means groups of workers seek to gain the higher social status of the traditional core professions.

But there is more than money and status at stake in having professional codes. There is also a sense of group purpose that not only justifies its existence to the larger society but also motivates its members.[20] Group norms expressed in such codes need not be public relations gimmicks or ideological window-dressing. They may in fact express the reasons that the profession is valued by society, and they may animate a great many individual deeds and intentions of professionals. To be sure, lawyers may perform *pro bono* work to burnish their firm's image with prospective clients — the *bonum* in question may be more their own than the public's. But they may also do *pro bono* work for reasons that attracted many into lawyering in the first place: performing a worthy service to society (in the form of justice for indigent

---

[19] The change in title of the stated norms of the American bar is instructive: from "Canons" (1908) to "Code" (1969) to "Rules" (1983) to "Laws" (2000).

[20] Caveats of course, apply to the strength or efficacy of such motivation: usually, if the group is functioning well, in most respects, etc.

clients), a public *bonum*. A sense that there are non-utilitarian standards for which one stands, and stands together with others, gives a different sense of purpose to one's life than pursuing work for self-interested reasons chiefly of an economic kind. This is what distinguishes a profession from a well-paying high-status job, and it is a feature shared with honor groups, for which a sense of personal honor is maintained fundamentally for non-utilitarian reasons, even though it doubtless usually has its benefits as well.

Professions often seem confused about the nature and purpose of their professional codes. At times they seem attracted by the business model of an organization's "mission statement." But codes are not purposive or teleological in this way. They seek neither profit-maximization nor institutional reputation or perpetuation. Second, codes can devolve to the merely technical level, specifying good professional behavior only as proficient skill or craftsmanship in a trade — good lawyering perhaps, but not necessarily being a good lawyer, or one who does much social good. Third, the codes may be assimilated to laws, backed by disciplinary and other coercive sanctions. There doubtless should be sanctions for violations of professional codes, but thinking of these codes as laws encourages a baleful form of legalism — leading members to think of cutting and trimming their behavior so as not to get convicted by the law's letter, but not living in the spirit behind the code (cf. Atkinson, 1995). Honor groups know better.

Professional codes should be seen in the same light as honor codes, in several ways. They should voice a group's aspirations as well as its minimal expectations; honor codes contain ideals as well as requirements. They should be manifest in behavior that can be monitored as well as inscribed in personal character; personal honor faces both outward to community as well as inward to the individual. They should enable group solidarity through respectful dealing with other group members; honor groups exist in, through and with such solidarity. And they should express a regard for other people (at least for other group members) that transcends those others' usefulness to one's purposes; the regard honorable people have for one another is not utilitarian.

Professional codes are often viewed as pieces of applied ethics — applications of morality's universal principles to particular settings. The codes then have all the force (urgency, stringency, ultimacy) of moral principles, albeit highly specific ones. Elucidation of the codes may then be handed over to ethical generalists or applied ethical specialists — to philosophers who are not necessarily group members. But viewing professional codes as honor codes casts a different light: Principles of honor may look like moral principles but they are not (cf. Chapter 4 above); they are relative to time, place and tradition, not timelessly universal. Of course they may, in various ways, have absorbed or be constrained by moral rules, but qua rules of honor they are not necessarily moral. Understanding, applying and adjudicating honor codes, therefore, is not a job for the ethical generalist or specialist — though formal training in ethics may sharpen one's thinking — but rather for someone who intimately understands the honor group's distinctive practices and traditions. Viewed in this light, professional codes express, though only partially and feebly, a professional group's concrete values, and to understand, apply and adjudicate them requires intimate (insider) acquaintance with the profession's form of life. Explicating and applying — as well as amending or even transforming — a professional code is therefore up to the profession's "elders," those persons sagely versed in its practices, traditions, and ideals. It is also up to them to inculcate the code in new members, whose formal intellectual training is necessary but not sufficient for understanding and applying the code in full and *in concreto.*

IV. THE LAW

Views about the law are as disputatious as legal cases, though not for the same reasons. Legal cases are contentious because in an adversarial system they are competitive and consequential: there are adjudicated winners and losers, winning matters and losing costs. Reflections on the law are contentious because the law is a very large, complex and changing social institution or set of institutions, naturally subject to a variety of interpretations, especially concerning the proper roles of key players such as judges and lawyers. Though proper understanding of the law is important, at least to scholars, judgments about winning and losing interpretations are inconclusive. Obviously we cannot settle these complex matters here, but instead will try to illuminate from the standpoint of honor one central issue in the interpretation of the law.

A central tension in so-called "legal ethics" concerns lawyers' zealous advocacy of client interests in an adversarial legal system, what Geoffrey Hazard calls "the partisanship principle" (Hazard, 1991, 1245).[21] In order to protect and advance their client's interests, lawyers become advocates, and as such they apparently — may or must but at any rate will — use means at odds with common morality: impugning the credibility of adverse and vulnerable witnesses known to be truthful; allowing or even encouraging clients to perjure themselves (perhaps by willfully suspending disbelief of client stories); emitting smokescreens of possibility to obscure actual or likely fact; or burying opponents under mountains of legal process — ceaseless discovery, endless motions. Lawyers have the common reputation — some would say well earned — of doing and saying (or withholding) almost anything in sole

---

[21] Daniel Markovits calls this tension "the central preoccupation of legal ethics," and he properly notes that while "not all lawyers are adversary advocates, even in an adversary system," nonetheless adversarial thinking permeates the entire system (Markovits, 2008, 1–2).

pursuit of the supposed interests of their individual clients, at the occasional expense of wider social goods like truth, justice and good-will. "Simply put, lawyers must lie and cheat" (Markovits, 2008, 5). There are basically two paths usually taken to resolve this tension.

Some argue that, appearances to the contrary, there really is no tension: lawyers are actually acting ethically in their zealous advocacy; they are zealous because they *morally ought* to be zealous. Lawyers practice perfectly proper role morality in an adversarial legal system, and this system is itself morally justified. The adversarial system is justified, argues Monroe Freedman, because it better preserves and protects fundamental individual rights founded on human dignity — not perfectly but better than alternative legal and non-legal systems (Freedman, 1966, 1975, 1990). Within this system, lawyers play vital but circumscribed roles. For an adversarial system to achieve its ends, parties to legal proceedings need knowledgeable advocates, and the more zealous the advocacy, the better the outcome, both for the individual client in the short run and for society in the long run. Lawyers do their moral duty in advocating for their clients just as tirelessly, vigorously, and single-mindedly as possible. What is ordinarily morally impermissible — e.g. lying — is actually morally permissible, even sometimes required, for a lawyer playing his proper legal role. Despite appearances, therefore, zealous advocates are justified in playing their partisan role to the hilt.

Others, however, hold that the role of a zealous advocate is precisely what it appears to be — morally dodgy or even impermissible. They seek to reduce the tension with ordinary morality by carefully circumscribing legitimate advocacy. David Luban, for example, says that ". . . the role of legal hired gun is morally untenable" (Luban, 1988, 166), and he seeks to restrain zealous advocacy chiefly by professional codes of responsibility interpreted as codes of ethics and written into enforceable law. Restricting lawyers' zeal through legally enforced codes of ethics is the way to reconcile morality and law.[22] Anthony Kronman speaks of this tension as a "spiritual crisis," a "crisis of morale" (Kronman, 1993, 204) attendant on the eclipse of an earlier ideal of the "lawyer-statesman" that Kronman would like to revitalize even though he thinks it unlikely that this can be done due to the baleful influences of misguided legal theory, mega-law firms, and bureaucratized courts. The only hope he sees for practicing lawyers is to live and work as general practitioners in a small community (Kronman, 1993, Chapter 7) — small hope indeed! William Simon likewise seeks to constrain zealous advocacy by putting it in contextual service of justice. "Lawyers should take those actions that, considering the relevant circumstances of the particular case, seem likely to promote justice" (Simon, 1998, 138).

---

[22] Luban also allows for the provision of ideals (Luban, 1988, 158), but the heart of his proposal lies in legally compelling lawyers to act morally.

None of these proposed solutions seem very stable: Unfettered advocacy injures the very sense of justice it claims to promote; justice is not only protection of individual rights but also fair, open and honest relationship with others. Legal constraints seem ineffective and may only promote legalistic cynicism. Moral constraints seem tenuous, controversial and likewise ineffective. Still, the tension between adversarial advocacy and ordinary morality remains.

Nor is a solution to this tension to be found in altering one's conception of morality. Even if the traditional consequentialist (Utilitarian and other) and deontological (Kantian) approaches to morality rely too heavily on rules and must be supplemented or replaced by a virtue-ethics approach that focuses on character, the argument remains within the bounds of morality, seeking moral virtues and habits as well as or instead of moral principles. The problem is that such appeal seems inadequate twice over: the application of moral norms, whether principles or virtues, is unclear in legal practice, and there seems to be no effective motivation to embrace the supposed moral solution other than individual choice or imposition of legal coercion.

Potentially more promising is the depiction and appeal via "stories" of actual or fictional legal heroes — Oliver Wendell Holmes, Jr., perhaps, or Atticus Finch — as exemplars of good lawyering. But once again morality intrudes, as when Tom Shaffer provides a moral encomium to "The Man from Maycomb, Alabama" (i.e. Atticus Finch in *To Kill a Mockingbird*; Shaffer, 1985), and tells stories of heroes in concrete contexts as a way of displaying and inculcating moral character (Shaffer, 1987, Chapter 1). Such characterization of lawyerly life remains a branch of (applied) ethics, however sensitively and imaginatively applied.

All these approaches, I suggest, suffer from the same defect: they misconstrue the nature of the problem as a clash between morality and lawyers' roles in an adversarial legal system. They all hold that what lawyers do — and sometimes reluctantly feel compelled to do — seems at odds with common morality, and one or the other has to give way. (Given the very lucrative nature of legal work today, the fear is that zeal either overcomes moral scruple or induces rationalization that zeal *is* scrupulous.) In short, they equate legal *professional responsibility* with legal *ethics*.[23]

But things look quite different from the standpoint of personal honor. If lawyers belong to honor groups, then "codes" or "laws" of professional responsibility are the groups' honor codes and consist of the principles honor group members share in common. Commitment to these principles

---

[23] There is another, opposite error to which some legal thinkers succumb (cf. Markovits, 2008, 10), that of thinking of the legal profession in terms of the law, specifically the law of lawyering. But just as honor codes are not reducible to legal codes, adherence to which is secured by (threat of) punishment, so the law itself is not a good model for a professional code, even for lawyers.

is rooted in the mutual regard members have for one another. "Professional" lawyers, then, are not merely technically competent, skillful and successful at winning cases — they are also, and more deeply, members of a profession who are loyal to their peers, who trust those peers, and who seek to be trusted in return. In a legal profession, lawyers pursue advocacy just as zealously as their commitment to code and loyalty to peers permit — no more, and perhaps no less — precisely because that is what belonging to this honor group means. The constraints on their zeal are constraints of professional honor.

What are these constraints of honor? First, they are relative to the particular honor group, and one may expect some local differences. Even when two honor groups are subgroups of the same wider honor group, and therefore share that larger group's common code, they may differ in how they understand, interpret and apply the common code, as well as adding rules and practices of their own. For example, the "same" professional code of lawyering will be applied differently in different contexts of legal practice, among different subgroups: differently in a large corporate law firm and in a "country lawyer's" office, differently in large cities and small towns, differently in different legal specializations.

Second, the motivations of lawyers to follow these constraints will reside primarily in peer regard — one's professional "face," so to speak — and only secondarily in individual existential commitment to moral principle or concern for acting lawfully. Members of honor groups care about their common honor code because they care about their fellow honor group members, and they express that care for peers through their commitment to the code. This motive of concern for highly regarded others' regard can be quite powerful.

Third, the rules regarding insiders and outsiders may differ. Lawyers may find it more difficult to lie to other lawyers than to non-lawyers, e.g. just as peer regard is more important to an honor group member than "what others think" — i.e. what outsider others think.

Fourth, the particular ways in which a sense of honor may constrain legal practice has been well described by Brad Wendel in a series of articles (especially 2001, 2002, 2003a, 2003b). "The key to the functioning of nonlegal sanction mechanisms is the value of a lawyer's reputation" (2002, 970), and this reputation may easily be construed as a matter of honor. To ensure that "a lawyer's word is her bond" (971) it helps to have a relatively small community (whether of small-town practices, legal specialties, or working groups within large firms), or at least considerable ongoing transactions where lawyers come to know one another well enough to appreciate that competing fairly, civilly, even courteously is not a liability but an asset. Credibility is a "valuable asset" (972) because it enables work to be done efficiently and smoothly, and it furthers clients' interests as well as smoothes a lawyer's life. In addition, "nonlegal sanctions can reach behavior that would be difficult to regulate using legal sanctions," as in "expensive and abusive discovery" (979).

V. MORAL CONCERNS

Such are some of the implications of regarding lawyering in terms of personal honor. I think this point of view helps us to see things we might otherwise overlook, or misinterpret, or under-appreciate. In particular, it helps to refocus the tension most find in zealous advocacy: Instead of asking directly about the moral or ethical limits of partisanship in an adversarial system, we should look at how the profession (or sub-profession) understands, limits and encourages such zeal as the expression of its actual code, having all the force of an honor code. Of course we — or, more to the point, members of the legal system — might think the limits too loose or tight, and then we or they are free to inject moral as well as other kinds of argument in an effort to amend or transform the group's code in our favored direction. But we should not confuse a professional code with morality. Legal professional responsibility is not legal ethics.

But this is not a very comfortable point of view, for it reduces the available justification for professional practices. Everyone would like to be able to justify his or her behavior — and morality trumps honor when it comes to justification. So a defense of lawyerly or other professional practice in terms of morality would seem preferable to appeals to honor. But perhaps what we would like is not the same as what we can have. Perhaps (some) professional honor isn't morally defensible after all.

Nevertheless, there is hope. An honor group determines its own code, and this code is liable to change over time with the admission and influence of new honor group members or changes in the wider society. New members are free to seek to amend these rules, and society is often able to push for reforms, though both can only work through means permitted in the honor group — especially, in a profession, through ongoing conversation among members regarded as equals. So advocates of unfettered zealous advocacy in the law are free to argue for their point of view, as are those who favor some form of regulation. I don't think this is simply a matter of power politics, but also, and more fundamentally, of waging and winning an argument in and with a tradition (MacIntyre, 1984a, 222). The code can change, and ethical considerations can alter its vector of change. Members of the honor group may decide that they deeply desire their honor code to be a morally defensible one, a form of *moral honor*. It is up to them to make it so.

Finally, to the extent that a profession such as the law is like an honor group, to that extent its code matters greatly to its members. Those who think that economic or bureaucratic factors largely determine behavior implicitly belittle the power of commitment to principle. But those with a sense of honor know better, and an honorable professional will resist being driven, solely or primarily, by money, power and status.[24] Indeed, if the argument of this chapter is correct, "honorable professional" is redundant. Resisting such interests is precisely what professionals do *as professionals.*

[24] Ironically, money, power and status are "honors" under different concepts of honor — chiefly conferred and positional honors. Here, personal honor not only doesn't equate to these other concepts of honor, it stands in stark opposition to them.

Part III

———

HONOR'S FUTURE

Clearly, honor's reach is very wide, extending not only to the disparate areas we have just examined in Part II, but to many others as well.[1] It provides a woefully under-appreciated vantage point for understanding the human condition, including the condition of contemporary Western humans. But honor's ubiquity is not the end of the story. My concern is with honor not only as a widely applicable descriptive concept but also as a potentially useful normative concept, and I still must take two steps to reclaim honor as a concept for us, a value we might value. First, I must defend honor against the formidable bill of indictment laid out in the Introduction (Chapter 1), for unless there are ways of deflecting or rebutting these very significant accusations, honor's ubiquity will only make it seem all the more terrible. Second, I must make out a more positive case for personal honor in the twenty-first century. It is not enough simply to escape the dark side and realize how honor is not ineligible; there must be positive reasons for wanting to use honor to guide our lives. I take up the former task in this chapter, the latter in the next.

———

[1] Consider, for example, the following from the standpoint of personal honor: intentional religious communities (not just sects or cults), Utopian groups, women's cooperatives, clubs, labor unions and guilds, social fraternities and sororities, civic and trade associations — perhaps most kinds of voluntary association.

154

Chapter 11

IN DEFENSE OF HONOR

In this chapter, I will consider each of the seven powerful criticisms previously leveled against honor and show that they do not eliminate honor from our serious normative consideration, though they do limit and constrain the kinds of honor that are viable for us. In this limited defense of honor, I will make generous use of the distinctions among the six concepts of honor, the distinction between concept and conception, and the variety of conceptions of personal honor. In effect, I am searching for versions of moral personal honor that are "live options" for us today (James, 1975 [1907], 14).

Some will view this defense as a whitewash of honor.[1] But it is far from complete exoneration: honor as an historical phenomenon is simply too stained by excess and deficiency to escape very considerable condemnation. I agree with many of the criticisms of historical examples of honor, and I can understand why some want to have nothing more to do with honor of any kind. They are, however, throwing the baby out with the bathwater, for there are forms of honor not subject to their complaints. Others will admit our defense may succeed in removing objectionable elements from the concept of honor but hold that in doing so nothing remains that is distinctively honorable; the concept of honor is altered beyond recognition — a philosophical bait and switch. Again, I respectfully disagree. Rather than generically condemning or wholeheartedly embracing all things labeled "honor," I seek instead to make clear the kind of honor that is eligible and potentially attractive for contemporary enlightened citizens of the world.

I. Honor is Shallow Reputation

This complaint is frequent and accurate — but only as directed against conferred honor. Conferred honor is indeed shallow, the applause of others on

---

[1] Interesting term, "whitewash," in both its parts, especially from the standpoint of honor!

their own terms, and only a fool would seek it at all costs, or want reputation as such, regardless of its basis. To be sure, there are a lot of fools out there, not least in our own time. Many seek fame without regard to its source, unable to distinguish fame from infamy, a good name from notoriety. "Say what you want about me, just be sure to spell my name correctly," seems to be the motto of foolish self-promoters in our time.

But conferred honor is not the only concept of honor. Recognition honor, for example, doesn't lie in the eye of the beholder; the reputation it demands is tethered to excellence. Perhaps the person who has the excellence doesn't seek or demand recognition, and would maintain the excellence even if unrecognized; nonetheless, others owe that recognition, and whether or not it means anything to the honoree, it certainly does add something to the honorer's life. Moreover, recognition honor is only as shallow as the excellence it honors; paying appropriate public attention to great excellence is not only a duty but also a considerable good, albeit a supplementary and dependent good.

More centrally to our case, however, personal honor is far removed from shallow reputation, even though some may think it little more than that.[2] To be sure, the respect of others *is* deeply important to anyone with a sense of personal honor, but this respect is neither shallow nor heteronomous.

On the first point, the respect of others matters because it is the regard of fellow honor-group members qua honorable according to the honor code they all share, and this regard may run quite deep — deep not only in commitment to the honor code, but deep also in the principles the code contains or defers to. Perhaps in some honor groups the code is shallow, arbitrary, even repellent. But surely not in all. In the case of *moral honor*, the code contains or is constrained by the very principles of morality. So moral personal honor is no less deep than morality itself.[3]

On the second point, personal honor is not necessarily and not usually heteronomous: it is anchored in the individual as well as tied to others, and at its best is a matter of free personal commitment to the code and freely given loyalty to other members of the honor group, a respect for their regard of oneself that is fully compatible with personal autonomy. Rather than being simply located in individual or group, honor is a *bridge concept*, linking individual character to communal regard. In a bridge concept, both termini are essential, as is their linkage. A person of honor is impossible apart from an honor group and its members' mutual regard, but equally so an honor

---

[2] Perhaps this criticism is most often made by outsiders: Utter other-dependence (seeking reputation and preserving face) may be all that personal honor looks like to those who don't belong to the honor group and don't share its sense of honor. Insiders have a deeper and more sympathetic view.

[3] Parallel comments could be made about religious honor — and doubly about moral religious honor.

group is impossible apart from persons of honor and their individually achieved characters.

So while many forms of honor are doubtless shallow and slavishly other-dependent, this is not true of (some versions of) personal honor. Whatever else might be wrong with personal honor, reputation mongering is not a major concern.

II. Honor is Confined to Limited Social Conditions

Here the complaint is that even personal honor cannot be a human universal because it is too closely tied to certain social conditions, ones that are increasingly absent in modern (or postmodern) industrial mass societies.[4] Personal honor, some hold, takes root only in traditional societies with clearly defined and even rigid social roles and rules, and such societies are necessarily small and inegalitarian, and usually patriarchal and violent. Since we neither can nor would want to live in such societies, honor cannot be a value for us. I will take up the particular worries about size, inequality, violence and patriarchy shortly. Here I want to focus on the more general claim that honor is not an anthropological universal, but a concept applicable only to certain kinds of societies. In this view, not all societies are or can be "honor societies." Only those formed under and sustained by certain contingent (and vanishing) conditions are eligible. So honor cannot be a normative concept for those of us who live in quite different social conditions.

It must be granted at the outset that many of the most vivid cases of honor are also cases of societies satisfying the usual conditions of rigid roles, small size, hierarchy, patriarchy, violence, and the like. Landed gentry in the Old South, nobility in the Ancien Régime, clans in the Balkans, Bedouin nomadic tribes, warrior groups everywhere — all illustrate the pattern, more or less. Honor flourishes under these conditions. But are these conditions necessary for honor, or is the connection only a contingent (albeit common) one? Can honor occur or flourish only under these conditions, or may it equally exist and flourish under social conditions more attractive to us?

The historical and anthropological evidence undoubtedly shows that certain forms of honor flourish under such conditions, but it doesn't follow that honor can exist or flourish *only* under these conditions. One should not mistake particular instances of a concept for its entire range of potential

---

[4] Consider the cluster of studies of "Mediterranean Honor," ably synthesized by Peristiany and Pitt-Rivers (Peristiany, ed., 1965; Pitt-Rivers, 1968; Peristiany and Pitt-Rivers, eds., 1992); or Peter Berger's well-known argument that honor is "obsolescent" in modern mass societies (Berger, 1970); or Alasdair MacIntyre's different argument to much the same conclusion in the Lindley lecture (MacIntyre, 1984b).

exemplification. So-called "Mediterranean honor," for example, may indeed, display honor quite vividly and memorably. But the limits and liabilities of this display are not necessarily the limits and liabilities of personal honor as such. Put another way, the vivid examples are surely all conceptions of the concept of personal honor, but they are not the only possible conceptions, and indeed not the only actual ones as well. The concept also covers more benign conceptions, and various elements thought important to one conception may be differently conceived, or even absent, in another. Earlier I traced the features that do seem essential to the concept of personal honor: a sense of honor, an honor group, an honor code, mutual recognition and respect, trustworthiness, loyalty, and the like. But none of these features is necessarily connected to the features many find distinctive — and dangerous if not despicable — in some honor groups: rigid roles, hierarchy, elitism, violence, gender oppression, etc. It seems possible for honor groups to arise and endure under different social conditions, ones without the negative features moderns find so odious, antique, or irrelevant.

Still, even though personal honor in general isn't bound to unsavory social conditions, it does have at least two disquieting essential features — small size and relativity — that I will consider in the next two sections.

III. Honor Groups are Necessarily Small

Size matters to honor groups: the mutual personal recognition and respect so crucial to a sense of personal honor cannot exist if the honor-group members don't know one another in fairly intimate ways so that they can discern and judge the honorability of their peers. In large anonymous mass societies, where nobody knows your name nor cares about your character, shame evaporates and honor withers.

To be sure, in a mass society individuals may have their own idiosyncratic codes of conduct — call them *private codes* — that are perhaps nourished in private associations freely chosen by independent individual adults. But these private codes are not and cannot be codes of honor, because they are either not shared or not shared in the way honor codes are shared. An individual's private code may be the same as, or largely overlap with, the private codes of other individuals; but this agreement, or even identity, of content has a different basis from a shared honor code: not the necessary mutual regard of peers but the accidental harmony of independent-minded individuals. Consider morality, which is often supposed to be capable of promoting social harmony because its rules apply equally to everyone and can be freely adopted by every individual. But even if morality commands respect for all moral agents, and hence for this particular person, and all who accept morality respect every individual, including this particular person, nevertheless moral respect is due and given out of universal principle, not necessarily out of concrete concern for this particular person and for her regard of oneself.

So honor groups must be relatively small, small enough to permit on-going mutual personal regard. But what's wrong with such a size constraint upon honor groups? Four worries come to mind: (a) Honor cannot unite large groups, such as nation-states, as a whole; (b) small honor groups can't exist (harmoniously or at all) within mass societies; (c) honor groups invidiously and arbitrarily exclude many from membership; (d) small groups are inherently elitist. (The first two worries concern possibility, the latter two desirability.) Let's take these points in order.

First, while it is true that a diverse mass society can't itself be a single honor group, there are various mitigations. For one, different honor groups may share roughly the same honor code, and such overlapping and interlocking subgroups could constitute a mass society. Also, the same person could belong to more than one honor group, internally harmonizing their different codes. Moreover, if an honor group is prestigious in a society (it has positional honor), its rules and customs may be adopted by other groups, even if these other groups aren't themselves honor groups in a strict sense; a prestigious honor code can spread even to those who lack a full sense of honor. Furthermore, where the honor groups in a society are moral ones, they will not conflict in morally important ways, and so even honor groups with different honor codes may be able to cooperate and get along. Lastly, there may well be a form of political honor — patriotism — that overlays other kinds of honor commitments: loyalty to (the constitutive rules of) a certain kind of political régime and its citizens creates and sustains its own distinctive form of honor. Patriotic support of the régime unites even when it is instanced somewhat differently in different honor groups.

Second, those who think honor groups can't exist in mass societies are making the now-familiar error of conflating the concept of personal honor with some conceptions of this concept. For example, they may have in mind an honor society that is hierarchical and patriarchal, and cannot see how such an honor society can co-exist with an egalitarian society. They are right that an inegalitarian honor group can't comfortably exist in a wider egalitarian society, but they are wrong in thinking that no form of personal honor group can exist in such an environment. For such subgroups to be successful in this environment their codes shouldn't conflict with egalitarian principles, e.g. gender equality. But there is no reason why these subgroups couldn't still be honor groups, with all the formal features of the concept of personal honor, e.g. a common sense of honor, a common code, mutual respect, and the like. Honor groups *can* exist in egalitarian societies.

Third, if honor groups are to remain small enough to enable mutual regard, the entrance requirements for the group must ensure either that only a limited number are eligible or that not all eligible members will actually have a chance to join. The former tack is often tried, e.g. where ties of blood or kinship go proxy for the true honor code in screening potential members: only those with the right lineage are entitled to claim to be honorable according to the group's code. But this restriction is arbitrary and hypocritical; the proxy properties don't necessarily reflect the honor requirements ("noble birth" doesn't guarantee nobility of character), and group members know this at some level, leading to self-deception or self-doubt that undermines their commitment to their own principles of honor.

The latter tack is the proper line to take: Any honor code — or at any rate, any *moral* honor code — will set out principles that many more people can follow than can be accommodated in any one particular honor group. Many may be called, but few can be chosen. How should members and non-members think about this arbitrary and accidental exclusivity? Certainly neither should view it as demarcating some deep divide of moral virtue or fitness for virtue; honor capability is widespread, and honor may be widely desired. The line dividing members from non-members, then, is not a judgment of honor-capability, much less of interest or accomplishment in honor. It is simply a necessary limit on group size that permits an honor community to function at all. In a moral honor group, members should be proud of their membership, and feel fortunate and glad to be in the group; and non-members should find membership desirable, even if they recognize that they cannot join for purely adventitious reasons. But being in or out of the honor group should not be grounds for invidious treatment or contempt by insiders, nor for malicious envy or spite by outsiders.

Fourth, there is doubtless a natural tendency towards elitism in any voluntary social group. Contrary to Groucho Marx's quip that he wouldn't want to belong to any club that would accept him as a member,[5] voluntary group membership ordinarily implies a sense of pride in membership (as well as a sense of ownership of the group's principles), and it is natural to think that the groups one chooses to join are superior to groups one chooses not to join.[6] When personal honor is at stake, it is therefore natural to think that members of one's group have a monopoly, or at least a surplus, of virtue, and that outsiders are deficient in honor, or even incapable of honor.

But honor groups are not necessarily elitist in any bad way. There is nothing wrong with thinking well of one's own group, so long as the perception is accurate. One's group may, in fact, be good enough to be superior to other groups, or individuals outside of the group, in certain respects, on the whole and for the most part. But this self-congratulation must be scrupulously honest, for self-deception is a constant danger. One shouldn't blind oneself

---

[5] Groucho's contrariness, after all, is what gives his quip traction.

[6] Moreover, associated positional and conferred honors may provide potent reasons for thinking one's group is superior; but these reasons are irrelevant.

to the faults within the group nor to the virtues outside the group. One shouldn't overlook outsiders' capacities for, and sometimes attainment of, the very virtues insiders take pride in achieving. No individual or group has the exclusive franchise for virtue — nor for honor.

IV. Honor is Relative

Personal honor is relative to time and place in several ways: First, its honor code is particular and distinct, containing rules with a local history and interpretation that may not be found in other honor groups, much less outside them. Second, its membership will be arbitrarily limited in size, even if it admits the honor-potential of at least many non-members. Third, not all belong to honor groups, nor even want to belong; not everyone values honor. Of course, some will not find these relativities problematic, but some will, especially if they embrace more universal and ultimate perspectives, particularly those of morality and religion: Moral principles are thought to be universally valid, unlike local honor codes, and religious norms claim ultimacy. But the relativity of honor doesn't render it ineligible for moral and religious approval.

First, morality. Honor codes are not necessarily moral. They may omit some moral rules and may add some non-moral ones, even some immoral ones. And it does not seem to be a moral requirement that there be honor groups at all, although also there is no general moral prohibition of such groups. But at the same time, honor codes are not necessarily immoral; they need not contain any rules that violate moral requirements, and they may even bind the members to moral requirements — such we have called *moral honor codes*. Moreover, honor may add something important to morality: A sense of honor links one to others more concretely than individual commitment to the abstract principles of morality.[7] Honor rules may be, and may be thought to be, ways of specifying universal moral obligations in particular social contexts (with a particular history, environment, population, etc.). So honor's relativity is not necessarily at odds with morality's universality.

Second, religion. Honor codes are not necessarily religious, and religions are not necessarily honor groups. Religion presses towards, or expresses, ultimate concern,[8] a sense of absolute requirement, an unconditional

---

[7] Even an ideal moral community, such as Kant's Kingdom of Ends, is still a (possible) group of possible people, not an actual community of particular actual persons who actually mutually recognize one another.

[8] I borrow the phrase from Paul Tillich: "Faith is the state of being ultimately concerned . . . it demands the total surrender of him who accepts this claim, and it promises total fulfillment even if all other claims have to be subjected to it or rejected in its name." (Tillich, 1957, 1.) Tillich's "concern" is very broad, and embraces the commitment to an honor code as well as loyalty to

devotion to the highest; and honor seems less than ultimate, absolute, and unconditional. But again, honor is not necessarily irreligious; commitment to honor codes and communities need not compete against religious or ultimate commitments. Indeed, honor may even *structure* religious communities and their theologies, such that religious requirements are viewed as matters of honor (and conversely). Honor communities may also be receptive to religious revelation, may help to interpret and construe such revelation, and may be effective vessels for its promulgation. So the relativity of honor is not necessarily a threat to religion's claims of ultimacy.

Hence honor's various kinds of relativity are not necessarily worrisome as such. It would be worrisome, of course, if something relative were taken to be absolute, if local honor codes overrode moral requirement, or if commitment to honor usurped religious devotion. But once again these are worries not about the concept of honor as such, only about certain conceptions of honor and their instantiations.

V. HONOR IS INEGALITARIAN

This is a variant of the previous complaint. Morality is deeply egalitarian, and so are many religions in some respects.[9] Each person equally possesses the dignity of moral worth; each is an inestimably valuable child of God. This sense of equality goes very deep, affecting all areas of human concern. For example, it is deeply rooted in liberal democratic political thinking: every person not only has a stake in her political arrangements but also has a fundamental right to help design any such arrangements and to participate fairly in its structures and processes. It is also fundamental for Biblical and Quranic senses of justice: A society is judged by its treatment of the least well off, who count equally with their socio-economic "betters." It is also ingredient in some feminist thought, where oppressive patriarchy and male domination involve unfair because unequal treatment of men and women. Any set of values that denies such fundamental equality is ineligible for moderns. But honor seems inegalitarian: its code is for members only; its membership is exclusive; its structure seems hierarchical; and it appears to elevate some above others by "honoring" them.

Let's take up this last point first, for in many ways it's the easiest to answer. It trades on confusing different concepts of honor. Positional honor is indeed concerned with social elevation, achieving success or enjoying status "above" others, to which may be added the plaudits and gifts of conferred honors.

members of an honor group.

   [9] To the extent that a religion is not egalitarian, it will be faced with the same complaints here discussed with respect to honor.

But all this elevation has little or nothing to do with personal honor. Personal honor groups may, but need not, be at the top of the social heap; as deviant they may even be reviled by the wider society. Moreover, honor group members are "better" than others only if their code is superior and they exemplify it to a superior degree. But none of this implies that others cannot or do not achieve as much, and honor groups must be wary of claiming too much for their code — humility and modesty might in fact be desirable parts of any honor code, as necessary corrections to an all-but-inevitable *hubris*.

To be sure, honor groups *are* exclusive in at least one sense: not everyone may join, even if they wanted to. This form of exclusivity follows from the size constraints mentioned earlier (cf. Section III above), which are necessary to preserve the mutual regard essential to personal honor groups. But such exclusivity is not the snobbish exclusion of some simply to be able to gloat over one's own presumed superiority.

Many think personal honor is inegalitarian because they associate such honor with hierarchical societies: a military elite, an aristocratic class, a caste system, a patriarchy. Honor doubtless often flourishes in such hierarchies, protecting the privileges of the powerful. But personal honor is not essentially tied to such hierarchies. Indeed, there is a surprisingly strong sense in which personal honor groups are more fundamentally committed to *equality* than to *inequality*.

Within the honor group, equality reigns: All members are presumed equally honor-capable, all are held to the same code of honor, each is equally and finally responsible for her own honor, all are called to mutually respect one another, and all are fully entitled to the respect of everyone. All this equality is bedrock for any honor group, and it is thoroughly consistent with various forms of inequality. Some may fulfill the inherent honor ideals more fully (paragons of personal honor, who thereby deserve recognition honor), some may have position or office within the group entitling them to greater than average rewards for service to the community (even a community of equals needs leaders), and some may play special roles in founding and safeguarding the group (such as sage arbiters of honor disputes). But none of these possible inequalities is as fundamental as the equality of honor-group members.

But what about outsiders? Don't members of honor groups regard themselves as superior to outsiders? Don't people who value personal honor preen themselves on their superiority to those who have no sense of honor? Perhaps they do, but perhaps also the prideful culprit is not their sense of personal honor but something else — a desire for positional or conferred honor. It may be that everyone wants to think herself better than others — but this is not the fault of honor. The only legitimate complaint of inequality against personal honor would be if it required those with a sense of honor to value themselves more highly than those without such a sense — to regard honor as an indispensable or at least superior-making virtue, lacking which one is inferior or even defective. But there is no reason to think that honorable persons must have this sense of superiority, much less adopt a supercilious air. Humility is a possible part of an honor code, and we can see once again why its inclusion might be desirable.

VI. Honor is Steeped in Violence

The archetypical honor group, and possibly the ancestral honor group, is a warrior society, whose members are fighters, skilled in the arts of deadly violence. Their honor code includes bravery in battle, perseverance against odds, stamina through stress, loyalty to one's "band of brothers," skill in the use of weapons, and a willingness to sacrifice oneself for others. But it is a code with a fearsome aim: to make effective fighters, enforcing their will through violence. This recourse to violence is the essence of warriors in war, of course, but it also infects warrior societies in peacetime, producing men who are accustomed to getting their way through threat and violence, leading to the oppression of many by a physically powerful few.[10] Honor in many societies today continues to require, and to be reinforced by, violence: witness the thousands of "honor killings" every year by male relatives intent on restoring family honor sullied by the supposed sexual misbehavior of women they presume to have the right to control. Recall also the blood feuds in many parts of the world that may continue for decades or longer, all to avenge and thus restore the lost or damaged honor of some family or clan. And remember duels, still acceptable in some parts as the most honorable way of responding to a personal insult.

There are four primary worries here: (i) the honor of warriors is the glorified archetype of honor, and all other honor groups admire and emulate its recourse to violence; (ii) honoring warrior honor leads to a general culture of violence, a society that believes "the final solution" to all problems is a violent one; (iii) honor requires violence to maintain itself, so that insults or challenges to honor can be removed or answered only by resorting to violence; and (iv) violence is needed to maintain the oppressive power of honor groups. These are formidable worries indeed, and honor can at best only partially avoid their sting. But I will argue that personal honor does not *require* violence, however frequently and variously honor groups have had recourse to violence.

---

[10] The gender of warriors will be considered in the next section; patriarchy is sustained by violence, domestic and otherwise, just as wars are fought with violence, and the same gender typically "wins" in both cases.

(i) Warrior honor may well be the earliest and most prominent kind of honor. It will likely be found wherever people (nearly always men) make a life out of fighting together against an outside enemy. Since nearly all societies sometimes do feel the need to defend themselves against aggressive others, warrior honor will be found in nearly all societies. Moreover, most societies bestow conferred honors upon their valiant defenders, who risk life and limb to save the group, and warriors may occupy very high, perhaps the highest, positions in society. So the violent honor of warriors looms large in any social and political history.

But the first question is whether *all* honor must emulate warrior honor in its recourse to violence. Is warrior honor a necessary part of any honor, or, more plausibly, is warrior honor an ideal form of honor, such that all other forms of honor can only mimic and shadow its features, particularly its use of violence? I think not. Rather, the violence attendant to warrior honor is a function of war, not of honor. *Wars* are necessarily violent, but *honorable persons* are not, nor are *honorable warriors*! Honorable warriors are violent in war, but not necessarily in other contexts. Violent means are indeed essential to fighting wars, but the end of war is not fighting but something else: peace, freedom, resources, power, territory, glory, and the like. Honorable warriors on occasion must pursue those ends by violent means — they must kill and be liable to be killed — but the violence is not an end in itself, and should only be a last resort of those who command and control the warriors. When violence is unnecessary, less efficient than non-violence, or forbidden in kind, then warrior honor requires something other than violence. Moreover, just because honorable warriors are occasionally (though sadly necessarily) violent, that doesn't mean that members of other honor groups must or even may be violent: their codes of honor may differ precisely in this regard (regarding recourse to violence on some occasions), with no detriment to the honor of either.

So if warrior honor is indeed the archetype of personal honor, it is only because it is the earliest kind of honor group and because it so clearly fulfills the basic requirements of personal honor — a sense of honor, a shared honor code, mutual regard — but *not* because personal honor as such requires recourse to violence.

(ii) Violence can spread from the thrall of war to the seductions of peace. If violence is viewed as a laudable way to solve external problems, it can come to seem an acceptable way to solve internal problems: a way to defeat or repel the aggressor within as well as the enemy without. A society bent on turning all problems into wars may find that along with focus, energy, mobilization and commitment, it also purchases widespread legitimation of violence. This is militarism run amok.

But recourse to violence need not spread. It is possible to circumscribe the legitimate contexts and aims of violence — justly fighting just wars, for example, and humanely coercing only law-breakers — so as to prevent violence from taking over a whole society. Without disrespecting military honor, other forms of personal honor may be valued more (and given not just recognition honor but also conferred and positional honor). More positively, conferring honors on warrior valor is compatible with not embracing warrior honor as the only, or even the highest, form of personal honor. Risking one's life in military service of one's country is indeed honorable, but so is risking one's life in political or other non-violent service to others.

(iii) Personal honor does seem to require, or at least to permit, violent defense of honor. How else, one might think, *could* one respond honorably to an insult to one's honor than by violence, say in a duel? How else could one respond honorably to the (dishonorable) murder of one's kin than in violent kind, by killing the killer's kin? Isn't honor necessarily committed to violent satisfaction and vengeance? No. Even though violence is a frequent recourse, it is not a necessary one; there are other, non-violent ways of preserving, defending and restoring one's honor, at least in some honor groups

Perhaps this can be seen most clearly with *insult*. An insult is a public accusation of dishonor, and that accusation cannot be allowed to stand without permitting it to achieve what it claims: its target's dishonor. Unless the accusation is removed or the accuser defeated, there will not be full public recognition of the accused person's honor. But how can this be done? Unilateral protestation of innocence won't cancel the accusation. Entreaties to the accuser will likely fall on deaf ears.[11] Insulting reply may tarnish the accuser, but it doesn't really bleach the stain of the original insult. Suing for libel or slander shows one doesn't consider the insult a matter of honor, but only an interest protected by law. What alternative remains open to the honorable insulted party, then, except recourse to violence? Surely someone who is unwilling to risk violence in defense of his honor either is guilty as charged (i.e. dishonorable) or else doesn't truly care about honor.

To the contrary, there *are* non-violent ways to defeat or negate insults, ways that are honorable in at least some honor groups. Arguing one's case (in the proper honor forum, on the proper occasion, and in the proper way) with and to one's honor peers may work — they may come to see the accusation as baseless and false, and then the person who loses public honor is the insulter, not the insulted. In addition, confronting

---

[11] Even when presented with evidence contrary to the accusation, the accuser may find it hard to summon forth the necessary public apology, for in doing so he diminishes the honor of his accusation.

one's accuser (again in the proper context, manner, etc.) may also help, by requiring him to "put up or shut up," to show that his accusation is not baseless or false.[12] Even when violence is permitted, forbearing violence may display greater honor (courage, resilience, a thick skin) than resorting to violence.

Likewise honorable justice for a blood offense doesn't require violent personal revenge. Sometimes honor may be satisfied by leaving criminal, especially capital, cases to the legal authorities, even though most honor groups prefer extra-legal disposition of such cases.[13] Other times the weight of shame or the power of shunning or ostracism (a kind of social death, but not necessarily a violent one) might be vengeance enough, especially since they enforce group solidarity through their exclusion of the dishonored person.

(iv) No one can deny that violence, or its threat, is the ultimate or even frequent prop of oppression. But however necessary violence is to maintaining oppression, it is inessential (and in a certain sense even inimical) to groups that value personal honor. No doubt many honor groups have employed, and will continue to employ, violence to maintain their position in society. But their positional honor is not their personal honor, and confusing the two is actually harmful to personal honor. Proper public recognition of personal honor by the wider society does not entail being given a high position in society, nor the conferred honors that usually accompany such positions. In fact, personal honor has no proper business maintaining or defending positional honor, with or without violence.

Even so, a worry persists. Whether or not personal honor requires violence, the fact remains that very many oppressors have draped themselves in a cloak of honor to justify the violence they use to maintain (and extend) their power over others. Southern white honor, for example, became charged with controlling slaves; Islamic male honor with controlling women; Russian aristocratic honor with controlling serfs. Surely where there's all this smoke there must be some fire? There is. Many honor codes contain rules for the unequal, unfair and oppressive treatment of outsiders: fundamental equality for members, but equally fundamental inequality for non-members. Granted, there are often extensive rules of hospitality for taking in and taking care of strangers.

---

[12] This tactic works best, of course, where the charge is baseless and false and where one can demonstrate this publicly by commonly accepted methods of proof.

[13] "The Kanun says: 'Forgive, if you see fit; but if you prefer, wash your dirty face.'" (*The Code of Lekë Dukagjini*, 1989, Book Eight ["Honor"], §595). "Dirty face" is a vividly apt metaphor for dishonor, and the essential point for honor is that the individual dishonored, and he alone, has the right and responsibility to wash his own face, to remove the dishonor that has befallen him. That one's face can be cleansed only through violence is another matter, one that is common but not essential to honor.

But there are also rules that permit or require lesser regard of those outside the honor group — a lesser regard that often finds expression in permitting violence for lesser cause, even for non-honorable cause. It is important to realize that such invidious treatment of insiders and outsiders is not a necessary part of an honor code, even while appreciating how tempting such invidious rules are. They starkly demarcate and enforce the boundaries of the group, and thereby increase its solidarity and enhance its social position. Doubtless there are other ways to strengthen group solidarity, identity and cohesion, but having different rules for insiders and outsiders is an all-too-tempting route.

So while honor groups are not necessarily oppressive and not necessarily violent, they frequently are both, and just as frequently they justify their violent oppression in terms of honor. This conflation may be understandable, but it is most unfortunate. It constitutes one of the foremost obstacles to accepting, or even tolerating, honor in our times. But it is not an absolute veto, for two reasons. For one, non-violent (and therefore non-oppressive) honor groups are possible, because honor doesn't essentially depend on the use of violence. For another, an honor group may use violence not for purposes of oppression, but for just cause, such as the legitimate defense of an essentially non-oppressive community. Honor without violence, or at any rate without oppressive violence, may still be an attractive possibility, as we shall argue in the next chapter.

VII. Honor is Patriarchal

As ancient as honor's bond to bloody violence is its link to sexual and gender oppression; in fact, many would claim the two are united at the hip. Many vivid examples are readily available, such as the "honor killings" of women who have violated a group's sexual code, which involves men thinking they must "defend the honor" of "their" women — allegedly protecting but actually controlling and subordinating those women. Or consider the treatment of women as chattel, the restriction of women to less reputable (i.e. less "honorable") lines of work, the sexual mutilation of women, the confinement of women to households, restrictions on women's dress, suttee, and so on. It is not just that women are held — often fiercely held — to a standard of sexual purity from which men are excused. They are, of course, frequently so held: women must remain pure and chaste at all times, while men are free, if not expected, to cast a wayward eye and sow their wild oats, to cite just two of many euphemisms. But this is only part of the problem.

Beneath the sexual double standard lies a deep gender disparity that assigns different rules of honor to males and females. It is almost as if men and women were members of different honor groups, except that their rules and their lives are so intimately intertwined and both think they are committed to upholding the invidious rules as matters of honor. Male honor is rooted in accomplishment, status, power and violence; female honor has to do almost exclusively with sexual purity. This social fact is reflected in language. The *Oxford English Dictionary* lists only one gendered meaning of "honor," but it speaks volumes: "3.a. (Of a woman) Chastity, purity, as a virtue of the highest consideration; reputation for this virtue, good name." There is no comparable definition of honor said "of a man." Chastity before marriage, fidelity in marriage, and subordination throughout to men, is demanded of women because this *is* their honor, while honor for men involves other matters altogether. The two gendered honors converge in male control of female sexuality, which is extended to nearly all areas of life. So honor is complicit in patriarchy, gender oppression, and sexism, and no contemporary feminist would want to have anything to do with such a notion. Or would she?

Perhaps she might, once she realizes that honor does not require either a sexual or a gender double standard. Let's take the sexual double standard first. It is one of those properties widely associated with personal honor, but its association is contingent, not necessary. Any honor code will likely have something to say about sexual behavior, because this is such a prominent feature of human life, but there is no reason essential to honor that requires different rules of sexual conduct for males and females. It may be honorable, according to a given honor code, for men to display different sexual behaviors than women — but it need not be. A double standard may, but need not, be part of a group's honor code.

But what about the gender double standard? Isn't it required by honor? Must not men and women be treated differently from the standpoint of honor? On the contrary. There is deep pressure from the very heart of honor for *equal* treatment, for a *single* standard for all. As we have seen, personal honor is fundamentally egalitarian concerning all members of an honor group: all are members because, and only because, they follow the same rules and mutually regard one another as honorable. Proper regard by honor peers is deeply treasured because it is respect by those one most respects, the same kind of respect both given and received. The regard of inferiors is worth much less than that of equals, if it is worth anything at all. True personal honor, in other words, can only be among equals. If there is any kind of double standard (of gender, race, class, etc.), then the parties are unequal. Inequalities within the honor group are due not to honor, but to something else, to something external to honor as such. An honor code need not elevate the status and interests of one gender over another, and it should not do so if it wants both genders to be full members of the honor group.

Still, honor usually *is* gendered. Why? Many are the speculations. Some would trace the problem to common male traits such as aggressiveness, competitiveness, and violence. Males aggressively and forcibly pursue their perceived interests, not just their private personal interests but their race, class and gender interests as well. Seeking privilege — including fame, fortune and identifiable offspring — males dominate whomever they can, often resorting to brute force to subdue their supposed "inferiors," control their reproduction, and usurp their labor, all to serve their own male ends. Some consider these supposed male traits innate or genetically programmed; others regard them as culturally trained; most consider them a complex mixture of both nature and nurture. These traits are bundled together and wrapped in a skein of honor — patriarchal honor. But this cannot be the whole story, for it is entirely one-sided: why would women submit to patriarchy? Male interests are doubtless served, but are females mere powerless victims? Some might argue that female interests in security, provision, and defense against predators (including especially predatory male humans!) are great enough to accept the control and domination by males: a Faustian bargain, to be sure, even if one thought it worthwhile or necessary.

But all this is sheer speculation, and none of it is essential to our limited defense of honor. Regardless of how and why honor groups throughout history have contained sexual and gender double standards, the fact remains that no such double standard is required by personal honor as such. Honor is not *essentially* gendered.

Conclusion

In this chapter, we have seen that honor's unsavory reputation is not totally deserved — nor of course is it totally undeserved. No one can deny that many historical honor groups are deeply infected with undesirable qualities, however contingently those qualities may be attached to personal honor as such. What, then, should we do with the concept of personal honor? Several important alternatives are open to us: (i) We could follow Berger's lead and pronounce personal honor to be factually "obsolete," unavailable to us even if we wanted to employ the concept. (ii) We could promote honor's obsolescence by refusing to think in its terms, discarding the concept of personal honor and filling our own normative space with more acceptable concepts. (iii) We could update our conceptions of personal honor, scrubbing them of undesirable connotations, or perhaps we could create a new, improved version — a conception of honor for us.

The first alternative is belied by honor's persistent ubiquity, as I have argued in Part II. The word "honor" may not always be used in contemporary culture, but the concept remains applicable because its content is deeply embedded in many of our practices; it needs only to be named in order for us to recognize that honor is not, and probably never will be, obsolete in human history.

The second alternative is attractive to many, and certainly contributes to their lack of interest in honor. Those who have suffered at the hands of honor groups with immoral conceptions of honor certainly have a right not only to protest and rebel but also to attempt to eliminate such practices by disabling, demoting or destroying concepts such as honor that give them protective cover. Such an approach is understandable, but I think it excessive and unnecessary.

The third alternative seems possible, but it will be desirable only if there are some good reasons for retaining some conception of personal honor in the modern world. What does such a conception have to offer us? Does it have any important features that are missing in the proposed replacements for honor? Does the revitalized conception of personal honor still have important normative work to do for us today? Here we are on slippery ground, for by proposing a new conception it may look as if we are adopting an entirely new concept, not reinvigorating an old one. It is not always easy to say when conceptual alterations leave off and replacement of concepts begins. My claim that the central features of personal honor do not require inequality, sexism, violence and the like is debatable, but honor without these features will seem unreal to many, not something properly called "honor." So be it. I do not want to haggle over names. But I do think that the concept I have called "personal honor" — which does not have the objectionable features in any necessary or essential way — has considerable promise, by whatever name it may be called. It is both continuous with much traditional usage and also full of promise for contemporary practice. So I persist in calling it "honor," and I propose a conception of that concept of honor for us.

____

Chapter 12

HONOR FOR US

Our defense of honor in the previous chapter has produced this result: the concept of personal honor is not rendered ineligible for us by all the familiar woes of militarism, violence, elitism, patriarchy, and the like. Recall now our earlier distinction (in Part I) between concept and conception: conceptions various specify concepts, so that there can be different conceptions of the same concept. The negative features treated in Chapter 11 doubtless belong non-contingently to various *conceptions* of personal honor, but, I have argued, they are not part of the *concept*; it is at least possible for there to be other conceptions of personal honor untainted by these features. Still our defense of honor shows only that honor is not dead on arrival; it does not follow that honor is a live option for us, a lively possibility we should take seriously today. Is there anything about the concept of personal honor that might make it a concept not only worth studying but also worth having, using, and living?

It is important not to recommend honor on the wrong grounds or for inadequate reasons. For example, we should not try to sell personal honor because of the conferred or positional honors that often accompany it. Personal honor should ride on its own horse or not at all. Nor should personal honor be retained solely out of piety for tradition; what was compelling to our ancestors may not be good enough for us when we think it through. Nor, finally, should personal honor be recommended solely by the attractive virtues of many honorable people — their courage, loyalty, honesty, and integrity — if these admirable features can be obtained in other ways that don't require honor, especially if these other ways are easier and less costly than honor.

Of course, the most potent appeal of honor would derive from intimate acquaintance with particular groups and individuals whose lives attract us precisely because they embody conceptions of honor. We should find it worth studying the concepts their lives exemplify if we first found those lives deeply worth living on account of their honor, and for no further reason. I believe there are such groups and such individuals, but it will take more than a philosopher's abstractions to give them flesh and vitality. So the reader will have to find her own examples — though I also believe her search will be illumined by the results of this book.

Nonetheless, there are other forms of attraction. In this chapter, I aim to provide a different kind of incentive for taking the concept of honor seriously as not only an object of study but also a value worth living. I seek to make the concept attractive for *conceptual* reasons. The concept of personal honor has, I hope to show, certain distinctive features that should commend it to thoughtful contemporaries, not least to philosophers. These conceptual features should be at once attractive on their own, independently of external payoffs; distinctive among other normative concepts jostling for our attention; and deeper than any particular conception of honor but attaching to the concept of honor as such. Perhaps there are no features meeting all three conditions. Nonetheless I will propose five candidates.

I. Overcoming Dichotomies

First, personal honor is not only a Janus-concept, looking simultaneously in different directions, but it is also a relatively *thick* normative concept[1] that bridges and overcomes a number of stultifying dichotomies in contemporary thought. I shall consider four such dichotomies, though this list is far from exhaustive.

1 **Inner/Outer**:[2] Honor is often disparaged as "merely external," consisting in one's reputation, or the regard of others, and not something inherent in a person. But this criticism applies only to conferred or recognition honor; what about personal honor? Is it inner or is it outer? Neither alternative makes sense by itself: personal honor is not solely an inner condition, for it requires commitment to a shared honor code and loyalty to other members of an honor group; nor is it solely an outer condition, for the recognition among members is mutual, and any recognized member must possess the requisite kind of internal condition, an effective sense of honor. The only solution to this puzzle is to see that personal honor essentially embraces *both* inner and outer: Personal honor cannot exist without both inner disposition and outer connection; it is not simply located[3] "inside" or "outside" an honorable

---

[1] A thin normative concept like good contains little if any descriptive content, while a thick normative concept like cute or cruel is richer in such descriptive content.

[2] Cf. G. Taylor, 1985, Chapter 3, for parallel remarks, though she considers only what we have called conferred, recognition and status (achievement) honor, and doesn't distinguish these from personal honor; or rather, she seems to think they are what personal honor is in so-called "honor societies."

[3] Cf. Whitehead, 1927, 64, on the fallacy of simple location.

person, but resides in both, because they are related in certain ways.

Sometimes we are tempted to think of character traits, especially those we call virtues, solely as a matter of a person's internal constitution: they are a person's enduring habits of mind, feeling and action that may arise in a particular social context but once acquired thereafter belong to someone independently of that context. We think someone is honest or courageous, for example, quite apart from what others think or do. Whether or not this is true of some virtues, it clearly cannot be true of the virtue of personal honor. Personal honor is possible only in a particular kind of social context: it requires allegiance to a publicly shared set of principles of action, the honor code, and loyalty to a publicly and mutually recognizable set of particular persons, the honor group. Moreover, this context is more than just a place to learn such allegiance and loyalty; it is also the place where these qualities can and should be displayed, and it is the only such place in which they make sense.

But equally, personal honor cannot be reduced to what others think or how they act towards an individual. Others cannot force or impose their code of honor upon someone; she must make the code her own, or else in following the code she cannot be doing so in an honorable way. An honorable person must be able not only to recognize the code of honor and to apply it in practice — she must also be personally *committed* to the code, and this means internalizing the code quite deeply (cf. Section IV below). A person who follows the code only to achieve other ends, e.g. of conferred or positional honors, lacks the appropriate virtue of personal honor.

So personal honor is a thick normative concept that overcomes the inner/outer dichotomy neither by choosing either term nor by denying both, but rather by affirming both as essentially related in one virtue, an effective sense of personal honor. This should appeal to those who find the inner/outer dichotomy confining and unrealistic.

2 **Guilt/Shame**: This dichotomy is often paired with inner/outer, and when applied to personal honor it suffers the same fate: neither makes sense by itself because both are essential to honor, and related intimately. Guilt and shame are variously described, contrasted, and evaluated by different authors looking through different disciplinary lenses; a quick survey will help to map most of the terrain:

- Social psychologist June Price Tangney thinks empirical research shows that the two "emotions of self-blame" have different objects: guilt looks to transgressive behaviors, shame to the transgressive self. So conceived, ". . . the weight of scientific evidence indicates that guilt is the more moral, adaptive response to sins and transgressions in a contemporary human society that is more egalitarian than hierarchical in structure" (Tangney, 2007, v. 2, 872).

- Family therapists Merle Fossum and Marilyn Mason define shame as "an inner sense of being completely diminished or insufficient as a person. It is the self judging the self." Guilt, on the other hand, is the "developmentally more mature . . . feeling of regret one has about behavior that has violated a personal value." "While guilt is a painful feeling of regret and responsibility for one's actions, shame is a painful feeling about oneself as a person" (Fossum and Mason, 1986, 5).

- Psychologist Silvan Tomkins unconventionally thinks shame is a fundamental affect hard-wired into human biology; its "innate activator" is "the incomplete reduction of interest or joy," perhaps because one is viewed as "strange" (Sedgwick and Frank, 1995, 134–5). "Shame turns the attention of the self and others away from other objects to this most visible residence of the self [i.e. one's face], increases its visibility, and thereby generates the torment of self-consciousness" (136).

- Anthropologist Ruth Benedict considers shame to be the violation or feeling of violation of cultural or social values, while guilt is the violation or feeling of violation of one's internal or personal values. Shame and guilt characterize whole cultures and condition the emotions of their members. "True shame cultures rely on external sanctions for good behavior, not, as true guilt cultures do, on an internalized conviction of sin. Shame is a reaction to other people's criticism" (Benedict, 1989 [1946], 223).[4]

- Philosopher Gabriele Taylor appeals to the anthropologists' distinction between a "shame-culture" and a "guilt-culture," where the former but not the latter thinks "public esteem is the greatest good and to be ill spoken of the greatest evil," and where such esteem is based on success or failure in living up to the group's code. She further identifies this public esteem with honor (Taylor, 1985, 54). Even though its only concern is for "public reputation," shame is over a loss so great as to amount to "total extinction of the individual that existed as a member of the group, it is total loss of identity" (56).

- Philosopher Bernard Williams takes shame to be a self-regarding emotion based on the experience of loss of power and diminishment of self by "being seen, inappropriately, by the wrong people, in the wrong conditions" (Williams, 1993, 78; cf. Jenkins, 2006, Chapter 7). This feeling is "bootstrapped" via cultural forms and agents to an ethical sentiment that makes use of an "internalized other" (84). Guilt, which points toward what has happened to others, is not independent of shame, which points to what the person has become; and both "serve to bind people together in a community of emotion" (80).

---

[4] Incidentally, Benedict thinks that honor in a non-honor culture can be "living up to one's own picture of oneself" (223) — but this is integrity, not honor.

- Philosopher Richard Wollheim considers shame a reflexive "moral" emotion that arises in response to a change in one's sense of self, felt as threat and insecurity, in relation to others (Wollheim, 1999, 151). Shame and guilt differ in a number of respects: Shame is for the kind of person we have become, the ideal we have failed to live up to, that brings a desire to change and a wish that others should forget what we have become, and is conveyed by a look. Guilt is for injunctions we have transgressed, brings a desire to repair or compensate, a wish that others should forget what we have done, and is conveyed by words or a voice (155–6). Wollheim is dubious about regarding whole cultures as "guilt" or "shame" cultures, believing that psychology will only lose insight should it "coarsen itself into the image of sociology" (157).

All these accounts have some merit, all have drawbacks and oversights, but none does full justice to the concept of personal honor we have explored. Personal honor demands a different construal of shame and guilt — but also repays us with a distinctive perspective on shame and guilt as ordinarily understood. The account briefly goes as follows: *Guilt* is a person's contravening some principle she holds, while *shame* is being deficient or deviant in the eyes of others; guilt is "inner," shame is "outer." In addition, subjective and objective senses of each may be distinguished: *subjective guilt and shame* are what are believed and felt by the individual, while *objective guilt and shame* exist in relation to a person's principles and society independently of whether they are recognized. Hence someone can *be* guilty (of breach of some principle) without *feeling* guilty (about that breach), and conversely; and likewise for being and feeling shamed.[5]

Understood in this way, both guilt and shame are intimately implicated in an effective sense of honor. Guilt arises when someone contravenes or fails to live up to the code of honor (objective guilt) or feels he has done so (subjective guilt). Guilt exists and is rightly felt insofar as the person has truly violated the code he truly embraces as his own (it contains at least some of the normative principles by which he endeavors to live).[6] Shame occurs when someone deviates from social expectation, or feels he has done so. If these are *honor expectations* (the expectations of an honor group concerning matters of honor), they are shared by all individual members, including the shameful person. But the shame of dishonor goes beyond failing to live up to the shared code; it is also

---

[5] Additionally, feeling shamed is not the same as feeling ashamed (G. Taylor, 1985, 53); but we shall not pursue this point.

[6] This is another way of saying that personal honor is internal to the person: the code is his code and not merely someone else's.

letting down one's fellow honor-group members.[7] Shame exists and is rightly felt insofar as the person is truly a member of the honor group, and insofar as she values their evaluation of herself as her own.

It follows that the motivation to honor is complex. It is neither a simple self-regard (looking only to principles one has autonomously adopted independently of others) nor a simple other-regard (looking only to principles held by others and adopted heteronomously by oneself). It is both, and both are intimately inter-related: in violating one's own principles one is also violating the principles of others, and conversely; and in being subject to the disapproval of others one is also subject to self-disapproval, and again conversely. Honor is a thick concept that helps us to comprehend this and other complexities of guilt and shame.

3   **Individual/Community**: It is tempting to succumb either to a hyper-individualism or to a totalizing communitarianism. On the one hand the individual is supposed to exist, or to define herself, quite independently of social context; what is deepest and most valuable in a person, her very identity, her true self, is hers no matter where and when she lives, if not in origin or inspiration then in essential possession: she may have discovered or chosen or formed who she is in a certain social context, but then she possesses this identity in a way that doesn't depend on remaining in that context. Her self, if not her sense of self, is essentially ahistorical. On the other hand, the community absorbs individuality: An individual is nothing more than a social construction, whether as an independent "self-made man" or as a dependent role-player. His deepest identity is the node he occupies in a complex social web, its coordinates fixed by the permissible social relations. His self, if not his sense of self, is essentially historical.

Once again personal honor overcomes the dichotomy: an honorable individual can exist only in a particular community of honor, but equally a community of honor can exist only as composed of honorable individuals; honor is not simply located in either individual or community. A person of honor can be honorable only according to some honor code and therefore in some honor group; but the honorable individual is not thereby totally assimilated to a group function, for each member must make the code his own in his own distinctive way, with individual commitment and interpretation. Likewise, an honor group can exist

---

[7] Two complications: The shame of dishonor is not simply how present, actual honor-group members view one, for (i) they may not be aware of the infraction, and (ii) potential as well as actual members also have a stake. Perhaps the "other" in whose eyes one is shamed is an amalgam: idealized actual and potential fellow members. In addition, one's own (idealized) self enters in: the "other" is also oneself as identified with the honor group both individually and collectively (on "the internalized other," cf. Williams, 1993, 88).

only in and through individuals with effective senses of honor who mutually recognize one another as fellow members, but this doesn't mean that the community is nothing more than the sum of its individuals, for what those individuals share, and the way they share it, is also vital. The thick concept of honor enables us to affirm both individual and community.

4 **Equality/Hierarchy**: Many have judged honor to be essentially tied to some form of hierarchy, both within and outside the honor group, and to be a matter of fulfilling the expectations of the differing hierarchical roles. Contrarily, I have stressed the fundamental egalitarianism of personal honor. How can honor be both? Part of the answer lies in the distinction between conferred, positional and recognition honor on the one hand, and personal honor on the other: The former not only permit but encourage and may even require hierarchical distinctions. Only excellences should be recognized, and excellences rise above the ordinary. Likewise conferred honors are normally bestowed upon those who have achieved something others admire, and thereby distinguished themselves above others. And positional honor demands inequality of achievement or status, sorting out social betters from social inferiors. But personal honor rests on the fundamental equality of all honor group members: all are equally capable of an effective sense of honor, all deserve and demand mutual regard from everyone else, all equally accept the same honor code, and all equally trust the honorability of others.

Yet the basic equality of personal honor is quite compatible with many kinds of inequalities, both within and beyond the honor group: (i) There may be differences in fulfillment of the honor code; some may exemplify the code to a greater degree and extent than their fellows, while others may be only minimally compliant. (ii) For purposes that have little or nothing to do with personal honor, an honor group may have a hierarchical organization; even the strictest democracy must elect leaders, and "officers" fulfilling special roles are set apart from the rest. (iii) Some group members may be better than others at discerning points of honor and interpreting the local code, and so the group may defer to their wise judgments in difficult cases; even so, a deeper equality remains: each member of an honor group is ultimately responsible for managing her own honor, including when and whether and how to defer. (iv) Honor groups may be highly esteemed by others and so showered with conferred honors and given elevated positions in society, but these bestowed honors are not essential to personal honor. In sum, personal honor's egalitarian foundation permits what human nature seems bound to seek: hierarchical differences. So honor can be both equal and unequal, in a variety of ways.

Once again we see that the concept of personal honor is a thick concept that helps overcome a wide variety of stultifying dichotomies. This conceptual feature should attract everyone interested in moving beyond such dichotomies.

II. SELF-REGARD[8]

Next, personal honor connects deeply, and intriguingly, with the roots of self-regard, with the fundamental ways in which a person regards herself. Immediately, we encounter a thicket of difficult questions: What *is* this self whom one regards? What kind of an entity is a self, if indeed it is any one kind of thing at all? What makes a self one and distinct from another? How is a particular self the same entity over time, the same self now as then? How are selves formed, and how destroyed? What are the conditions necessary for there to be selves and for selves to thrive? How is a self to be apprehended? Do others see the same self as oneself, and do they look at the same factors? What kind of value, if any, do selves have inherently, and how valuable are they?

This is not a book on the self, so I don't propose plunging into this tangle of issues. Rather, I will explore a narrower topic: self-regard. How should someone regard herself — i.e. her self? There are of course many vantage points for addressing this question, ranging all the way from extreme self-elevation (creating one's own value in the very act of evaluating oneself) to extreme self-abasement (submitting to the judgment of others that one has little to no inherent value). But what about the vantage point of personal honor? How should an *honorable* person regard her self?

It is important to note straight off that the self-regard of an honorable self is not arbitrary or unguided; it rests on, and is constrained by, essential ingredients of honor. This self-regard must always look to the honor code and to the honor group: Have I faithfully kept the code, lived up to its requirements and expectations? Have I been loyal to my fellow members, trusting their honorability and caring about their trust of mine? Honor therefore provides standards as well as a vantage point for self-regard. But there are complications.

One complication is *interpretation*. Rules such as those contained in honor codes are not algorithms for automatons. No set of rules applies itself; people must apply those rules, and in doing so, people must judge when, whether and how a rule applies. Such application inevitably involves interpretation — interpretation of the meaning of the rules, both singly and collectively, as

---

[8] In this and the next section we take up further aspects of the individual/community dichotomy considered previously.

well as interpretation of the context in and to which the rules are applied. Some capacity for proper interpretation is ingredient in an effective sense of honor, for without it a person cannot be responsible for managing his own honor, and without the ability to manage his own honor a person cannot be honorable. Moreover, as we have argued, this capacity and responsibility for interpreting the honor code for oneself is presumed equal among all honor group members. Still, there are differences in discernment: some are better interpreters of the code and its application than others, due to greater intelligence, experience or other qualities. These are the *sages of honor*, to whose insight and judgment honor groups often defer when difficult questions of interpretation and application arise. Even so, the views of sages must be ratified by others in the group in order to constitute valid interpretation of the honor code, and there will always be other possible interpretations.

Second, there may be some leeway in the *extent* of the honor code's application: its jurisdiction, if you will.[9] Most honor codes are not easily confined to only a few aspects or areas of life. Honor tends to spread, to expand to the point where just about *everything* one does is within honor's purview.[10] But if honor's jurisdiction is everywhere — at home and abroad, between and beyond families, and concerning those outside as well as those inside the honor group — then it may come to seem unmanageable and even unbearable. Here there is room for leniency and compassion in application, and perhaps even for "*honor holidays.*"[11] An overly zealous honor rigorist may find herself trapped and made miserable by absurdly high expectations. Still, honor's demands are not to be circumscribed on that account alone.

Third, *self*-regard in an honor group should ideally coincide with *other*-regard, not just because others share the same code and its applications, but also because an honorable person cares about and carefully monitors the regard of honorable others. Part of what it means to have an effective sense of honor is that one does care, and care deeply, about what honorable others think of one. This means that self-evaluation of a person cannot be at wide variance with communal evaluation of that person — unless, of course, one or the other thoroughly misapprehends the situation. Practically speaking, this ideal coincidence of self-regard and other-regard means that one has a mirror in the eyes of others, and they in yours.

---

[9] In using such a term as "jurisdiction," I highlight one of the many parallels between honor and law. Yet they are in the end quite different domains, and I don't want the parallels to overshadow the differences.

[10] There may be very good reasons for so-called "Honor Systems" to restrict their jurisdiction: Only as limited, for example, to cases of cheating on course work might an academic Honor System survive; moreover, one might think, better some honor than none, and perhaps this minimum will inspire honorable behavior beyond the confines of the system. Nevertheless, these restrictions in jurisdiction are artificial, not inherent in the nature of personal honor.

[11] Cf. William James on "moral holidays," i.e. needed respites from the burdens of morality, "to let the world wag in its own way" (James, 1975 [1907], Lecture II, 41).

Honorable selves care about other selves, and especially about how those others regard them. Why? Isn't this a weakness, an objectionable dependency on others? Not necessarily. Concern for the regard of others may be deeply rooted in human nature and development. At birth we are utterly dependent beings who must rely on the care of others. We could not live, much less thrive, without their care, and so we become intensely interested in our care-givers and how they regard us. In short, we care about others and their regard because they have first cared for us, and we extend that care from immediate to wider family and beyond. Honor's concern for other-regard develops from this natural human foundation of care for care-giving others.

Fourth, honor's self-regard includes but goes beyond recognition honor. If virtues are excellences and personal honor is a virtue, then personal honor deserves public recognition, and much of that recognition lies in the words and deeds of other honor-group members. Even so, there is more than public recognition of excellence involved in the mutual regard of honor-group members. Obviously, taking notice of and having negative regard for dishonorable acts is not recognition (in this technical sense), yet it is required of all members as a matter of honor. They must neither ignore nor approve of deviations from the code. But further, their regard goes beyond recognition of excellence and notice of fault: it encompasses all the many ways in which respect is shown, through paying attention to, sympathizing with, deferring to others, as well as standing by them in distress, standing up for them in trouble, and standing up to them when they act dishonorably. It would be an odd social group in which regard for others only manifested itself in recognition of their excellences.

Fifth, the regard (by self and by others) in question is not superficial but goes to the heart of one's sense of self, of one's "identity" in the sense of self-concept. An effective sense of honor is perceived by self and others alike as something very nearly constitutive of oneself, such that losing one's honor would be a loss more grievous than most, perhaps even worse than the loss of life itself. An honorable death is far preferable to a dishonorable life, because the former somehow preserves, or at least doesn't harm, the self that counts, the self that identifies itself with honor. For an honorable person, a self dishonored would mean not only guilt for contravening important principles and shame in the eyes of others, but also revulsion for oneself.[12]

So the concept of personal honor illumines the roots of self-regard in important ways. With honor, self-regard no longer seems like the boot-strapping creation of one's own value so one can value oneself — there are shared standards. With honor, self-regard is no longer narcissism because one

---

[12] Of course, a dishonorable person, as such, would not feel these things. It is only an honorable person who will be repelled by the very thought of herself as dishonorable. This is an essential part of her sense of honor.

joins a community of regard — there are significant others. And with honor, one's sense of self transcends mere life and even one's own self — there is commitment to honor itself. The self-regard of an honorable person is rooted in care for others, and provides a patterned yet personal way of expressing that care.

III. COMMUNITY

In an individualistic age, the concept of personal honor opens up new ways of conceiving and connecting to community. Honor is a deeply communitarian virtue without losing its grounding in individual character. Moreover, it permits a variety of communities that differ significantly in the kinds of character they foster, even while it requires a deep concern for the regard of others.

Our age is individualistic not just in encouraging greed, fetishizing narcissistic exhibition and excess, and celebrating mere idiosyncratic "uniqueness" as if it were a value in itself. It is individualistic also in how it thinks about an individual's relation to the wider community. This comes out in many ways. Some, for example, think a social group is nothing but a collection of individuals; some hold that governments exist solely to protect the liberty rights of its individual citizens; some maintain that every allegiance and commitment (including commitment to morality) is to be tested ultimately by reference to self-interest. Such views have little appreciation of concepts like personal honor, and their prevalence doubtless contributes to the lack of interest in honor for us. But things look very different from the standpoint of honor.

Personal honor is possible only in and through a certain kind of community, an honor group, and it rests upon and fosters a certain kind of concern for that community. There is commitment to a shared code of honor, of course, but this is in some respects a lesser linkage. More important is the mutual regard of others, the commitment to a common social practice of having regard for the behavior and character of others, and for their similar regard of oneself. This mutual regard rests on a basis of care for *particular* others — care for their welfare, to be sure, but even more care for their regard of oneself. For a person with an effective sense of honor, it matters profoundly what these others think and how they feel, not least what they think and how they feel about one's self but not because it is in one's interest to gain their approval. Others' views of oneself matter because those very others matter to oneself.

There are many ways in which honorable others matter to someone with an effective sense of honor. I will highlight six of them.

- **Equality**: is fundamental (cf. Section I above). Honor-group members are and regard one another as equals in honorability if not in actual achievement of honor, and this egalitarian regard conditions all other relationships, including any hierarchical ones. Doubtless there are inegalitarian forms of attachment and affection (for example, familial ones) that can generate community, but a fundamentally egalitarian community has its advantages, not least because the fundamental worth of each individual to the community is equally affirmed — there can be no doubts or quarrels about lesser or greater, about rank or status, in a community of personal honor.
- **Reciprocity**: follows from equality plus care for others: one will seek to be regarded by others as one regards them (and oneself), and one will treat and regard others as they wish to be treated and regarded. One might think of this as the *Golden Honor Rule*: Do unto others (other honor-group members, at least!) as you would have them do unto you. Since everyone is equally bound by this principle, all are thereby assured of equal and reciprocal respect from all.
- **Respect**: is owed all other honor-group members and it is what an honorable person demands as her right — it is an important part of proper self-respect to insist on the respect of respected others. Such respect is neither affection for special persons nor esteem for their attractive features nor recognition of anyone's excellences. Rather, it is a fundamental awareness of another's worth that give such worth its due. Worth in the context of honor is an intrinsic value that is neither granted to everyone nor reducible to use or interest; rather, it is a person's honorability. Such respect is prominent in an honor group; it undergirds all other relations (personal, commercial, political, etc.); and it thereby strengthens the community.
- **Mutuality**: is present in the fundamental respectful regard of honorable people for honorable others. No one is or feels alone in this regard; rather it is a common regard that grows in strength through being mutual. The regard is reciprocal and it is public, so it is also reflexive: one's respect for others is reflected not only in their respect for oneself but also in their communicated awareness of one's respect for them, and so on.
- **Publicity**: Honor's mutual and reciprocal regard is overt and publicly demonstrated, not hidden to view. Of course, there is public embrace of the honor code and trust of other members. But there are more subtle matters: word and gesture, tone of voice and manner of address, assistance given and acknowledged, judgments made and communicated — all these and innumerable other forms of public interaction express and reinforce an honor group's bonds of commitment and loyalty. Community is thereby strengthened.
- Finally, **solidarity**: grows out of the special loyalty and care honor-group

members have for one another as well as their commitment to common principles. Honor-group members stand together — sometimes literally shoulder to shoulder with comrades in battle but also sometimes figuratively in supporting those comrades in peacetime pursuits: business deals, perhaps, or personal ventures, or religious quests. Honor-group members also stand up for one another when attacked, threatened or challenged: "all for one and one for all." And they stand by one another, comforting them in affliction and supporting them in adversity.

In all these and myriad other ways honor groups create and constitute very strong communities. But such community need not come at the cost of conformity, either within one honor group or across honor groups. Within a single honor group, there may be plenty of room for individuality in expressing and enacting common commitments and loyalties. No one faces exactly the same situations as another, and each individual is responsible not only for his own commitment to the common code and loyalty to other members but also for how to interpret that code and display that loyalty in those varying situations. Across honor groups there is further variation. Since different honor groups may have different honor codes, and since different codes mold different characters, a common respectful concern for others may find expression in the cultivation of different kinds of character. Some honor groups, for example, may extol the martial qualities and consider emotional display as weakness, while others may prize the sympathetic qualities and think lack of emotion is dangerous repression. Both kinds of group, however, achieve community through caring for others — caring that is equal, reciprocal, respectful, mutual, and public.

The major problem of community for honor groups is not one of achieving internal solidarity — that is an essential and outstanding feature of such groups — but of reaching out beyond the community in a respectful fashion. To be blunt, members of honor groups are often snobs, disdaining outsiders as unworthy of the respect they owe and gladly give to fellow members.[13] Some might think that snobbery is the necessary price of honor solidarity, but this is a mistake. Honor groups can display genuine respect for non-group members both as a matter of their own honor code and in recognition of others' potential membership (their actual exclusion is merely accidental). Honor groups do not need to reinforce their proper sense of solidarity by withholding respect from non-members, much less by reviling them.

At its heart, honor constitutes community neither through self-interest nor through shared characteristics such as kinship, race, ethnicity, gender and religion. Its bond is a matter of voluntary commitment to principle, the

---

[13] Of course, they may still display good manners to the outsider — not out of respect to the outsider but out of concern for the regard of fellow members.

honor code, as well as trust and loyalty willingly extended to the honor-group members, the people who instantiate that code. This kind of community does not squeeze the individuality out of individuals, but allows many differences to thrive within the limits of mutual respect — differences in tastes and talents, plans and projects, behaviors and beliefs that are compatible with their shared code of honor. A community of honor doesn't necessarily or steadily pursue the common good, but it does permit that goal, and likewise with the happiness of individuals. Honor groups may endure and they may allow individuals to flourish, but they must remain honorable come what may.

IV. Anti-Consequentialism

Personal honor is a non-consequentialist virtue; its structure does not involve consideration of consequences. Indeed, it is anti-consequentialist — consideration of consequences is excluded in important ways. Here I intend "consequences" in a very broad sense, encompassing any effect on self or others, proximate or remote, quantifiable or not, that results from decisions, actions or character-states of a person. I will focus on the consequences of people having some conception of personal honor and living in accordance with that conception.

One might suppose personal honor could be recommended in terms of its consequences: in an academic honor group, no worries about cheating and relative freedom from theft; in warrior honor groups, the unflagging support of one's buddies, every one doing his duty; in sport, a "level playing field" in terms of fair play; in the legal profession, quicker and more efficient proceedings; and so on. Equally, one might seek to criticize honor groups on the basis of the personal and social havoc they often wreak: macho males, gender oppression, violence, snobbery and the rest. Such consequentialist appeals, both positive and negative, have undoubted force. Yet they all fail to come to grips with the nature of personal honor, which can neither be analyzed nor lived in consequentialist terms. This may be seen in various ways.

People who understand and use the concept of personal honor in their lives are thereby committing themselves to thinking in certain ways — and to not thinking in other ways — about what they should do and become (or not do and not become). When something is a matter of honor, and what honor requires can be ascertained, questions of what will happen to self or others simply don't come up: If honor requires something, then one must just do it or cease being honorable. Reckoning the costs and benefits is simply not something an honorable person will do when it is a matter of honor.[14]

---

[14] Of course, such consequentialist calculations are permitted, and undeniably useful, to an honorable person where honor is not at stake. Likewise a person from one honor group may

This point may be put another way: Personal honor excludes consideration, much less calculation, of interests. By "interest" I mean an object of desire in a broad sense: anything that anyone wants (independently of personal honor itself). Consideration and adjustment of interests can be very subtle, complicated and rewarding, but it is not what the concept of personal honor allows.[15] Doubtless living an honorable life does often promote many interests (e.g. security, reputation, social position), but these are irrelevant when thinking in terms of personal honor. Honor's claims are independent of the tug of desire, or rather they are independent of desires other than wanting to be honorable. Of course an honorable person wants to be honorable, but this desire is not based on interests and indeed excludes them from consideration.

Honor's appeal is not to the good independently conceived. To be sure, honorable people will find honor inherently good, not good because of its results (apart from the condition of being honorable). To follow an honor code because of the non-honor good it brings to self or others is to fail to be sufficiently motivated by honor. It doesn't follow that the good of honor must outweigh all other goods, just that its good isn't a function of those other goods. A person may decide that, all things considered, a life of honor is less important than a life without honor, or that a life of honor is not supremely important. But what she cannot do is to use honor as a means to other goods while still retaining the good of honor. Being honorable means forgoing such a purpose — indeed forgoing even thinking about such a purpose.

Honor therefore resists being viewed as something useful even in Alasdair MacIntyre's way, as a means to realizing the goods internal to a practice.[16] Doubtless honor is useful to achieving the goods of the practice of honor, but this is saying only that honor is good as a means to the good of honor, which is an odd way of emphasizing the independent goodness of honor. The point is that honor is thoroughly anti-consequentialist in its very structure. To think in terms of personal honor is to think of the honor code and the regard of the honor group, not to think of means/ends, or costs/benefits, or goods/ills produced.

Such anti-consequentialist thinking as honor displays is unfashionable

---

weigh the value of another honor group in consequentialist terms. And outsiders to all honor may calculate the consequences of honor, all things considered. (Indeed, as Nat Goldberg has suggested to me, there might even be a form of consequentialism bent on maximizing honor. Still, it wouldn't be a matter of honor to do so!) My point is internal to honor: From the standpoint of a person of honor weighing a matter of honor — to her such consequentialist calculations don't count because they don't even arise.

[15] Other concepts of honor, for example conferred and positional honor, do allow such consideration. To obtain conferred honors, one may perform intricate calculations of what behaviors and beliefs are most likely to bring about the desired results. Needless to say, this is not a matter of personal honor.

[16] Cf. MacIntyre, 1981 (1e), 178.

in a society where anything — and even anyone — is believed to have its value measured by people's desires, and often a market price measured by its exchange value. Likewise, it will seem odd to public policy makers who think they must always and solely calculate — or at least consider and weigh — costs and benefits. It will frustrate game-theoretical analysts who stipulate consequentialist thinking for their hapless players (as in Prisoner's Dilemma games). And it will seem mysterious to those who think all normative justification must be rooted in self-interest.[17] How, then, could we accept such a non-consequentialist concept as personal honor?

We could, of course, depict honor's benefits, knowing that these can only be achieved, paradoxically, by suspending the very kind of thinking that warrants thinking in terms of honor's benefits. Or we could point to honorable individuals and communities even outsiders find admirable, and ask: wouldn't you like to be like them, even knowing full well how profound a change in your current thinking would be required to become like them? Or perhaps we could appeal to other non-consequentialist concepts a person already possess, such as certain (not all!) conceptions of justice, care, and love, and express the point of honor in parallel fashion.

But all such appeals may fail for those who find non-consequentialist thinking quaint and old-fashioned, and who are resolutely committed to some consequentialist mode of thought (come what may?). They will find honor's ubiquity troublesome, its appeal mysterious, and its non-obsolescence inexplicable. My only hope is that they might find themselves engaged with and by honorable people, and perhaps be given incentive to explore what an honorable life is all about. If they do become so engaged, perhaps they will come to appreciate some merits of anti-consequentialist thinking.

V. Honor's Distinctiveness

Honor is often confused with other virtues such as honesty, integrity, and civility, but it is a distinct virtue, and it is worth distinguishing even though its value is not only a matter of its distinctiveness.

Honesty is often defined by what it is not: it is not lying or not concealing one's beliefs, intentions, and feelings. More positively, honesty is presenting to others only what one is to oneself, and perhaps holding nothing back. It is allied to *sincerity*, which is believing what one presents to others. An honest person can be trusted, for there is no duplicity in his words, no hidden agenda behind his actions, no concealment of true feelings, no false front.

---

[17] Even John Rawls, in the course of taking Utilitarianism to task in *A Theory of Justice*, used such thinking within his favored version of the initial situation, the infamous "Original Position," to justify as well as to explicate his two principles of justice.

But honor is not the same as honesty. An honorable person certainly is loyal to fellow members of the honor group and can be trusted by them, but whether she will always be honest toward them (not to mention toward outsiders) depends on the particulars of the honor code in question. The code may prescribe universal honesty, but often will not. There are many occasions on which (full) honesty is not required, and may even be forbidden, by honor codes — nearly always to enemies but sometimes even to fellow members, where delicacy is needed to maintain polite appearances. Of course, not being honest is not the same as being dishonest. Doubtless an honorable person is rarely *dis*honest, at least with other honor-group members, for that would imply an untrustworthy character. But honesty isn't always the best policy from the standpoint of honor, even to other honor-group members.

Integrity is often equated with honor: "a man of honor" and "a man of integrity" sound synonymous to many today. But they are quite distinct. Integrity means wholeness, coherence, and integration in at least four ways: (i) a person with integrity has a coherent set of principles that fit together without contradiction or conflict; (ii) these principles encompass the whole person, without exempting large segments of life, and are firmly embraced; (iii) a person of integrity lives what she believes; whereas an honest person says what she believes, a person of integrity does what she says; and (iv) a person of integrity lives in harmony with his environment.

But honor is not the same as integrity. To be sure, *dis*honorable persons lack integrity, and a truly honorable person possesses as much integrity as his honor group permits; but still, integrity doesn't imply honor. On the first point, dishonorable behavior is an indication of lack of acceptance of a relevant honor code,[18] and so of course there will be lack of coherence between the code and a person's beliefs and actions. On the second point, normally an honor group does prize one form of integrity, seeking members who fully embody and embrace its code. Yet integrity may be blocked or diminished in an honor group, in several ways: if the honor code is incoherent or not fully coherent, if it doesn't extend fully to all aspects of life, or if it requires duplicity of thought, word and deed on many occasions. On the third point, one shouldn't presume that only principles of honor are coherent or can structure an entire life. It is possible for someone to live by a coherent set of principles that are idiosyncratic or only accidentally shared with others, and hypocrisy is not the exclusive possession of honor groups.

Civility usually accompanies honor, especially when dealing with fellow honor-group members. Honor involves respecting others, and being civil is a way of publicly showing respect to others. But civility often has a meaning beyond mere manners: it refers to the way people act towards one another on

---

[18] Must the person who is judged dishonorable accept the code he violates? Or is it only the judgment-maker who must (at least profess to) accept that code?

civic occasions, i.e. when interacting with one's fellow citizens. Here respect for others requires accepting and promoting others' full participation in public life. Civility in this sense is a political virtue. Now a political group and an honor group may coincide, each with exactly the same set of members, so that every citizen is expected to be an honorable person, and vice versa. But they coincide only *per accidens*, not essentially. The honor of citizens, I argued earlier (Chapter 8), may be viewed as patriotism, and patriotism is indeed tightly linked to civility — treating one's fellow citizens with patriotic honor implies treating them civilly. But a citizen may belong to honor groups other than the countrywide one, and these other groups may have codes that limit civility toward all. Indeed, one's honor group may require or permit snubbing outsiders in order to reinforce the group's presumed elite status. Honorable people are not necessarily civil, and vice versa — civility towards other citizens may be narrow and shallow, and it is quite compatible with incivility towards outsiders.

So, whether construed on a personal or on a political level, civility is not the same as honor, even when some conception of honor requires civility. But honor doesn't have to require civility; civility — even civility to fellow honor-group members — is not an essential part of any honor code. The code, for example, could call for considerable competition within the group — rough talk, sharp elbows, scant deference — or at least allow for this kind of incivility on occasion.[19] An honor group will find ways of respecting one another and achieving trust and loyalty, but civility is not the only route to this end. In honor groups, respect for other members means respecting them as equally honorable in terms of the group's code, and whether this respect includes being civil depends entirely on what the code prescribes: often civility, but not always civility.

Personal honor, therefore, is a distinctive virtue, and it shouldn't be confused with its frequent associates. One may, of course, seek to recommend honor on the ground of the conceptual company it keeps, but being clear about its distinctiveness is a better way. Personal honor is distinctive in the premium it places on commitment to principle (the honor code), loyalty to others (members of the honor group), and the kind of concern it has for the regard of those honorable others. Perhaps that is distinction enough to compel a closer look — and maybe even admiration and adoption.

---

[19] Cf. The Homeric heroes in the *Iliad*, especially their trash-talking in war councils, where for example Achilles bitingly insults Agamemnon, knowing he retains his warrior honor — his personal honor — because he can out-fight his expedition's nominal leader — who retains positional honor even when his personal honor is called into question.

Conclusion

Let's put together the case we have made for personal honor in this book. First, as our conceptual analysis in Part I showed, the concept of personal honor is distinct from a number of other concepts often labeled "honor" (Chapters 2–3) and in particular should not be conflated with morality or religion (Chapter 4). Clarity about this distinctive concept sharpens our focus on its distinguishing features, for good and for ill. Second, as Part II illustrates, the concept of personal honor is descriptively useful in interpreting and understanding a wide range of human life, including contemporary culture from the military and sports to politics and the professions. Honor-like behavior is very widespread, perhaps even humanly universal, and concepts that illumine it should be taken seriously. Third, as we argued in the preceding chapter (Chapter 11), personal honor is not ineligible for us; various negative features often associated with honor are not essential components of the concept, only features of certain historically contingent conceptions of that concept. Fourth, while personal honor isn't the same as morality, still honor isn't necessarily *im*moral; personal honor can be moral in some conceptions of this concept. Indeed, indeed, the very standards of honorability that we proposed in Chapter 5 to assess deviant honor codes and groups point towards moral honor as honor's best instantiation. Presumably some form of moral honor will be most attractive to us today. Fifth, as we argued earlier in this chapter, the concept of personal honor possesses certain attractive features: it overcomes various fruitless dichotomies; it connects deeply with the roots of self- and other-regard, with a person's sense of self and with her commitment to community; and it is a distinctive concept, non-consequentialist at its core and different from (though complementary to) other virtues so prized by moderns such as honesty, integrity and civility. These points together constitute a reasonably strong conceptual case for honor's contemporary salience.

To be sure, large problems remain. One would like to know, for example, how honor fits into the good life, a life that is good, all things considered, for the person who lives it. How important *is* honor among life's goods? How does the virtue of honor connect to other virtues — is it one among many, a controlling virtue, or even a meta-virtue? What is the psychology of honor — does its need for others' regard open one to darker dependencies? Exactly how does honor relate to fundamental human concerns such as morality and religion?

But practical concerns may be even more challenging: Are there in fact any honor groups today that are both eligible and desirable? Could one form such an honor group, if there were none to join? What are the necessary social and personal conditions, the opportunities as well as the obstacles, to creating honor groups today? I think that there are indeed desirable honor groups in our contemporary world, though they don't always use the word "honor" to name themselves. Some academic honor systems approach this status, but so do some other kinds of social experiments — religious orders, so-called "cults," realistically Utopian communes, and, perhaps surprisingly, some feminist communities.[20] It would be worth looking at such groups through the conceptual lens of this book. Better still, we might try creating such groups that appeal to us out of whatever social materials we find to hand. We might then discover that honor becomes a concept for us as we make it our own. There is nothing essential to the concept that prevents our doing so. That's why in the end honor's future for us is up to us.

---

[20] In her 2005 senior honors thesis at Washington and Lee University, "'The possibility of life between us': honor as a feminist ethical concept," Susan Somers has vividly depicted in terms of personal honor the N Street Village in Washington, DC, a women's collective that provides housing and other services for homeless women.

SELECTED BIBLIOGRAPHY

This list contains only those works mentioned in the text, and offers but a glimpse of the vast iceberg of writings on, about, of, for and against honor, from a very diverse range of professional, ideological and personal perspectives.

Aase, Tor, ed. 2002. *Tournaments of Power: Honor and Revenge in the Contemporary World.* Aldershot, England: Ashgate.

Abu-Lughod, Lila. 1986. *Veiled Sentiments: Honor and Poetry in a Bedouin Society.* Berkeley, CA: University of California Press.

Adams, Marilyn McCord. 1992. "Symbolic Value and the Problem of Evil: Honor and Shame," in *Interpretations in Religion*, Shlomo Biderman and Ben-Ami Scharfstein, eds. Leiden: E. J. Brill, 259–82.

Adamson, Christopher. 1998. "Tribute, Turf, Honor and the American Street Gang: Patterns of Continuity and Change since 1820," *Theoretical Criminology* 2, 1 (February), 57–84

Adkins, Arthur W. H. 1960. *Merit and Responsibility: A Study in Greek Values* Chicago, IL: University of Chicago Press.

Akers, Ronald Louis. 1973. *Deviant Behavior: A Social Learning Approach.* Belmont, CA: Wadsworth.

Anderson, Elijah. 1992. *Streetwise: Race, Class, and Change in an Urban Community.* Chicago, IL: University of Chicago Press.

———. 1994. "The Code of the Streets," *Atlantic Monthly* 5, 81–94.

———. 1999. *Code of the Street: Decency, Violence, and the Moral Life of the Inner City.* New York: W. W. Norton.

Anderson, John P. 2003. "Patriotic Liberalism," *Law and Philosophy* 22:6, 577–95.

Anderson, M. 1992. *Imposters in the Temple: American Intellectuals are Destroying our Universities.* New York: Simon & Schuster.

Anderson, Scott. 1999. "The Curse of Blood and Vengeance," *The New York Times Magazine* (December 26), 28–35, 44, 54, 56–7.

Aquinas, St. Thomas. *Summa Contra Gentiles* (Dominican Fathers translation). London: Burns Oates & Washbourne, n.d. III.1, 28, 63.

———. *Summa Theologiae* (Blackfriars translation). London: Eyre & Spottiswoode; New York: McGraw-Hill, 2a2a3: Vol. 39 (Qs 80–91) 1964, tr. Kevin D. O'Rourke.

Aristotle. 1985. *Nicomachean Ethics*, tr. Terence Irwin. Indianapolis, IN: Hackett.

Arnold, Peter J. 1997. *Sport, ethics and education.* London: Cassell.

Ashcroft, Jeffrey R. 1994. "*Honor imperii — des riches ere*: the idea of empire in Konrad's *Rolandslied*," in *German Narrative Literature of the Twelfth and Thirteenth Centuries: Studies Presented to Roy Wisbey on his Sixty-Fifth Birthday*, ed. Volker Honemann *et al.*(Tübingen: Niemeyer, 139–56.

Atkinson, Rob. 1995. "A Dissenter's Commentary on the Professionalism Crusade," 74 *Texas Law Review* 259.

Axinn, Sidney. "Honor, Patriotism, and Ultimate Loyalty" in. *Nuclear Weapons and the Future of Humanity* Avner Cohen, ed. Totowa, NJ: Rowman & AllanHeld, 273–88.

———. 1989. *A Moral Military*. Philadelphia, PA: Temple University Press.

Barber, Bernard. 1963. "Some Problems in the Sociology of the Professions," *Daedelus* 92 (Fall), 669–88; reprinted in Callahan, 1988.

Barth, Karl. 1961. *Church Dogmatics*, III/4. Edinburgh: T & T Clark, §56, "Freedom in Limitation," pp. 647–85.

Barton, Carlin A. 2001. *Roman Honor: The Fire in the Bones*. Berkeley, CA: University of California Press.

Basler, Roy P., ed. 1953. *The Collected Works of Abraham Lincoln*. New Brunswick, NJ: Rutgers University Press.

Bayles, Michael D. 1989. *Professional Ethics*, 2e. Belmont, CA: Wadsworth; reprinted in Callahan, 1988, 7–11.

Beatty, Joseph. 1992. "For Honor's Sake: Moral Education, Honor Systems, and the Informer-Rule," *Educational Theory*, 42/1 (Winter), 39–50.

Becker, Howard Saul. 1966. *Outsiders: Studies in the Sociology of Deviance*. New York: The Free Press.

Beckman, Svante. 1990. "Professionalization: Borderline Authority and Autonomy in Work," in Burrage & Torstendahl, eds., pp. 115–38.

Benedict, Ruth. 1946. *The Chrysanthemum and the Sword: Patterns of Japanese Culture*. Boston, MA: Houghton Mifflin.

Bennett, John B. 1998. *Collegial Professionalism: The Academy, Individualism, and the Common Good*. Phoenix, AZ: American Council on Education/Oryx Press.

———. 2003. *Academic Life: Hospitality, Ethics, and Spirituality*. Bolton, MA: Anker.

Bennett, Walter. 2001. *The Lawyer's Myth: Reviving Ideals in the Legal Profession*. Chicago, IL: University of Chicago Press.

———. 2002. *The Lawyer's Myth: Reviving Ideals in the Legal Profession*. Chicago. IL: University of Chicago Press.

Benson, C. David. 1992. "The Lost Honor of Sir Gawain," in *De Gustibus: Essays for Alain Renoir*, John Miles Foley, J. Chris Womack and Whitney A. Womack, eds. NY: Garland, 30–9.

Berger, Peter. 1970. "On the Obsolescence of the Concept of Honour," *European Journal of Sociology*, xi, 339–47, reprinted in *The British Journal of Sociology*, xi (1970), 149–58.

Best, Geoffrey. 1982. *Honour Among Men and Nations: Transformations of an Idea*. Toronto: Toronto University Press.

Best, Joel. 2004. *Deviance: Career of a Concept*. Belmont, CA: Wadsworth/Thomson Learning.

Black-Michaud, J. 1975. *Cohesive Force: Feud in the Mediterranean and the Middle East*. Oxford: Basil Blackwell.

Blok, Anton. 1974. *The Mafia of a Sicilian Village*, 1860-1960. New York: HarperCollins.

———.2001. *Honour and Violence*. Cambridge: Polity; Malden, MA: Blackwell.

Boehm, Christopher. 1984. *Blood Revenge The Anthropology Of Feuding In Montenegro And Other Tribal Societies*. Philadelphia, PA: University of Pennsylvania Press.

Bonanno, Bill. 2000. *Bound by Honor: A Mafioso's Story*. New York: St. Martin's Press.

Bonnano, Joseph (with Sergia Lalli). 1983. *A Man of Honour: The Autobiography of a Godfather*. London: Andre Deutsch.

Borgatta, Edgar F. and Montgomery, Rhonda J. V., eds. 2000. *Encyclopedia of Sociology*. Detroit, MI: Macmillan Reference.

Braudy, Leo. 2003. *From Chivalry to Terrorism: War and the Changing Nature of Masculinity*. New York: Alfred A. Knopf.

Bryant, Clifton D., ed. 1990. *Deviant Behavior: Readings in the Sociology of Norm Violations*. New York: Hemisphere.

Bryant, Clifton D. and Peck, Dennis L., eds. 2007. *21st Century Sociology: A Reference Handbook*. Thousand Oaks, CA: Sage Publications.

Bridges, George F. and Desmond, Scott A. 2000. "Deviance Theories," in Borgatta and Rhonda, eds.

Burke, Michael D. and Roberts, Terence J. 1997. "Drugs in Sport: An Issue of Morality or Sentimentality?" *Journal of the Philosophy of Sport* XXIV: 99–113.

Burlingame, Michael. 1994. *The Inner World of Abraham Lincoln*. Urbana, IL: University of Illinois Press.

Burrage, Michael and Torstendahl, Rolf, eds. 1990. *Professions in Theory and History: Rethinking the Study of the Professions*. London: Sage Publications.

Burton, Steven J., ed. 2000. *The Path of the Law and Its Influence: The Legacy of Oliver Wendell Holmes, Jr.* Cambridge: Cambridge University Press.

Butcher, Robert, and Schneider, Angela. 2001. "Fair Play as Respect for the Game," in Morgan, Meier and Schneider, eds., 2001, 21–48.

Cahill, Stephanie Francis. 2000. "Motion Warriors," *ABA Journal* 88:28f.

Cairns, Douglas L. 1993. *Aidôs: The Psychology and Ethics of Honour and Shame in Ancient Greek Literature*. Oxford: Clarendon.

Calhoun, Craig, Chris and Rojek, Bryan, Turner, eds. 2005. *The Sage Handbook of Sociology*. London: Sage.

Callahan, Joan C., ed. 1988. *Ethical Issues in Professional Life*. New York: Oxford University Press.

Callan, Eamonn. 2006. "Love, Idolatry, and Patriotism," *Social Theory and Practice* 32:4, 525–46.

Campbell, Barth L. 1998. *Honor, Shame, and the Rhetoric of 1 Peter*. Atlanta: Scholars Press.

Campbell, J. K. 1964. *Honour, Family, and Patronage: A Study of Institutions and Moral Values in a Greek Mountain Community*. Oxford: Oxford University Press.

Carlin, Jerome E. 1966. *Lawyers' Ethics: A Survey of the New York Bar*. New York: Russell Sage Foundation.

Carnovan, Margaret. 2000. "Patriotism is not Enough," *British Journal of Political Science* 30, 413–32.

Carter, Stephen L. 1996. *Integrity*. New York: Basic Books.

———. 1998. *Civility: Manners, Morals, and the Etiquette of Democracy*. New York: Basic Books.

Cast, David J. 1977. "Liberty, Virtue, Honor: A Comment on the Position of the Visual Arts in the Renaissance," *Yale Italian Studies*, 1:4, 371–97.

Chereso, C. 1960. *The Virtue of Honor and Beauty according to St. Thomas Aquinas*. River Forest, IL: Aquinas Library.

Christoph, Siegfried. 1982. "Conflict Resolution and the Concept of Honor in Wolfram's *Parzival, Colloquia Germanica* 15:1–2, 32–45.

———. 1995. "Honor, Shame and Gender," in *Arthurian Romance and Gender: Selected Proceedings of the XVIIth International Arthurian Congress*, ed. Friedrich Wolfzettle. Amsterdam: Rodopi, 26–33.

Clark, Ian. 1988. *Waging War: A Philosophical Introduction*. New York: Oxford University Press.

Gjeçov, Shtjefën, ed., and Fox, L., trans. 1989. *The Code of Lekë Dukagjini*. 1989. New York: Gjonlekaj Publishing.

Cohen, Albert K. 1966. *Deviance and Control*. Englewood Cliffs, NJ: Prentice-Hall.

Cohen, Sheldon M. 1989. *Arms and Judgment: Law, Morality, and the Conduct of War in the Twentieth Century*. Boulder, CO: Westview.

Collette, Carolyn P. 1994. "Criseyde's Honor: Interiority and Public Identity in Chaucer's Courtly Romance," in *Literary Aspects of Courtly Culture*, selected papers from the Seventh Triennial Congress of the International Courtly Literature Society. Cambridge: D. S. Brewer, 47–55.

Collins, Randall. 1990. "Market Closure and the Conflict Theory of the Professions," in Burrage and Torstendahl, eds., pp. 24–43.

Cordner, Christopher. 1994. "Aristotelian Virtue and Its Limitations," *Philosophy* 69:269 (July), 291–316.

———. 1997. "Honour, Community, and Ethical Inwardness," *Philosophy* 72 (July), 401–15.

Council, Norman. 1973. *When Honor's at the Stake: Ideas of Honour in Shakespeare*. New York: Harper and Row.

Crisp, Roger. 1996. *How Should One Live? Essays on the Virtues*. New York: Oxford University Press.

Crisp, Roger, and Michael Slote. 1997. *Virtue Ethics*. Oxford: Oxford University Press.

Curzer, Howard J. 1990. "A Great Philosopher's Not So Great Account of Great Virtue: Aristotle's Treatment of 'Greatness of Soul,'" *Canadian Journal of Philosophy* 20:4 (December), 517–38.

———. 1991. "Aristotle's Much Maligned *Megalopsychos*," *Australasian Journal of Philosophy* 69:2 (June), 131–51.

Dancy, Jonathan. 2004. *Ethics Without Principle*. New York: Oxford University Press.

Darwall, Stephen, ed. 2003. *Virtue Ethics*. Malden, MA: Blackwell.

Davis, Michael. 1999. "Is Higher Education a Prerequisite of Profession?" *International Journal of Applied Philosophy*, 13:139–48.

DeSilva, David A. 1995. *Despising Shame: Honor Discourse and Community Maintenance in the Epistle to the Hebrews*. Atlanta: Scholars Press.

Dewey, Horace W. 1968. "Old Muscovite Concepts of Injured Honor (*Beschestie*)," *Slavic Review* 27:4, 594–603.

Dixon, Nicholas. 2001. "Rorty, Performance-Enhancing Drugs, and Changes in Sport," *Journal of the Philosophy of Sport* XXVIII: 78–88.

Dobel, J. Patrick. 1999. *Public Integrity*. Baltimore, MD: Johns Hopkins University Press.

Dodge, David L. 1990. "The Overnegativized Conceptualization of Deviance: A Programmatic Exploration," Reading 3 in Bryant, 1990, pp. 77–97.

Dombrowski, Daniel. 1992. "On Why Patriotism is not a Virtue," *International Journal of Applied Philosophy* 7:1, 1–4.

Donald, David Herbert. 1995. *Lincoln*. New York: Touchstone.

Downes, David. 1999. "Crime and Deviance," Ch. 11 in *Sociology: Issues and Debates*, Steve Taylor, ed. London: Macmillan, pp. 231–52.

Downes, David, and Rock, Paul. 1995. *Understanding Deviance: A Guide to the Sociology of Crime and Rule-Breaking*, 2e rev. Oxford: Clarendon [1e 1982].

Dubish, Jill. 1986. *Gender and Power in Rural Greece*. Princeton, NJ: Princeton University Press.

Dupont, Florence. 1989. *Daily Life in Ancient Rome*. Oxford, NJ: Blackwell.

Dutton, Brian. 1979. "The Semantics of Honor," *Revista Canadiense de Estudios Hispánicos*, 4:1, 1–17.

Elfstrom, Gerald, and Fotion, Nicholas. 1986. *Military Ethics: Guidelines for Peace and War*. Boston, MA: Routledge and Kegan Paul.

Elliott, John H. 1995. "Disgraced Yet Graced: The Gospel According to 1 Peter in the Key of Honor and Shame," *Biblical Theology Bulletin* 25:166–78.

Elliott, Philip. 1972. *The Sociology of the Professions*. New York: Herder and Herder.

Emerson, Ralph Waldo. 1898. *The Conduct of Life*, Vol. IV of Riverside Edition of Emerson's Complete Works. London: Routledge.

Engeman, Thomas S. n.d. "Homeric Honor and Thucydidean Necessity," *Interpretation* 4, 65–78.

Fenster, Thelma, and Daniel Lord Smail, eds. 2003. *Fama: The Politics of Talk and Reputation in Medieval Europe*. Ithaca, NY: Cornell University Press.

Fischer, David Hackett. 1989. *Albion's Seed: British Folkways in America*. New York: Oxford University Press.

Fisher, N. R. E. 1979. *Hybris: A Study in the Values of Honour and Shame in Ancient Greece*. London: Aris and Phillips.

Fletcher, George P. 1993. *Loyalty: An Essay on the Morality of Relationships*. New York: Oxford University Press.

Fogarty, Robert S. 1990. *All Things New: American Communes and Utopian Movements, 1860–1914*. Chicago, IL: University of Chicago Press.

Foot, Philippa. 1978. *Virtues and Vices, and Other Essays in Moral Philosophy*. Oxford: Blackwell.

Fossum, Merle A. and Mason, Marilyn J. 1986. *Facing Shame: Families in Recovery*. New York: W. W. Norton.

Fotion, Nicholas G. 1990. *Military Ethics: Looking Toward the Future*. Stanford, CA: Hoover Institution Press.

Fraleigh, S. 1984. *Right Actions in Sport: Ethics for Contestants*. Champaign, IL: Human Kinetics.

Frankfurt, Harry. 2000. "The Dear Self," *Philosophers Imprint* 1:0 (January 2001).

Freedman, Monroe. 1966. "Professional Responsibility of the Criminal Defense Lawyer: The Three Hardest Questions," *Michigan Law Review* 64: 1469–84.

———. 1975. *Lawyers' Ethics in an Adversary System*. Indianapolis, IN: Bobbs-Merrill.

———. 1990. *Understanding Lawyers' Ethics*. New York: Matthew Bender.

Freeman, Joanne B. 2001. *Affairs of Honor: National Politics in the New Republic*. New Haven, CT: Yale University Press.

Freidson, Eliot. 1986. *Professional Powers: A Study of the Institutionalization of Formal Knowledge*. Chicago, IL: University of Chicago Press.

———. 1991. "Nourishing Professionalism," in Pelligrino, Veatch and Langam, eds., 193–215.

———. 1994. *Professionalism Reborn: Theory, Prophecy, and Policy*. Chicago, IL: University of Chicago Press.

———. 2001. *Professionalism, The Third Logic: On the Practice of Knowledge*. Chicago, IL: University of Chicago Press.

French, Peter. 1997. *Cowboy Metaphysics: Ethics and Death in Westerns*. Lanham MD: Lanhan MD: Rowman & Littlefield.

French, Shannon. 2003. *The Code of the Warrior: Exploring Warrior Values Past and Present*. Rowman & Littlefield.

Frevert, Ute. 1995. *Men of Honour: A Social and Cultural History of the Duel*, tr. Anthony Williams. Cambridge: Polity.

Fried, Charles. 1976. "The Lawyer as Friend in the Moral Foundations of the Lawyer-Client Relation," *Yale Law Journal* 85:8 (July), 1060–89.

Fussell, Paul. 1989. *Wartime: Understanding and Behavior in the Second World War*. New York: Oxford University Press.

Gabriel, Richard A. 1982. *To Serve with Honor: A Treatise on Military Ethics and the Way of the Soldier*. Westport: Greenwood.

Gaffney, James. 1993. "Patriotism: Virtue or Vice?" *Philosophy and Theology* 8:2, 129–48.

Galligan, Francis B. 1979. *Military Professionalism and Ethics*. Newport, RI: Naval War College Press.

Gambetta, Diego. 1988. *Trust: Making and Breaking Cooperative Relations*. New York: Blackwell.

Gilmore, David D., ed. 1987. *Honor and Shame and the Unity of the Mediterranean*. Washington, DC: American Anthropological Association, Special Publication #22.

Goldman, Alan H. 1980. *The Moral Foundations of Professional Ethics*. Totowa, NJ: Rowman and Littlefield.

Goldstein, Joshua S. 2001. *War and Gender: How Gender Shapes the War System and Vice Versa.* Cambridge: Cambridge University Press.

Goode, Erich. 1991. "Positive Deviance: A Viable Concept?" *Deviant Behavior* 12, 289–309.

———. 2007. "Deviance," in Ritzer, ed., III: 1075–82.

Gottfriedson, Michael R. and Travis Hirschi. 1990. *A General Theory of Crime.* Stanford, CA: Stanford University Press.

Gough, Russell Wayne. 1997. *Character Is Everything: Promoting Ethical Excellence in Sports.* Fort Worth, TX: Harcourt Brace.

Gray, J. Glen. *The Warriors.* 1998 [1959]. Lincoln, NE: University of Nebraska Bison Books.

Greenberg, Kenneth S. 1985. *Masters and Statesmen: The Political Culture of American Slavery.* Baltimore, MD: Johns Hopkins University Press.

———. 1996. *Honor and Slavery.* Princeton, NJ: Princeton, University Press.

Haas, Jonathan, ed. 1990. *The Anthropology of War.* Cambridge: Cambridge University Press.

Haber, Samuel. 1991. *The Quest for Authority and Honor in the American Professions, 1750–1900.* Chicago, IL: University of Chicago Press.

Habermas, Jürgen. 2001. "Constitutional Democracy: A Paradoxical Union of Contradictory Principles?" *Political Theory* 29:6, 766–81.

Halfon, Mark S. 1989. *Integrity: A Philosophical Inquiry.* Philadelphia, PA: Temple University Press.

Hanson, K. C. 1996. "How Honorable! How Shameful! A Cultural Analysis of Matthew's Makarisms and Reproaches," *Semeia* 68, 81–112.

Harré, Rom. 1990. "Embarrassment: A Conceptual Analysis," in *Shyness and Embarrassment.* ed. W. R. Crozier. Cambridge: Cambridge University Press, 181–204.

Hartle, Anthony E. 1989. *Moral Issues in Military Decision Making.* Lawrence, KA: University of Kansas Press.

Hatch, Nathan D. 1988. *The Professions in American history.* Notre Dame, IN: University of Notre Dame Press.

Hazard, Geoffrey. 1991. "The Future of Legal Ethics." *Yale Law Review* 1239.

Heermance, Edgar L. 1924. *Codes of Ethics: A Handbook.* Burlington, VT: Free Press.

Heidsieck, François. 1961. "Honor and Nobility of Soul: Descartes and Sartre," *International Philosophical Quarterly* 1 (December), 569–92.

Henberg, Marvin. 1990. *Retribution: Evil for Evil in Ethics, Law, and Literature.* Philadelphia, PA: Temple University Press.

Hirsi Ali, Ayaan. 2007. *Infidel.* New York: Free Press.

Hobbes, Thomas. 1968. *Leviathan,* C. B. Macpherson, ed. Harmondsworth: Penguin.

Hobbs, T. R. 1997. "Reflections on Honor, Shame, and Covenant Relations," *Journal of Biblical Literature* (Fall), 116:3, 501.

Holdaway, Simon, and Paul, Rock, eds. 1998. *Thinking about Criminology.* London, University College London Press.

Holmes, Robert L. 1989. *On War and Morality.* Princeton, NJ: Princeton University Press.

Horowitz, Ruth. 1982. "Adult Delinquent Gangs in a Chicano Community: Masked Intimacy and Marginality," *Urban Life* 11:1 (April), 3–26.

———. 1983. *Honor and the American Dream: Culture and Identity in a Chicano Community.* Brunswick, NJ: Rutgers University Press.

———. 1987. "Community Tolerance of Gang Violence," *Social Problems* 34:5 (December), 437–50.

Hume, David. 1994. *Political Essays,* Knud Haakonssen, ed. Cambridge: Cambridge University Press.

Hurst III, G. Cameron. 1990. "Death, Honor, and Loyalty: The Bushido Ideal." *Philosophy East and West,* 40/4 (October), 511–27.

Ignatieff, Michael. 1997. *The Warrior's Honor: Ethnic War and the Modern Conscience.* New York: Henry Holt.

Ingram, Attracta. 1996. "Constitutional Patriotism," *Philosophy and Social Criticism* 22:6, 1–18; reprinted in Primoratz, ed., 2002.

Jackson, J. A., ed. 1970. *Professions and Professionalization*. London: Cambridge University Press.

James, Mervyn. 1978. "English Politics and the Concept of Honour, 1485–1642," *Past and Present* Supplement 3, 1–92.

James, William. 1975 [1907]. *Pragmatism: a New Name for Some Old Ways of Thinking*. The Works of William James. Cambridge, MA: Harvard University Press.

Jankowski, Mártin Sánchez. 1991. *Islands in the Street: Gangs and American Urban Society*. Berkeley, CA: University of California Press.

Jenkins, Mark P. 2006. *Bernard Williams*. Montreal: McGill-Queens University Press.

Jenkins, Richard. 1998. "From Criminology to Anthropology? Identity, Morality, and Normality in the Social Construction of Deviance," in Holdaway and Rock, eds., 133–60.

Jensen, Gary F. 2007. "The Sociology of Deviance," in Bryant and Peck, eds., I: 370–9.

Johnson, James Turner. 1984. *Can Modern War Be Just?* New Haven, CT: Yale University Press.

Johnson, Lyman L. and Lipsett-Rivera, Sonya, eds. 1998. *The Faces of Honor; Sex, Shame, and Violence in Colonial Latin America*. Albuquerque, NM: University of New Mexico Press.

Kagan, Donald. 1995. *On the Origins of War and the Preservation of Peace*. New York: Doubleday.

Kalinke, Marianne E. 1973. "Honor: the Motivating Principle of the *Erex Saga*," *Scandinavian Studies* 45:2, 135–43.

Kant, Immanuel. 1948. *The Moral Law: Kant's Groundwork of the Metaphysics of Morals*, tr. H. J. Paton. London: Hutchinson University Library.

———. 1996. *The Metaphysics of Morals*, tr. Mary Gregor. Cambridge: Cambridge University Press.

Kanter, Rosabeth Moss. 1972. *Commitment and Community: Communes and Utopias in Sociological Perspective*. Cambridge, MA: Harvard University Press.

Kateb, George. 2000. "Is Patriotism a Mistake?," *Social Research* 67:4, 910–24.

Katz, Jack. 1988. *The Seduction of Crime: Moral and Sensual Attractions in Doing Evil*. New York: Basic Books.

Keating, James. 1964. "Sportsmanship as a Moral Category", *Ethics* LXXV (Oct.), 25–35; reprinted in Morgan and Meier, eds., 1988, 241–50.

Keegan, John. 1978 [1976]. *The Face of Battle: A Study of Agincourt, Waterloo and the Somme*. Harmondsworth: Penguin.

Keegan, John, and Holmes, Richard. 1985. *Soldiers: A History of Men in Battle*. London: Hamish Hamilton.

Keen, M. H. 1965. *The Laws of War in the Late Middle Ages*. London: Routledge and Kegan Paul.

Keller, Simon. 2007. *The Limits of Loyalty*. Cambridge: Cambridge University Press.

Kennedy, Roger G. 2000. *Burr, Hamilton, and Jefferson: A Study in Character*. Oxford: Oxford University Press.

Kephart, William M. and W. W. Zellner. 1994. *Extraordinary Groups: An Examination of Unconventional Life-Styles*. New York: St. Martin's Press.

Khouri, Norma. 2003. *Honor Lost: Love and death in Modern-Day Jordan*. New York: Atria.

Kiernan, V. G. 1988. *The Duel in European History: Honour and the Rein of Aristocracy*. New York: Oxford University Press.

Kimball, Bruce A. 1992. *The "True Professional Ideal" in America: A History*. Cambridge, MA: Blackwell.

Kitchen, Martin. 1968. *The German Officer Corps 1890–1914*. Oxford: Clarendon.

Kleinig, John. 2008. Review of Simon Keller, *The Limits of Loyalty*, in *Notre Dame Philosophical Reviews*, April 29.

Koehn, Daryl. 1994. *The Ground of Professional Ethics*. London: Routledge.

Kollman, Nancy Shields. 1999. *By Honor Bound: State and Society in Early Modern Russia*. Ithaca, NY: Cornell University Press.

Krause, Elliott A. 1996. *Death of the Guilds: Professions, States, and the Advance of Capitalism, 1930 to the Present.* New Haven, CT: Yale University Press.

Krause, Sharon. 2002. *Liberalism with Honor.* Cambridge, MA: Harvard University Press.

Kronman, Anthony. 1993. *The Lost Lawyer: Failing Ideals of the Legal Profession.* Cambridge, MA: Harvard University Press.

Krueger, Roberta L. 1985. "Love, Honor and the Exchange of Women in *Yvain*: Some Remarks on the Female Reader," *Romance Notes* 25:3, 302–17.

Kubrin, Charis E., Thomas D. Stucky, and Marvin D. Krohn, eds. 2009. *Researching Theories of Crime and Deviance.* New York: Oxford University Press.

Kuehn, Thomas J. 1980. "Honor and Conflict in a Fifteenth-Century Florentine Family," *Ricerche storiche* 10:2, 287–310.

Kultgen, John. 1988. *Ethics and Professionalism.* Philadelphia, PA: University of Pennsylvania Press.

Kumar, Krishan. 1990. "Utopian Thought and Communal Practice: Robert Owen and the Owenite Communities," *Theory and Society* 19/1 (February), 1–35.

Kuo, Simone. 1996. *Shao-Lin Chuan: The Rhythm and Power of Tan-Tui.* Berkeley, CA: North Atlantic Books.

Landon, Donald D. 1990. *Country Lawyers: The Impact of Context on Professional Practice.* New York: Praeger.

Laniak, Timothy S. 1998. *Shame and Honor in the Book of Esther* (Society of Biblical Literature).

Larson, Magali Sarfatti. 1977. *The Rise of Professionalism.* Berkeley, CA: University of California Press.

Lehman, Craig K. 1988. "Can Cheaters Play the Game?" in Morgan and Meier, 283–87.

Lendon, J. E. 1997. *Empire of Honor: The Art of Government in the Roman World.* Oxford Clarendon.

Levitas, Ruth. 1990. *The Concept of Utopia.* London: Philip Allan.

Liazos, Alex. 1972. "Nuts, Sluts, and Perverts: The Poverty of the Sociology of Deviance," *Social Problems* 20:103–20.

Limbrick, Elaine. 1981. "Glory, Fame and Honour in the 'Essais' of Montaigne," *Review of the University of Ottawa* 51 (October-December), 695–704.

Liska, Allen E. 1981. *Perspectives on Deviance.* Englewood, NJ: Prentice-Hall.

Little, Craig B. 1989. *Deviance and Control: Theory, Research, and Social Policy.* Itasca, IL: F. E. Peacock Publishers.

Lloyd-Jones, Hugh. 1990. "Honour and Shame in Ancient Greek Culture," in *Greek Comedy, Hellenistic Literature, Greek Religion.* Oxford: Clarendon Press.

Lofland, John. 1969. *Deviance and Identity.* Englewood Cliffs, NJ: Prentice-Hall.

Luban, David. 1988. *Lawyers and Justice: An Ethical Study.* Princeton, NJ: Princeton University Press.

Lumkin, Angela, Stoll, Sharon Kay, and Beller, Jennifer M. 1994. *Sport Ethics: Applications for Fair Play.* St. Louis, MO: Mosby; [2e, 1999 WCB/McGraw-Hill.]

MacIntyre, Alasdair. 1984a. *After Virtue: a Study in Moral Theory*, 2e. Notre Dame, IN: University of Notre Dame Press [1e 1981, London: Duckworth].

———. 1984b. *Is Patriotism a Virtue?* (Lindley Lecture). Lawrence, KS: University of Kansas Press. [Reprinted in Primoratz, ed., 2002.]

———. 1988. *Whose Justice? Which Rationality?* Notre Dame, IN: University of Notre Dame Press.

MacLeod, Jay. 1995. *Ain't No Makin' It.* Boulder, CO: Westview.

McCabe, David. 1997. "Patriotic Gore, Again," *Southern Journal of Philosophy* 35:2, 203–23. [Reprinted in Primoratz, ed., 2002.]

McCall, Nathan. 1994. *Makes Me Wanna Holler: A Young Man in America.* New York: Random House.

McConnell, Terrance. 1993. *Gratitude.* Philadelphia, PA: Temple University Press.

McGrath, James, and Anderson, Gustaf E., III. 1993. "Recent Work on the American

Professional Military Ethic: An Introduction and Survey," *American Philosophical Quarterly* 30 (July), 187–208.

McIntosh, Peter C. 1979. *Fair play: Ethics in Sport and Education.* London: Heinemann.

McNamara, Peter, ed. 1999. *The Noblest Minds: Fame, Honor, and the American Founding.* Lanham, MD: Rowman & Littlefield.

McNamee, Maurice Basil. 1960. *Honor and the Epic Hero: A Study of the Shifting Concept of Magnanimity in Philosophy and Epic Poetry.* New York: Holt.

Malina, Bruce J. 1993. *The New Testament World: Insights from Cultural Anthropology*, 2e. Louisville, KY: Westminster/John Knox Press.

Malina, Bruce J. and Neyrey, Jerome H. 1991. "Honor and Shame in Luke-Acts: Pivotal Values of the Mediterranean World," in Jerome H. Neyrey, ed., *The Social World of Luke-Acts: Models for Interpretation.* Peabody, MA: Hendrickson, 25–65.

Mandrell, James. 1992. *Don Juan and the Point of Honor: Seduction, Patriarchal Society, and Literary Tradition.* University Park, PA: Pennsylvania State University Press.

Maraniss, David. 1999 *When Pride Still Mattered: A Life of Vince Lombardi.* New York: Simon & Schuster.

Margalit, Avishai. 1996. *The Decent Society.* Cambridge, MA: Harvard University Press.

Markell, Patchen. 2000. "Making Affect Safe for Democracy? On 'Constitutional Patriotism,'" *Political Theory* 28:1, 38–63.

Markovits, Daniel. 2008. *A Modern Legal Ethics: Adversary Advocacy in a Democratic Age.* Princeton, NJ: Princeton University Press.

Marshall, S. L. A. 1947. *Men Against Fire: The Problem of Battle Command in Future Wars.* New York: William Morrow.

Mauss, Marcel. 1967. *The Gift: Forms and Functions of Exchange in Archaic Societies*, tr. Ian Cunnison. New York: W. Norton.

Metzer, Yehuda. 1975. *Concepts of Just War.* Leyden: A. W. Sijthoff.

Meyer, Kathleen J. 1986. "The Ambiguity of Honor in Gottfried's *Tristan*: lines 17694–17769," *Neophilologus* 70:3, 406–15.

Mickel, Emmanuel J., Jr. 1975. "The Theme of Honor in Chrétien's *Lancelot*," *Zeitschrift für romanische Philologie*, 91:3–4, 243–72.

Miller, William Ian. 1990 *Bloodtaking and Peacemaking: Feud, Law, and Society in Saga Iceland.* Chicago, IL: University of Chicago Press.

———. 1993. *Humiliation: and Other Essays on Honor, Social Discomfort, and Violence.* Ithaca, New York: Cornell University Press.

———. 1997. *The Anatomy of Disgust.* Cambridge, MA: Harvard University Press.

Milne, A. A. 1934. *Peace with Honour.* New York: E. P. Dutton.

Moore, Wilbert E., with Gerald W. Rosenblum. 1970. *The Professions: Roles and Rules.* NY: Russell Sage Foundation.

Morgan, William J, and Meier, Klaus V., eds. 1988. *Philosophic Inquiry in Sport.* Champaign, IL: Human Kinetics Publishers.

Moxnes, Halvor. 1996. "Honor and Shame," in Richard L. Rohrbaugh, ed., *The Social Sciences and New Testament Interpretation*, 19–40. Peabody, MA: Hendrickson.

Müller, Jan-Werner. 2007. *Constitutional Patriotism.* Princeton, NJ: Princeton University Press.

Nathanson, Stephen. 1988. "In Defense of 'Moderate Patriotism'," *Ethics* 99:3 (1988/89), 535–52 [Reprinted in Primoratz, ed., 2002.]

———. 1993. *Patriotism, Morality, and Peace.* Lanham, MD: Rowman & Littlefield.

Nelson, Robert L., Trubek, David M., Solomon, Rayman L., eds. 1992. *Lawyers' Ideals/Lawyers' Practices: Transformations in the American Legal Profession.* Ithaca, NY: Cornell University Press.

Neu, Jerome. 2008. *Sticks and Stones: The Philosophy of Insult.* New York: Oxford University Press.

Neuschel, Kirsten B. 1989. *Word of Honor: Interpreting Noble Culture in Sixteenth-Century France.* Ithaca, NY: Cornell University Press.

Neyrey, Jerome. 1998. *Honor and Shame in the Gospel of Matthew.* Louisville, KY: Westminster John Knox Press.

———. 1999. *The Social World of Luke-Acts.* Peabody, MA: Hendrickson Publishers, ed.

Nisbett, Richard E. and Cohen, Dov, 1996. *Culture of Honor: The Psychology of Violence in the South.* Boulder, CO: Westview.

Nitobe, Inazo. 1907. *Bushido: The Soul of Japan.* New York: G. P. Putnam's Sons.

Nozick, Robert. 1981. *Philosophical Explanations.* Cambridge, MA: Harvard University Press.

Nussbaum, Martha C., with respondents, ed. Joshua Cohen. 1996. *For Love of Country: Debating the Limits of Patriotism.* Boston, MA: Beacon.

Nye, Robert A. 1993. *Masculinity and Male Codes of Honor in Modern France.* New York: Oxford University Press.

Oates, Stephen B. 1984. *Abraham Lincoln: The Man Behind the Myth.* New York: Harper and Row.

———. 1994. *With Malice Toward None: A Life of Abraham Lincoln.* New York: HarperPerennial.

Offer, Avner. 1995. "Going to War in 1914: A Matter of Honor?" *Politics and Society,* 23 (June), 213–41.

Oldenquist, Andrew. 1982. "Loyalties," *Journal of Philosophy* 79:4, 173–93; [Reprinted in Primoratz, ed. 2002.]

O'Neill, Barry. 1999. *Honor, Symbols, and War.* Ann Arbor, MI: University of Michigan Press.

Paskins, Barrie, and Dockrill, Michael. 1979. *The Ethics of War.* Minneapolis, MN: University of Minnesota Press.

Patterson, Orlando. 1982. *Slavery and Social Death: A Comparative Study.* Cambridge, MA: Harvard University Press.

Pearson, Kathleen M. 1988. "Deception, Sportsmanship, and Ethics," in Morgan and Meier, eds., 1988, 263–5.

Pelligrino, Edmund D., Veatch, Robert M., and Langan, John P., eds. 1991. *Ethics, Trust, and the Professions: Philosophical and Cultural Aspects.* Washington, DC: Georgetown University Press.

Peltonen, Makku. 2003. *The Duel in Modern England: Civility, Politeness and Honour.* Cambridge: Cambridge University Press.

Peristiany, Jean G., ed. 1965. *Honor and Shame: The Values of Mediterranean Society.* London: Wiedenfeld and Nicholson.

Peristiany, J. G. and Pitt-Rivers, Julian, eds. 1992. *Honor and Grace in Anthropology.* Cambridge: Cambridge University Press.

Philp, Mark. 2007. *Political Conduct.* Cambridge, MA: Harvard University Press.

Pitt-Rivers, Julian. 1968. "Honor," *International Encyclopedia of the Social Sciences,* ed. David Sills, 503–8.

Primoratz, Igor, ed. 2002. *Patriotism.* Amherst, NY: Humanity Books.

Putnam, Daniel. 1995. "In Defence of Aristotelian Honour," *Philosophy* 70 (April), 286–8.

Rawls, John. 1971. *A Theory of Justice.* Cambridge, MA: Belknap.

———. 1999. *The Law of Peoples.* Cambridge, MA: Harvard University Press.

———. 2001. *Justice as Fairness: A Restatement,* ed. Erin Kelly. Cambridge, MA: Belknap.

———. 2005. *Political Liberalism* (expanded ed.). New York: Columbia University Press.

Readings, B. 1996. *The University in Ruins.* Cambridge, MA: Harvard University Press.

Reddy, William M. 1997. *The Invisible Code: Honor and Sentiment in Postrevolutionary France 1814–1848.* Berkeley, CA: University of California Press.

Redfield, James M. 1975. *Nature and Culture in the Iliad: The Tragedy of Hector.* Chicago, IL: University of Chicago Press.

Richards, Norvin. 1992. *Humility.* Philadelphia, PA: Temple University Press.

Ritzer, George, ed. 2007. *The Blackwell Encyclopedia of Sociology.* Malden, MA: Blackwell Publishing.

Robin, Ron. 1995. *Scandals & Scoundrels: Seven Cases that Shook the Academy.* Berkeley, CA: University of California Press.

Rodriguez, Luis J. 1993. *Always Running: La Vida Loca, Gang Days in L.A.* Willimantic, CT: Curbstone Press.

Rosen, Bernard. 1987. "Honor and Honor Codes," *Teaching Philosophy* 10 (March), 37–48.

Rosenberg, D. 1993. "Sportsmanship Reconsidered," *International Journal of Physical Education* 30(2), 15-23.

Rudd, Andy. 1998. "Sport's Perceived Ability to Build Character," PhD dissertation in Education in College of Graduate Studies, University of Idaho.

Sagarin, Edward. 1975. *Deviants and Deviance: An Introduction to the Study of Disvalued People and Behavior.* New York: Praeger.

————.1990. "Positive Deviance: An Oxymoron," Reading 4 in Bryant, 1990, 98–111.

Schaar, John. 1981. "The Case for Patriotism," in *Legitimacy in the Modern State.* Piscataway, NJ: Transaction Publishers, 285–311.

————. 2002. "The Case for Covenanted Patriotism," in Primoratz, ed., 2002.

Schleiermacher, Friedrich. 1967. *Christmas Eve: Dialogue on the Incarnation,* tr. Terence N. Tice. Richmond, VA: John Knox Press.

Schneider, Jane. 1971. "Of Vigilance and Virgins: Honor, Shame and Access to Resources in Mediterranean Societies," *Ethnology* 10:1–24.

Schneider, Johannes. 1972. s.v. '*timê*' in Gerard Kittel and Gerard Friedrich, eds., Theological Dictionary of the New Testament. Grand Rapids, MI: Eerdmans, 8:169-80.

Schneider, Peter. 1969. "Honor and Conflict in a Sicilian Town," *Anthropological Quarterly* 42:130–54.

Schur, Edwin M. 1971. *Labeling Deviant Behavior: Its Sociological Implications.* New York: Harper and Row.

————. 1980. *The Politics of Deviance: Stigma Contests and the Uses of Power.* Englewood Cliffs, NJ: Prentice-Hall.

Sedgwick, Eve Kosofsky and Frank, Adam. 1995. *Shame and its Sisters: A Silvan Tomkins Reader.* Durham, NC: Duke University Press.

Sessions, William Lad. 2004. "Sportsmanship as Honor," *Journal of the Philosophy of Sport,* XXXI.

————. 2007. "Honor and God," *The Journal of Religion,* 206–24.

Shabani, Omid A. Payrow. 2002. "Who's Afraid of Constitutional Patriotism? The Binding Source of Citizenship in Constitutional States," *Social Theory and Practice* 28:3, 419–43.

Shaffer, Thomas L. 1985. *American Legal Ethics.* New York: Matthew Bender.

————. 1987. *Faith and the Professions.* Provo, UT: Brigham Young University Press.

Shakur, Sanyika, a.k.a. Monster Kody Scott. 1993. *Monster: The Autobiography of an L.A. Gang Member.* New York: The Atlantic Monthly Press.

Shapin, Steven. 1994. *A Social History of Truth: Civility and Science in Seventeenth-Century England.* Chicago, IL: University of Chicago Press.

Sharp, Gene. 1973. *The Politics of Nonviolent Action.* Boston, MA: Porter Sargent.

————. 1985. *National Security through Civilian-Based Defense.* Omaha, NE.: Association for Transarmament Studies.

Shay, Jonathan. 1994. *Achilles in Vietnam: Combat Trauma and the Undoing of Character.* New York: Atheneum.

Sherman, Nancy. 2007. *Stoic Warriors.* Oxford: Oxford University Press.

Shulstad, Raymond A. 1986. *Peace is My Profession: A Soldier's View of the Moral Dimension of U.S. Nuclear Policy.* Washington, DC: NDU Press.

Simon, William H. 1998. *The Practice of Justice: A Theory of Lawyers' Ethics.* Cambridge, MA: Harvard University Press.

Slusher, Howard S. 1967. *Man, Sport, and Existence: A Critical Analysis.* Philadelphia, PA: Lea and Febiger.

Smith, David Horton. 1996. "Teaching a Course on Deviant Groups: A Neglected Aspect of Deviance," *Teaching Sociology* 24:2 (April), 177-88.

Sokolowski, Robert. 1991. "The Fiduciary Relationship and the Nature of the Professions," in Pelligrino, Veatch and Langan, eds., 1991.

Solomon, Robert C. 1992. *Ethics and Excellence: Cooperation and Integrity in Business.* New York: Oxford University Press.

Sommers, Christina Hoff. 2000. *The War Against Boys: How Misguided Feminism is Harming our Young Men.* New York: Simon and Schuster.

Sorley, Lewis. 1998. *Honorable Warrior: General Harold K. Johnson and the Ethics of Command.* Lawrence, KS: University of Kansas.

Southern, R. W. 1990. *Saint Anselm: A Portrait in a Landscape.* Cambridge: Cambridge University Press.

Stansell, Gary. 1996. "Honor and Shame in the David Narratives," *Semeia* 68:55–79.

Stevens, William Oliver. 1940. *Pistols at Ten Paces: The Story of the Code of Honor in America.* Boston, MA: Houghton Mifflin.

Stewart, Frank Henderson. 1994. *Honor.* Chicago, IL: University of Chicago Press.

Stirling, Pamela. 2004. "In the Public Domain," *The Listener* (Auckland, NZ), March 20.

Stockdale, James B. 1984. *Love and War: The Story of a Family's Ordeal and Sacrifice During the Vietnam Years, by Jim & Sybil Stockdale.* New York: Harper and Row.

———. 1993. *Testing Epictetus's Doctrines in a Laboratory of Human Behavior.* Stanford, CA: Hoover Essays, #6.

———. 1995. *Thoughts of a Philosophical Fighter Pilot.* Stanford, CA: Hoover Institution Press Publication, #431.

Suits, Bernard. 1967. "What is a Game?" *Philosophy of Science* XXXIV: 148–56.

———. 1978. *The Grasshopper: Games, Life and Utopia.* Toronto: University of Toronto Press.

Sullivan, Mercer L. 1989. *Getting Paid: Youth Crime and Work in the Inner City.* Ithaca, NY: Cornell University Press.

Sumner, Colin. 2004. "The Social Nature of Crime and Deviance," Ch. 1 in Sumner, ed. 2004. *The Blackwell Companion to Criminology.* Malden, MA: Blackwell, 3–31.

Swanton, Christine. 2003. *Virtue Ethics: A Pluralistic View.* New York: Oxford University Press.

Sykes, Charles J. 1988. *Profscam: Professors and the Demise of Higher Education.* Washington, DC: Regnery.

Tangney, June Price. 2007. "Shame," in Roy F. Bassmeister and Kathleen D. Vohs, eds., *Encyclopedia of Social Psychology*, 2 vols. Thousand Oaks, CA: Sage.

Taylor, Gabriele. 1985. *Pride, Shame, and Guilt.* Oxford: Oxford University Press.

Thomas, Emory. 1995. *Robert E. Lee.* New York: W. W. Norton & Company.

Thomson, Judith Jarvis. 2008. *Normativity.* Chicago, IL: Open Court.

Tillich, Paul. 1957. *Dynamics of Faith.* London: George Allen and Unwin.

Tittle, Charles R. 1995. *Control Balance: Toward a General Theory of Deviance.* Boulder, CO: Westview.

Tomio, Shifu Nagaboshi (Terence Dukes). 1994. *The Bodhisattva Warriors: The Origin, Inner Philosophy, History and Symbolism of the Buddhist Martial Art within India and China.* York Beach, ME: Samuel Weiser.

Tompkins, J. 1992. *West of Everything: The Inner Life of Westerns.* New York: Oxford University Press.

Trexler, Richard C. 1978. "Honor among Thieves. The Trust Function of the Urban Clergy in the Florentine Republic," in *Essays Presented to Myron P. Gillmore*, Sergio Bertelli and Gloria Ramakus, eds., 2 vols. Firenze: la Nuova italia Editrice, I:317–54.

Turnbull, Stephen, ed. 2000. *The Samurai Tradition*, 2 vols. Tokyo: Edition Synapse.

Turner, Bryan S. 2002. "Cosmopolitan Virtue, Globalization and Patriotism," *Theory, Culture, and Society* 19:1–2, 45–63.

Van Creveld, Martin. 1991. *The Transformation of War*. New York: The Free Press.

Vesey, Lawrence. 1988. "Higher Education as a Profession: Change and Continuities," in Hatch, 1988, 15–32.

Vigil, James Diego. 1988. *Barrio Gangs: Street Life and Identity in Southern California*. Austin, TX: University of Texas Press.

Viroli, Maurizio. 1995. *For Love of Country: An Essay on Patriotism and Nationalism*. Oxford: Clarendon.

Vollmer, Howard M. and Mills, Donald L., eds. 1966. *Professionalization*. Englewood Cliffs, NJ: Prentice-Hall.

Walcot, Peter. 1970. *Greek Peasants, Ancient and Modern: A Comparison of Social and Moral Values*. Manchester: Manchester University Press.

Wallace, James. 1978. *Virtues and Vices*. Ithaca, NY: Cornell University Press.

Walton, Douglas N.1986.*Courage: A Philosophical Investigation*. Berkeley, CA: University of California Press.

Walzer, Michael. 1977. *Just and Unjust Wars: A Moral Argument with Historical Illustrations*. New York: Basic Books.

Wasserman, Loretta. 1980. "Honor and Shame in *Sir Gawain and the Green Knight*," in *Chivalric Literature: Essays on Relations between Literature and Life in the later Middle Ages*, Larry D. Benson and John Leyerle, eds. (Studies in Medieval Culture, 14). Kalamazoo, MI: Medieval Institute Publications, 77–90, 164–69.

Wasserstrom, Richard A. 1975. "Lawyers as Professionals: Some Moral Issues," *Human Rights* 1, 1–24; reprinted in Callahan, 1988.

Watson, C. B. 1960. *Shakespeare and the Renaissance Concept of Honor*. Princeton, NJ: Princeton University Press.

Weber, Linda R. and Carter, Allison. 2003. *The Social Construction of Trust*. New York: Kluwer Academic/Plenum.

Welsh, Alexander. 2008. *What is Honor? A Question of moral Imperatives*. New Haven, CT: Yale University Press.

Wendel, W. Bradley. 2001. "Nonlegal Regulation of the Legal Profession: Social Norms in Professional Communities," 54 *Vanderbilt Law Review* 1955.

———. 2002. "Informal Methods of Enhancing the Accountability of Lawyers," 54 *South Carolina Law Review* 967–85.

———. 2003a. "Busting the Professional Trust: A Comment on William Simon's LADD Lecture," 30 *Florida State University Law Review* 659.

———. 2003b. "Regulation of Lawyers without the Code, the Rules, or the Restatement: Or, What do Honor and Shame Have to Do with Civil Discovery Practice?" 71 *Fordham Law Review* 1567–620.

Whitehead, Alfred North. 1927. *Science and the Modern World*. Cambridge: Cambridge University Press.

Williams, Bernard. 1993. *Shame and Necessity*. Berkeley, CA: University of California Press.

Wilshire, Bruce. 1990. *The Moral Collapse of the University: Professionalism, Purity, and Alienation*. Albany, NY: SUNY Press.

Wilson, Douglas. 1998. *Honor's Voice*. New York: Knopf.

Winchester, Simon. 2008. *The Man Who Loved China: The Fantastic Story of the Eccentric Scientist Who Unlocked the Mysteries of the Middle Kingdom*. New York: HarperCollins.

Wisley, Andrew C. 1996. *Arthur Schnitzler and the discourse of honor and dueling*. New York: Peter Lang.

Wolfgang, Marvin E. and Ferracuti, Franco. 1967. *The Subculture of Violence: Towards an Integrated Theory in Criminology*. London: Tavistock.

Wollheim, Richard. 1999. *On the Emotions*. New Haven: Yale University Press.

Wood, Gordon S. 2000. *"An Affair of Honor,"* *The New York Review*, April 13, pp. 67–72.

Woodruff, Paul. 2001. *Reverence: Renewing a Forgotten Virtue*. New York: Oxford University Press.

Wurmser, Leon. 1981. *The Mask of Shame*. Baltimore, MD: Johns Hopkins University Press.

Wyatt-Brown, Bertram. 1982. *Southern Honor: Ethics & Behavior in the Old South*. New York: Oxford University Press.

———. 1986. *Honor and Violence in the Old South*. New York: Oxford University Press.

———. 2001. *The Shaping of Southern Culture: Honor, Grace, and War, 1760s-1880s*. Chapel Hill, NC: University of North Carolina Press.

Young, David C. 1984. *The Olympic Myth of Greek Amateur Athletics*. Chicago, IL: Ares.

Zhi, Geng and Yiquan, Liang. 1987. *Shaolin Martial Arts*. Beijing: China Reconstructs Press.

academic honor 113–39
    academic integrity 124–5
    administrators 136–8
    honor systems 124–6
    faculty 127–36
        scholars/researchers 130–2
        teachers 127–30
    students 124–7
anti-consequentialism 144–7, 153, 185–7
appearance v. reality 13
applied ethics 86, 145, 147–8, 150
autonomy, 4, 120–1, 156, 177

bridge concepts 156, 173, 177, 179; *see also* Janus concepts

civility 188–9
commitment honor 20–1, 26, 36, 116
community 177–8, 182–5
concept v. conception v. category 2, 8, 79n. 31, 157–9, 162, 171, 172
concepts of honor 10–36
    compared 18, 19, 21, 22, 24–5, 33, 35–6
conferred honor 11–14, 36, 87, 113–14, 155–7, 186n. 15
    attributed basis 11, 12

"dark side" of honor, 4–6, 155–70
deontology 26, 88; *see also* anti-consequentialism
deviance 44–56
    v. derivation 45
    v. deviation 45, 50–1
    v. difference 44–5
    deviance theory (in sociology) 46–9
deviant honor 52–56

deviations from honor 50–1
distinctiveness of honor 187–9

elitism 18, 160, 163, 184
equality 32–3, 70, 86, 88, 162–3, 169, 172–3, 178–9, 183; *see also* inequality

fair play 84

game theory 98n. 2, 187
Golden honor rule 183
guilt v. shame 32, 174–7
    subjective v. objective 176

honesty 187–8
honor killings 5, 164, 168
honorability 30, 44, 53–5, 183
    standards of 54–5
honor codes 26–9, 51, 70–3, 87, 124
    v. codification 27
    v. private codes 158
    primary, secondary, tertiary codes 28
honor expectations 176
honor groups 26, 29f., 49f., 67, 88, 91–2, 101–2, 143–6
    conflict between 127, 132–6
    membership 34, 102, 161
    size 5, 34–5, 92, 94, 108–9, 126, 144, 158–61
honor taboo 1, 118–19

ideals 28, 54–5, 126–7, 147; *see also* principles
Iliad 51, 189n. 19
impartiality 105
individualism 120–3, 177, 182

inequality 5, 18, 20, 23, 32–3, 159, 162–4, 169, 178; *see also* equality
inner v. outer 12, 32, 53, 173–4, 176
insider v. outsider 27, 58–60, 63, 105, 163, 167–8
insult 31, 143, 166–7
    and challenge 31–2
    v. offense 31–2
    and violence 166–7
integrity 83, 85, 188

Janus concepts 26, 29, 32, 53, 173; *see also* bridge concepts

leadership 24n. 18

matters of honor 1, 26, 52–4, 67n. 13, 88n. 11, 126, 185–6
morality 37–41, 69–70, 78, 81, 86, 89, 90–1, 95, 105–7, 111, 147–8, 152–3, 158, 161
    moral honor 39f., 55, 78, 152, 156, 161
    moral religious honor 43
    what honor adds to morality 40–1, 161

normativity 2–3, 56, 173

obsolescence of honor 157–8
other-regard 181

patriarchy 6, 168–170
patriotism 97–112
    defined 99–101
    love of country 99
    as citizen honor 98, 101–4
    and morality 105–7, 109, 111
    v. nationalism 100, 103, 109
    strength of 104, 111–12
peripheral concepts of honor 10–25, 113–16
personal honor 26–36; *see also* civility, honesty, honor codes, honor groups, integrity
    ancestry 31
    attractive conceptual features 172–91
    authority 27, 39–40

    degrees of 35
    honor-capability 160
    loyalty 22, 34, 41, 68n1
    mutuality 29, 32, 88, 183
    publicity 29, 30, 88–9, 183
    reciprocity 70, 72, 183
    reliability 34
    responsibility 30, 33
    self-regard 30, 32, 179–82
    solidarity 31, 34, 68, 89–90, 147, 183–4
    trustworthiness 34, 74, 89
political honor 97–112
    of citizens 98
    of politicians 97
    of polities 98
positional honor 17–20, 36, 87, 115, 162–3, 167
    achievement honor 17–18, 32
        and social power 19
    status honor 18
principles 28; *see also* ideals
professions 140–53
    codes 130, 145–8
    criteria 140–3
    honor groups 143–6
    the law 148–52
        legal ethics 148f.
        professional responsibility 150
        zealous advocacy 148–51
    and morality 152–3

realpolitik 106–7
recognition honor 14–17, 36, 87, 115, 156, 181
    excellences 14, 16, 93
relativism 5, 14, 37, 54, 89, 93, 105, 161–2
religion 41–3, 161–2
    religious honor 42
    what honor adds to religion 42–3
reputation 4, 54, 155–7
respect 28, 30, 36, 38, 54, 70, 76, 88–9, 103–4, 137, 156, 169, 183
    v. deference 30
    v. esteem 30
responsibility 30, 54, 74, 179–80, 184

sages of honor 178, 180

self-regard 179–82
sense of honor 1, 26f., 87–8, 156,
176
sportsmanship, 82–96
honor code of competition 89
v. sports honor code 89n. 14
honor groups of competitors 91–2
"love of the game" 85, 92
as personal honor 86, 87–90
in self-policing sports 94

trust honor 22–4, 26, 36, 116

violence 4, 104, 164–8
virtue 26, 69

virtue ethics 2–3, 115

war 63–5
and gender 66n. 8, 78–81
surrender and captivity 72
warriors 62–81, 104–5
v. fanatical fighters 74
as honorable fighters 65–68
good warriors 68–70
judging warriors 76–8
motivation 73–6
v. sheer killers 73–4
treatment of enemy fighters 70–1
and violence 165
warrior codes 70–3

INDEX OF NAMES

Anderson, Elizabeth 106
Aristotle 19n. 12
Atkinson, Rob 145n. 15

Benedict, Ruth 175
Berger, Peter 4n. 10, 35, 117, 157n. 4, 170
Best, Geoffrey 63n. 3
Braudy, Leo 78n. 28

Campbell, Doug 117n. 7
Cohen, Albert K. 44

Dancy, Jonathan 37n. 2

Eggleston, Ben 145n. 15, 145n. 18
Emerson, Ralph Waldo 4

Forster, E. M. 103n. 10
Fossum, Merle A. 175
Freidson, Eliot 143

Gaffney, James 107
Gilligan, Carol 115
Goldstein, Joshua S. 78n. 28, 79–80
Goldberg, Nat 131n. 19, 186n. 14
Gough, Russell 86

Haber, Samuel 143
Hobbes, Thomas 22n. 15
Hume, David 38

Ignatieff, Michael 63n. 3

James, William 109, 155, 180n. 11
Jenkins, Richard 54n. 18

Kant, Immanuel 30, 39n. 3, 123

Kateb, George 100
Keating, James 83n. 5
Keller, Simon 99, 110
Kronman, Anthony 149

Lincoln, Abraham 16n. 9
Liska, Allen G 47–8
Lombardi, Vince 83
Luban, David 34n. 20, 149

MacIntyre, Alasdair 7, 37n. 2, 69n. 16, 84,
        106, 152, 157n. 4, 186
McCabe, David 107
Marx, Groucho 160
Mason, Marilyn 175
Müller, Jan-Werner 106

Nathanson, Stephen 106
Nussbaum, Martha 106
Nye, Robert A. 79n. 31

Oldenquist, Andrew 106

Rawls, John xi, 8n. 1, 20n. 13, 30,
        187n. 17

Sagarin, Edward 47n. 12
Schaar, John 100, 106
Schellenberg, John 9n. 3
Schleiermacher, Friedrich 14n. 6
Schur, Edwin M. 48
Shaffer, Tom 150
Shakespeare 3–4
Shapin, Steven 22n. 16
Shaw, George Bernard 100
Simon, William 149
Somers, Susan 191n. 20

Tangney, June Price 174
Taylor, Gabriel 173n. 2, 175
Thomas, Emory 35n. 22
Tillich, Paul 21n. 14, 161n. 8
Tomkins, Silvan 175
Twain, Mark 13n. 5

Van Creveld, Martin 81n. 34

Wendel, Brad 151–2
Westmoreland, William 80n. 33
Whitehead, A. N. 173n. 3
Williams, Bernard 175, 177n. 7
Winchester, Simon 131n. 20
Wollheim, Richard 176